WORKING TOGETHER

Also by Michael D. Eisner

Work in Progress

Camp

WORKING TOGETHER

Why Great
Partnerships
Succeed

MICHAEL D.
EISNER

with Aaron Cohen

HARPER
BUSINESS

An Imprint of HarperCollins*Publishers*
www.harpercollins.com

HarperCollins books may be purchased for educational, business, or sales promotional use. For information, please write: Special Markets Department, HarperCollins Publishers, 10 East 53rd Street, New York, NY 10022.

FIRST EDITION

Library of Congress Cataloging-in-Publication Data has been applied for.

ISBN: 978-0-06-173236-2

10 11 12 13 14   OV/RRD   10 9 8 7 6 5 4 3 2 1

Work and Love and Friendship
Two of Those Three Will Result in a Great Partnership
All Three Will Result in a Great Life

To all my great partners, my loving wife of forty-three years,
my three sons and their spouses, and my present and future
grandchildren, I dedicate this book.

And to Frank Wells.

CONTENTS

INTRODUCTION

I n May of 2008, I got a phone call from Bob Miller, the founding president of Hyperion Books, the publishing unit of Disney that we began in 1991.

"I'm leaving Disney and starting a new imprint at Harper-Collins," he said, "and you have to write a book for me."

Before I could decline—my natural first response—he plowed forward.

"How about a book about you and Frank?" he said. "A book about partners, and how partnerships work."

I did what I often do when I hear what I think is a great idea, even if nearly every fiber in me is saying that I'm too busy and too distracted to get involved. I answered quickly.

"Okay, I'm in."

Soon we hung up, and it occurred to me that I had suddenly committed to a lot of effort, a lot of time, and a lot of procrastination, a Mark Twain kind of procrastination ("I do not like work even when somebody else does it"). Eventually I called Bob back, and asked for two years to get the book done. The idea intrigued me for a number of reasons. First, my ten years with Frank Wells at Disney were the most successful of my career. Beyond the great vision we shared for the future, no one was more engaging than Frank, and no one's drive to support ideas—business and creative—was more insatiable. Along with a great group of executives we assembled, from inside Disney and our alma maters Warner Bros. and Paramount, Frank and I worked hard together and succeeded together. But the comfort, camaraderie, and connection, family friendship and intellectual fellowship, all came to a crashing halt Easter Sunday in 1994, when Frank died far too young in a helicopter crash during one of his many adventurous expeditions. After that tragedy, we carried on at Disney, producing more great animated movies, building new theme parks, and climbing new mountains, including one of the largest and most significant transactions of the time, the acquisition of Capital Cities/ABC and ESPN in 1996. I remained at Disney until 2005, working with a handful of new partners—some successfully, some very successfully, some not so much—but none of the arrangements ever worked as seamlessly and effortlessly as the one I had with Frank Wells. And in the days, weeks, and months following my phone call with Bob Miller, I spent more and more time wondering exactly why our partnership worked so well, what had actually made that connection so extraordinarily productive and made us so much more successful than we would have been working alone.

As I thought about it, I found myself wishing I was an art-ist rather than a weekend writer. Inspired perhaps by Marc Chagall, I would paint three canvases to make my point, all of a man riding a horse. The first would be a tiny man atop a giant horse, the second would be a giant man atop a tiny horse, and the third would be a man and a horse of equal sizes. In the first scenario, the horse would be too strong, and too uncontrollable for the man. The second would be equally unsuccessful, for a tiny horse can't move with a giant man weighing him down. But the third match would be perfect, with the man and horse able to move successfully in concert. The man represents intellect, the horse represents emotion. Both need to be equally balanced for any leader to succeed. The best combination, I've learned, comes from partnership, when two people balance each other, constantly reminding the other of the need to keep the conscious and unconscious in harmony, to make each other smarter, make each other better.

Since I'm not a painter, I came upon a different way to an-swer those questions in a book. Start with a look back at my time with Frank Wells, and then go to work and find some other partnerships that succeeded. I'd do some research, make a list, go talk to these partners, and hopefully learn more about how people work together. It turns out the list was easier to create than I first thought. The most successful and well-respected investor in the world, Warren Buffett, has a partner, Charlie Munger. The most successful figure to come out of the computer revolution, Bill Gates, famously worked with partners at Microsoft, and now, in his new job, saving the world (quite literally) with his foundation, he has perhaps his best partner yet: his wife, Melinda. In Hollywood, you'd be hard-pressed to find a more successful or well-liked movie and television production company than Imagine Entertainment—run by partners Brian Grazer and Ron Howard, who've won multiple Academy Awards and produced and directed dozens of movies and television series. One of the biggest retail chains in the United States, Home Depot, was started by a pair of visionaries, Bernie Marcus and Arthur Blank. In fashion, the great designer Valentino spent a half century atop his world flanked by an amazing partner, a man named Giancarlo Giammetti. In Los Angeles, among the most well-known and respected restaurant owners in town are a pair of chefs, Susan Feniger and Mary Sue Milliken, who've shown that despite the old saying, there is in fact room for two cooks in the kitchen. In finance, a company run by my childhood friend John Angelo and his partner, Michael Gordon, has been successful for decades managing billions of dollars, not only surviving the financial meltdown but growing during it. Partnership goes beyond the traditional definition of business as well. In sports, the most successful baseball manager of the last half century, Joe Torre, won his four World Series titles with a partner by his side, a man Yankee fans know well, his bench coach Don Zimmer. And even the best ongoing party of the last fifty years—the Studio 54 dance club in New York—was run by partners Ian Schrager and the late Steve Rubell, who shared not only enormous success but, for a year, a jail cell.

Writing the book required me to spend a lot of time with these people, interviewing them about their partnerships. I started the project while buying the baseball card company Topps, making a television show, working on movie projects, advising my three sons on thirty different projects (when they let me), and being an entrepreneur. So Jane, my wife of forty-three years, suggested I politely exit the project, and stop driving myself crazy. It served as a good first lesson about partnerships: always find a partner who's not afraid to tell you what they think. She was half right on this one: I started writing, and stopped thinking about why I didn't have the time.

Once I did that, I began to realize more and more that this project was not only interesting, but important and timely. If there is a single, central story to be written about business in the twenty-first century, it is, sadly and regrettably, a story dominated by a handful of individuals who infected the economy with deceit, manipulation, and amorality; essentially the death of honesty. From destructive failures like Enron to the sociopathic deception of Bernie Madoff to irresponsible banking and real estate executives and government figures, a lack of ethics has crippled the business world over the last decade. Partnerships, however, encourage a series of characteristics—trust, teamwork, a regard for someone else, and continuing checks and balances—that run counter to the factors that contributed to the sequence of economic messes of the last ten years. All in all, this is a perfect time to be encouraging partnerships devoid of envy, jealousy, and rivalry as a way to escape from the toxic culture that has given the business world a bad name, and to instead help people chart a new, often overlooked path toward a better way of working.

As you'll see in the book, the people I met were thrilled to talk about what they shared with their partners, and what had made their pairings so successful. So much of the business world is supposed to be about getting ahead of the rest of the field, and winning while someone else loses. And there are many, many stories in business of iconic individual achievers who stood tall atop their worlds. Yet the tales of these partnerships are not just about their spectacular success. They are about something else, something far more elusive. They're about learning to share, and how great sharing can be: sharing success and sharing failure, adrenaline and frustration, laughter and tears. It is far from easy, though, and each of the partnerships profiled in this book illustrates different ways of sharing, and different styles of working together. It is hardly as simple as dividing up power, authority, the spotlight, salary, stock options, and success down the middle. If it was this basic, this book would not be nearly as interesting. Instead, there are many different stories to tell, stories of pairs who are similar, and tales of duos who are different; partners who were the same age and partners who were born decades apart; two men and two women or one of each; loud and colorful characters, and modest and withdrawn figures. For all the contrasts, there is one common thread. Collectively, the stories you're about to read demonstrate the virtue of something that's often forgotten about, in business and in life: these are not just all successful people, they're also happy people. They enjoy getting up in the morning, they love what they do, and they are among the select and very fortunate few who have found that partnerships create happiness.

These are the tales of ten magical partnerships. These are ten stories that show why working together is better.

WORKING TOGETHER

FRANK WELLS AND I

Where I learned 1 + 1 = 3 (if not much more)

I still can't believe I said that," I told my wife. But like many things in life, you had to be there to understand the moment.

It had been eight hours earlier, a beautiful Saturday morning in September 1984 in Los Angeles. For the previous year and a half, Barry Diller and I had been riding a roller coaster at Paramount Pictures working for Marty Davis. Davis was the head of Paramount's parent company, Gulf & Western. I had spent eight years as the president of Paramount, brought there by Barry, whom I had been working for and with from the time we were twenty-four-year-old assistants at ABC in New York. Barry had been a mentor, a teacher, and a friend, but was about to leave Paramount to go to Twentieth Century-Fox, thanks to Davis, a man whom Barry found unbearable and who'd become the chairman of Gulf & Western following the death of the eccentric but brilliant, supportive, and even affectionate Charlie Blühdorn. Without Barry, my life at Paramount—long so satisfying creatively and personally—was looking like it would be much less pleasant. Although I never really knew Marty Davis well, I did know he'd told Jeffrey Katzenberg, my talented young head of production, that "Michael Eisner is like a kid playing with blocks on the floor." With delusional confidence in our performance, I had actually taken that as something of a compliment, but in some honest portion of my heart, I was pretty sure he didn't mean it so flatteringly. Furthermore, it appeared I would now be not only working with a tough boss but going at it alone—without someone to bond with about this potential common enemy. In such situations, I had learned, shared frustrations could actually lead conversely to more creativity, and more fun. But without Barry Diller as my partner, I found working for Davis a very questionable proposition.

Then, by fate or perhaps circumstance, just as I began to see firsthand the difference between Charlie Blühdorn and Marty Davis, I had been approached by another entertainment corporation—more than just a film company, more exciting, and with bigger challenges to meet. That company, of course, was Disney—then called Walt Disney Productions—which had long been struggling to grow since the death of its founder Walt Disney eighteen years earlier, and was now in search of new leadership.

I had first been quietly approached to talk about working at Disney in late 1983, but the timing was not right for them or me. Now, though, it was a year later, and the company was being attacked by corporate raiders. And on this late summer day, I found myself at the home of an attorney named Stanley Gold, a round, rather larger-than-life man with bright red glasses, a ubiquitous unlit cigar in his mouth, an odd sense of humor, and uncompromising loyalty to his one client, Roy E. Disney, Walt's nephew.

I had been summoned to Stanley's Beverly Hills home to bring this courtship to a conclusion, and determine whether or not I'd be joining the Disney company. Other relevant parties were in attendance, most notably a man named Frank Wells, who had run Warner Bros. a few years earlier before leaving Hollywood for a different kind of challenge: climbing the tallest peaks on each of the world's continents. He had scaled six out of the seven, and was now back looking to resume his entertainment career. Frank and I had crossed paths over the years a few times, but I didn't know him very well. He was, though, close to Stanley, and as we sat out on the terrace, the two of them were presenting what I knew was the latest plan for Disney's new leadership. It was very clear that the moment had arrived for decisions to be made. Time had run out on my hesitations and confusion about why I hated being at Paramount with Diller and Blühdorn gone, even as we remained atop the industry in motion pictures and television. The handwriting was on the Paramount wall, with an arrow pointing in Disney's direction. But one big part of the Disney plan made me uncomfortable.

"You and Frank," Stanley summarized, "will be co-CEOs. You will share power at the top of the company, and together report to the board of directors. You'll handle the creative side. He'll handle the business side. But you'll be equals."

"I really don't want to do this unless I'm the sole CEO," I heard myself saying. "I'm extremely flattered, of course, but I just don't think that arrangement makes sense."

There was an utter quiet in the room. As I would tell Jane

that night, I couldn't believe what I had just said. Sure, I believed what I was saying, but still: the most storied entertainment company in the world was offering me a parachute away from what threatened to become for me a Hollywood dungeon, and I was telling them their plan wouldn't fly.

Maybe, though, I had an instinct. Even if I was overplaying my hand, maybe, just maybe, it might work.

Less than three seconds later, Frank Wells broke the silence.

"Okay," he said. "You can be chairman and CEO, and I'll be president and COO."

If I had stunned myself by blurting out my own demand, I was, silently, at least doubly shocked by Frank's reply. After all, he had set up the plan that they proposed. Fortunately, I had learned early in my career to take yes for an answer. Too many times a person is told okay, and then says, "Really? You must be kidding. I can do that?" I knew when to say yes. So I simply said, "Great. I'm in."

But in the days and weeks ahead, I found myself wondering about Frank. What kind of person would spend his life so successfully climbing his way up the corporate ladder and then, at the very top, step aside for someone else—and someone else, for that matter, he didn't know very well? I had spent the previous twenty years working in a terrific partnership alongside Barry Diller, one of the most brilliant executives the entertainment world has ever seen, but now, this Frank Wells appeared to be a different sort of animal: an executive who could cede power just like that, and be as comfortable as a number two as he was as a number one. Could that really be true?

I was about to find out. Frank and I got the jobs, just as we had defined them that day on the terrace at Stanley Gold's house. We were headed into the toughest challenge of our professional lives, together. For the next ten years, that journey would be as exciting, enjoyable, rewarding, and triumphant as either of us could have dared to hope. From our first day in the office that fall, my partnership with Frank Wells taught me what it was like to work with somebody who not only protected the organization but protected me, advised me, supported me, and did it all completely selflessly. I'd like to think I did the same for Frank, as well as the company. We grew together, learned together, and discovered together how to turn what was in retrospect a small business into indeed a very big business.

We learned that one plus one adds up to a lot more than two. We learned just how rewarding working together can be.

■   ■   ■

This is a story that begins on opposite sides of the country, about two young men who couldn't have been much more different. You see, while I grew up in New York City, Frank was a navy brat from California who moved around a lot as a child before attending Pomona College and then going overseas to spend two years at Oxford as a Rhodes scholar. After I graduated from Denison University in Ohio, I lasted just two weeks in Europe. I thought I'd be a playwright in Paris, but solitary views of the Eiffel Tower and lonely nights at cafés weren't my thing. I came home and got a job at NBC as a clerk. I was ecstatic. There were people around.

Frank finished his education with a law degree from Stanford, and also spent two years in the army before becoming a lawyer with the well-known firm of Gang, Kopp & Brown (later Gang, Tyre, Ramer & Brown). He entered the studio entertainment side of the business in 1969 by joining Warner Bros., a client of his firm, and then worked his way up to company president a decade later. I had arrived in Hollywood from ABC in New York in the summer of 1973, joining Barry Diller so we could both be closer to the center of production at ABC after seven years together in New York City. Then, in 1976, I followed Barry again across town to become his second in command at Paramount Pictures, president to his chairman. Still, other than at industry functions, I didn't really cross paths with Frank until 1982, when we ran into each other skiing in Vail, Colorado, and decided to have dinner together with our wives. It was just after Frank had decided to take leave of the entertainment business to spend a year climbing those seven tallest peaks. That night, I met a man who was clearly adventurous, and clearly in need of something new. He had achieved a lot as a lawyer and a motion picture executive, but having found two executives (Bob Daly and Terry Semel, who would form their own example of a great partnership over the next two decades) to step into his job as head of Warner Bros., he was ready to move on. To me, though, the idea of climbing the world's highest mountains was at once fascinating and baffling, and as I am wont to do, I asked him roughly a thousand questions about his plans for an adventure, most of them variations on the theme: Who would be crazy enough to take that kind of risk? I learned several years later that he couldn't believe I asked all those questions. He told me nobody else bothered to ask more than one. He would say that he knew at that moment that I was the inquisitive type. (He may have used a different adjective.) Maybe what surprised me most was learning that his previous climbing experience amounted to having hiked to the top of Vail a handful of times. Frank wasn't exactly Lance Armstrong. This wasn't like Rocky training by running up the steps of the Philadelphia Museum of Art—to this day, I'm not even sure Frank trained much at all. In other words, this was not a finely tuned athletic specimen testing the limits of his body, even if he may have looked the part. (Years later, I'd confirm all this on our fifth day on the job at Disney, when Frank hit his head on every crossbeam on the inside of the Matterhorn theme park ride as we explored Disneyland.) What I learned that night at dinner was that he was a successful middle-aged executive who had simply decided to embark on an adventure. With a twinkle in his eye, he was very aware of what he was doing, and seemed to know what I had always believed: as long as you think and act as if you're coming from behind, you have a shot at staying ahead. I liked him immediately for that.

Back at Paramount, I suppose I thought about Frank from time to time while he was walking the ends of the earth—particularly when someone on his Everest expedition (the one mountain he failed to summit) died near the top. And though we crossed paths once or twice when he returned—actually cochairing a political event at one point—we remained business acquaintances rather than friends. Though we certainly got along well, I can't pretend that we ever talked about collaborating in the future. Still, Frank knew my work at ABC and Paramount and must have respected my accomplishments there, just as I respected his success at Warner Bros. And then, all of a sudden, there we were—on that terrace at

Stanley Gold's Beverly Hills house, talking as we looked out at a tennis court, swimming pool, and the backyard grass of a neighbor's house.

I learned later that Frank had stayed close to Roy Disney and Stanley Gold, hoping that some business opportunity would come up for him at Walt Disney Productions. He had come back from his trip a few months earlier and had been talking to them. He knew Roy always hated the way he was treated by his uncle's successors, Card Walker and Ron Miller. He also knew Roy had quit the Disney board over the frustration of being ignored. He had known Roy since they were in college together, had worked as his lawyer, and had turned over his law practice to Stanley at their firm when he moved to Warner Bros. And he also knew the Disney Company was in chaos and was being approached by corporate raiders, and that Roy was looking for revenge and a way to spare his father and uncle's company from being broken apart. Frank was looking for the next step in his own career, but then, with a kind of honesty to which the business world often seems allergic, suggested they talk to me. I'm still not sure whether it was because I had a pretty good record over the past two decades or because I had quizzed him incessantly about his mountaineering wanderlust at the Vail dinner years before. He hadn't simply said to them, "Well, I'm available," but instead offered the advice, "You should talk to Michael Eisner." And then, of course, his selflessness had culminated on the terrace.

Getting the job wasn't quite as simple as that, of course; we had to get the board of directors to approve the deal. This wasn't just a company making a leadership change—this was the Walt Disney Company, less than twenty years after the death of its founder, still never having brought someone in from outside the company family to run things. We in fact would be taking over for Walt's son-in-law, Ron Miller, who had been the CEO since 1980. But after some impressive votes of confidence by people like Card Walker and the investor Sid Bass, we got the jobs, and on Monday morning, September 24, 1984—just a few weeks after the conversation on Stanley Gold's terrace—I found myself driving to the Disney lot in Burbank to start my first day of work. The coverage in the press was enormous, surprising me greatly. During the rush to get our jobs, I had forgotten just how fond of, and interested in, Disney as a company the public was. It made me nervous. For years, I had avoided making deals out of ego and testosterone that would make the front page of the *Wall Street Journal*—only to appear a few years later on the business obituary page of the *New York Times*. As I drove to Burbank that day, I hoped that wouldn't be the fate of this experiment.

Lucille Martin, who had been Walt's secretary and then worked for Ron Miller, was there to welcome me into the office where Walt himself had once worked. I had been there for maybe ten minutes when Frank arrived with a big hello and sat down across from me. I pushed back my chair and began talking about what we had to do that day, figuring he'd respond and then head out, but after about fifteen minutes, something else became apparent to me.

"Frank," I asked him, "are we going to sit here together?"

"Well, yeah," he said. "I thought we would."

I wasn't sure how to react. Yes, I suppose partners who work together should be able to actually *work together*, but the whole idea made me uncomfortable. I need my privacy.

I made the point to Frank, and offered to go find another office, leaving this one to him.

"No, no," he said, jumping up. "You stay here, I'll go." And he walked to the room next door and sat down. Though Frank projected a tremendous, statesmanlike sense of calm and stability to everyone else that day, I—the supposed creative executive—could tell he was truly nervous starting this adventure. I liked that. For the first time, I saw that he was human—and this was going to work. Underneath that handsome, perfectly postured, military-son Rhodes scholar was real flesh and blood, so much more than I expected. Although we didn't share the same space, we came into each other's offices anyway about twenty times each over the course of that morning, sharing news and comparing notes from phone calls, a pattern that would repeat itself countless more times over the next ten years.

■   ■   ■

As I've alluded, I had come to Disney on the heels of another partnership, with Barry Diller—first at ABC, and later at Paramount. I first met Barry in 1966. From my first job as an usher at NBC, I had gone on to another entry-level job, this time at CBS. After working with another partner—my girlfriend and later wife, Jane—writing a hundred or so letters, I got an interview with Leonard Goldberg, the vice president of programming at ABC, who had to vet me before I could get a job as an assistant to another executive. I still remember the day well—forgetting to put on my best suit that morning; going home in the middle of the day to change before the interview; forgetting the keys to my apartment; begging the shared secretary in my CBS office, Ann Mastrogiacomo (Ann, where are you now? Write me at info@tornante.com), to bring the keys to my apartment; somehow getting to ABC on time. I was met by a young man, probably about my age, but prematurely balding and dressed in a suit much sharper than anything I had in my closet.

"Michael Eisner?" he asked me, and I nodded.

Without introducing himself, he took me into an office and interviewed me for twenty minutes, a meeting marked by the fact that every few minutes, a light would glow on his phone, and he would pick up an earpiece and silently listen in before putting it down and resuming the conversation. At dinner that night I described to my brother-in-law, who had grown up in the same building as Leonard Goldberg, my meeting with Leonard, the young, balding executive. Norman told me whoever that was, it absolutely was not Leonard Goldberg.

Only when I got the job and reported to work at ABC did I find out that I had been interviewed by Goldberg's assistant, who was exactly my age, and had been hired by the network out of the William Morris mailroom at the suggestion of his longtime family friend, the actress Marlo Thomas. His name was Barry Diller, and those pauses in the conversation had been him listening in on Goldberg's phone calls, common practice in those days to guide assistants in knowing what business to follow up on. Luckily that practice vanished at ABC shortly after I arrived.

For much of the next twenty years, I would work for or alongside Barry. More than forty years after that strange interview, we are still close friends. To this day, I don't know if there's anyone who taught me more about being an executive than Barry. From the start, as mere twenty-four-year-old executives, we were both relentlessly ambitious. I respected him enormously, and I think he respected me as well. But unlike Frank Wells and me, we were also competitive. We were both on our way up.

For the bulk of our working relationship, Barry ranked a notch ahead of me (well, maybe more than a notch—he was my boss, after all), whether it was among the batch of assistants at ABC or at the top of the food chain at Paramount. Because of that, I was sensitive sometimes to Barry treating me more as an employee than as a partner—particularly early on in our relationship, when he once shouted to me at the top of his voice down the hall, "Eisner!" wanting me to come into his office. I very simply walked into his office, closed the door, and told him, "It just isn't going to work for you to shout commands at me from one end of the hall to the other." Immediately he apologized. And that approach, I realized, was the way to deal with Barry—simply and directly. When there would be an issue of any kind, I would confront him about it, and it would be settled. He would do the same. I learned quickly: honesty, directness, and a certain amount of mutual respect go a long way.

There was also something else gained through all those frank and direct discussions about projects and politics in the company—a trust that put our relationship in a place others couldn't touch. When he hired me at Paramount, we were both working for the founder of Gulf & Western, a true original if there ever was one, Charlie Blühdorn. I say both because although I technically worked for Barry, Charlie acted like everybody worked directly for him. Charlie was totally brilliant—and completely unpredictable. Trusting no one, he'd constantly be calling people inside the company in an effort to get them to give him information maybe their colleagues hadn't. When I arrived at Paramount, I was quickly added to this call list, but Charlie stopped trying with me when he realized that everything he said to me, I'd relay to Barry. There was a joint, largely tacitly made agreement: no one was going to get between us and play one against the other. And that's what made us less boss and employee, and more partners.

At Paramount, with the movie studio in our hands, the partnership blossomed into success—success that derived from working so well together. When I wanted to take a risk with a film, Barry would be the cautious one, making sure it was the right call. When Barry wanted to kill a project, I would be there championing it, trying to find a reason to keep it alive. Our ability to go at each other, to agree and disagree, to be completely honest without having to worry about any conflicts having collateral damage—it gave us the ability to truly put our brains together. And so, at the end of the day, we always seemed to agree on everything. Getting to a decision on content and then what that content would cost wasn't always easy or pretty (remember what Woody Allen said: "If show business wasn't a business, it would be called show show"), but it got the job done—and, over our years at ABC and Paramount, resulted in television shows like *Happy Days*, *Laverne and Shirley*, *Taxi*, *Cheers*, *Winds of War*, *Roots*, and dozens more, and movies like *Saturday Night Fever*, *Raiders of the Lost Ark*, *Flashdance*, *Grease*, *Reds*, *Atlantic City*, *Ordinary People*, *Terms of Endearment*, and hundreds more. Creatively, we were in so many ways a perfect match, and I think the proof is in the results.

Together we were managing partners, programming partners, and ethical partners. Ethics are an interesting thing.
Often they are defined by the person on the wrong side of
an outcome; other times, by the media, or the law, or the
Bible, Torah, Koran, or other books of choice. But in almost
all ways, ethics are fairly obvious; and like Justice Potter
Stewart famously said about pornography, you know it when
you see it—and more important, you know it when you don't
see it. And it has always astonished me that there is so much
unethical behavior in business.

I learned ethics from my family, my father, my school,
my life; but I really learned it when I went to work for ABC,
and then Paramount. You may be surprised about what I'm
now going to say. The entertainment business is generally, in
my experience, one of the most ethical places I have found
in American business, at least a large part of it. Your word
is your reputation in broadcasting. There is no other way.
Transactions move too quickly for contract writing to follow immediate verbal assurances. Therefore, one lives by his
or her word. And it doesn't hurt that broadcasters, namely
television stations, need a government license to exist. That
creates an environment of honesty. The same could be said
for cable. The movie business, especially the studio business
and the talent agency businesses, are not far behind. People
in independent film work can be less honest and upfront.
The music business is still another notch below in that there
is little regulation, and a lot of very young and inexperienced
talent. But when you get to real estate, your word means little, and lawyers forget anything said by the principals when
the negotiations were conducted. I have at times had conversations with people I've been negotiating with in real estate

and reminded them of a deal we made on price. "Remember," I have said, "when we had lunch four months ago at the Four Seasons Restaurant in New York City, and you said such and such?" "No" is the response, "I don't remember having lunch with you that date. I think I was in Europe then."

There are differences in ethical behavior between any business where you have continuing relationships with the same people, and any business where you don't. In the first case, there is the pressure to be fair. Often in real estate you don't have that. Other businesses with frequent single-transaction relationships would be the same, I guess. When you never see a person again, he can cheat you all he wants. Barry Diller and I learned all that together at ABC and Paramount, and discovering this together was another shared experience that enhanced our partnership, and enlightened us further on how to do our jobs.

And while we did those jobs together, as partners, I was clearly the junior partner, and as the number-two executive, I often found myself becoming a buffer between Barry and the other executives at Paramount who didn't know how to deal with him, and stand up to him when he challenged them. When Barry would get them upset, I would make nice, almost acting as the mother of the family, protecting the children from the volatile and demanding father.

Everything changed when Charlie Blühdorn died in February 1983, after a battle with leukemia that he kept secret from all of us, even if we had known something was strange for several months leading up to it. Marty Davis took over as chairman of Gulf & Western, and immediately set about trying to take control of the company in a peculiar way: forcing every top executive who worked for him to replace his lieutenant with someone of Davis's choice. As you may have guessed, this meant he wanted me out, as well as every other "number two" throughout the many companies of Gulf & Western. Barry, though, putting his job on the line, said he wouldn't do that. We were both amazed this was happening; Paramount had been either number one or number two every year at the box office since we had been there. Of all the studios, we had been number one in profits every year. And we had five of the top ten shows on network television. I learned later that Barry did what he could to defend me, but the strain on us, on the company, and on our relationship was obvious. A few months later, Barry himself was negotiating to leave Paramount and go to Twentieth Century-Fox. He knew he couldn't work for Davis even if Davis continued to accept him. Davis, after all, had just been named by *Fortune* magazine as "the worst boss in America"!

Barry offered to take me with him, but when he introduced me to his new boss at Fox, Marvin Davis (no relation to Martin Davis), I felt we would be two fish jumping right back into the same frying pan. And the Disney conversations had just begun. Part of me wanted to continue in my partnership with Barry, but something new and different was on the horizon. Barry would make it work totally and completely for himself and for his career at Fox, starting a new network, and then moving on to QVC, the USA Network, and eventually his own empire of digital businesses, IAC. By September of 1984, of course, I would follow him out the door on my way to Disney. My days of working with Barry Diller were over, but there were bigger things in store for both of us. What we had learned from each other was immeasurable, but looking back, there's no doubt that one of the biggest lessons for me was realizing the value of great partnership.

■　■　■

After that first day at Disney—when Frank Wells briefly but unsuccessfully tried to sell me on the virtues of shared offices—everything seemed to take off at warp speed. Disney was ripe for all kinds of growth, and the story of how Frank and I led a great team of people to realize that growth has been told before. I was the unpredictable but excitable creative executive, always coming up with new ideas—some good ones, some off the wall. Meanwhile, Frank was a constantly steadying influence, and someone whom I instantly trusted to tell me when an idea was great and not so great. Me, the wild and creative CEO; Frank, the calm and soothing president, "controlling" me. Yes, it's a well-known story, but one with a significant problem.

The story's not true.

And to my chagrin, even just a few months ago at a dinner party, Sid Bass put it much more accurately.

"Everyone thinks Michael was the crazy one, and Frank was the straight one," Sid said. "Actually, they were both crazy."

Back to 1984: a few weeks into our time at Disney, I was at an event where I bumped into Bob Daly, who had worked at Warner Bros. with Frank. As we spoke, I couldn't resist taking his temperature. "Bob," I said, "is Frank different from how people perceive him, or am I missing something?" He looked at me for a second, and then burst out laughing uncontrollably, and started telling me stories that sounded familiar even after just several weeks of working with Frank. Bob told me how one time, he had mentioned offhandedly to Frank that Robert Redford might be good for a particular role in a movie, and before he had a chance to finish his thought, Frank was headed to his car, ready to drive out and do a "sell job" on Redford. The anecdote seemed to fit—in our frequent meetings, I had noticed that when I threw an idea out there, Frank would instantly become the idea's biggest cheerleader. A concept for an animated movie? Frank would instantly decide it was a winner. Should we build more hotels at Disneyworld in Orlando? Let's build a dozen. At one point Sid Bass and I were discussing whether I should host *The Wonderful World of Disney*. I was tentative. I even asked Barry Diller, and he warned me my life would never be the same. But Frank's response: "Absolutely! This company needs a public rudder." I am sure he thought that, but mostly he knew I wanted to try it, and he was behind me. Most anything, it seemed, that I could come up with, Frank would support with double the enthusiasm. And the response wasn't "Why do it?" but "You must do it," and "When in doubt, go for it."

I've since thought a lot about that period of getting to know each other that Frank and I went through in our first few months at Disney, and the purpose and the impact of Frank's instant support for me and my ideas for the company. What made him such a perfect partner? To start, Frank believed in me, and he believed in the ability of our team to succeed at Disney. Responding with instant passion about new ideas was just part of that overall support, and it invigorated the whole company. It was also simply a part of Frank's utter selflessness. Unlike for so many other people in Hollywood and elsewhere, for Frank Wells, it wasn't about getting credit for the successful idea—it was about simply succeeding. Sure, Frank wanted respect, and would get as annoyed as anyone when he was taken for granted by others in the company, but he would vent only to me—nobody else—and not often.

In another unlikely scenario for the business world, Frank also wasn't that interested in the spotlight. For so many other people, Frank's job would have been a means to an end; a temporary landing spot on the way to an official CEO's job somewhere else. But being the president of Disney was what Frank, in his fifties when the job started, wanted; he was happy to see someone ten years younger than him, me, hungry to be out front. Frank was a man who had succeeded at essentially everything he had done from the time he was in high school, and he was entirely secure and at ease with himself. There were never any hurt feelings or ego trips or secret signals of discontent between us: one or two—it didn't matter. We were partners, and life was always about the decisions themselves, and what made sense for the company. As Warren Buffett will explain a lot better than I can, the spotlight accommodates one person a lot easier than two. But it takes real trust and understanding for both partners to be satisfied with that arrangement, and from the start, Frank and I enjoyed exactly that.

Frank's approach did reveal his only bit of insecurity—toward creative decisions. Years earlier, after first starting on the business side of the motion-picture industry, Frank had been thrust into the creative executive's chair at Warner Bros. In that area, he'd never felt entirely comfortable as the person making those final content calls. His few mistakes about movie choices really upset him. So after his adventures above 25,000 feet, returning to Hollywood, he saw part of the Disney job as a perfect next step. Along with the rest of our team, I thought Frank's concerns about his own creative abilities were nonsense, and therefore he was always consulted on significant decisions. He had to be consulted, because from the first day until the last, we had one constant conversation going. And his role in every decision-making process took particular advantage of his strengths.

And finally, there was also this inescapable reality: partners have to like each other. That's how ego disappears, and that's what prevents others from getting between partners. That's what creates that foxhole, with two people fighting the world together to achieve something special, fighting their competitors, fighting to protect each other, being friends, and keeping the institution together. Every day with Frank Wells was fun, every day a new adventure. If the yin-and-yang perception of us that people had was wrong, the sense of partnership that we had was totally spot-on.

After more than forty years in the entertainment business, I've analyzed the practices and policies and strategies that direct the way I operate. When I give speeches, I call my theory "creativity in a box." Picture a box, with a creative idea at the center, and its size represented by the finances—how much the idea will cost to produce. In business, the trick is not only to come up with the idea, but to determine the size of the box—how much should be spent on it. This, of course, is based on how much profit you think it can make. Now, the most important thing that goes into creative success is having the people who can come up with the great ideas. But the next most important thing is often overlooked: having people who will enable those great ideas, and support those creative people—manage the creativity with real economic foresight. It's not an easy thing to do—in every instance, it is a lot safer to say no, and it takes a special and gutsy kind of leader to say yes. That leader alongside me, that coach and that cheerleader at Disney, was Frank. Together with the countless movie and television show ideas and theme parks that he helped push forward, he supported me on smaller but memorable decisions as well, like the use of top-quality architects for new hotels at our theme parks and other projects, and moving Disney animation into the computer age at a large expense. He also was passionate about our compulsive desire for corporate synergy, even having the audacity to name a hockey team after one of our movies (*The Mighty Ducks*). Frank was the one who helped push, pull, and enable all those ideas, managing the managers of all of creative and financial in the boxes of our projects. He was the catalyst who found a way to bring them to life. And he was thrilled to do it.

Still, all this was just one part of his job. Frank also handled . . . well, everything else.

■   ■   ■

It's inevitable in any work environment, and certainly all the more so in Hollywood: there are always going to be people working for you upset about something. At Disney, they went to Frank, and he would take them to lunch and find a solution to the problem. (He'd also eat off their plates. Seriously. Frank was the quickest and most voracious eater I've ever met, and had no qualms about eating off someone's plate, even if he barely knew them.) When he got back, I'd always hear about what had transpired, and how Frank had found a way to make everyone happy again. He liked helping people, and he was a great problem-solver. He had to fire our general counsel—and the next day the guy asked Frank to be best man at his wedding. I still don't understand how that happened. And these kinds of issues were only one kind of problem Frank solved: he also would plunge himself into areas of crisis—like the French outcry over the American cultural "invasion" of Disneyland Paris, and our early financial situation (*situation* defined as excessive costs against disappointing revenue) with the park—and find paths to solutions. Nearly two decades after his work on that project, I'm sure he'd be proud to know that Disneyland Paris is not only still the most-visited destination in all of Europe, but profitable as well.

The fact that Frank did so much of this type of work, I think, is why a somewhat clichéd character portrait of him as a buttoned-down, dealing-only-with-the-boring-details executive emerged. But you don't solve as many problems as Frank did, and keep peace in such a large kingdom, with a quiet and nondescript style. An energy and unpredictability emanated from him every time he walked into a room, sat down at a dinner table, or offered a hearty hello to you in a 2:00 a.m. phone call (he was notorious for "forgetting" time differences when he traveled, but easy to forgive because of the excitement that always accompanied the call). He was also willing to do anything to make a deal. One famous story that dates back to his days at Warner Bros. involves his negotiations with Clint Eastwood (who'd later become a close friend) for *Dirty Harry*. To settle a sticking point holding up the deal, Frank agreed to play tennis against Clint to settle it. (Clint won.) Even when it didn't involve playing a movie star in tennis, Frank embraced the process, and always wanted to find a way to finish a deal, make a movie—start something new.

At Disney, we used to joke that along with president and chief operating officer, another of his unofficial titles was vice president of *mishegoss*, a Yiddish word that essentially means "craziness." But amid that craziness was one simple constant: a real sense of what was right. To this day, I've never heard anyone say that Frank Wells did them wrong, and I don't think I ever will. When something about a deal or opportunity or recommendation didn't feel quite right ethically, when it didn't pass our institutional judgment—whether legal or not—we'd pass. We knew that a lawyer's justification wasn't necessarily real justification. Frank didn't care if we were told others were doing it, or it was the accounting fashion of the day; if it wasn't right, it wouldn't sell, and it was not for us. I called it the "smell test"; an odor is an odor. Frank called it ethics. Go to Frank's office, come up with a solution, and you'd walk out knowing you were doing the right thing. On our first afternoon at Disney, Frank asked me to write a $15,000 check to the company—in case for some reason there was any kind of clerical error with our expenses, we had already handled that up front with the company. We did that every year, knowing that being Caesar's wife—above suspicion—was the right kind of model, for both moral and practical reasons. Somehow in school, you take a test and are later graded on it. Often in business, you're graded before you actually take the test. And always in business, there's a more practical argument for being ethical, and even for telling the truth: morality pays. It just does. And it's also so much easier to remember the truth.

Maybe the most important thing Frank did as the "VP of *mishegoss*" was to use his platform to execute our maniacal desire for synergy across all company lines. I insisted that each division "help the other fellow," an archaic and clichéd but true virtue I had learned at summer camp decades earlier (chronicled in my book *Camp*, which you can get on Amazon or eBay for probably three dollars—or less). For the Disney company, "help the other fellow" meant the movie division would create a film . . . that could be become a theme park ride or attraction . . . that could become a consumer product . . . that could become a television show . . . that could become a film sequel . . . that could become a cable show . . . that could become an international attraction . . . that could be remade as a foreign film . . . that could be turned into a musical . . . it goes on and on. But to accomplish that, everybody had to cooperate with each other, with no place for jealousy, and no competition between divisions.

That's an unlikely reality in corporate America. When I worked at Gulf & Western, it had been easier to buy a book from Simon & Schuster, a GW company, if you were outside the company than it would be if you were at Paramount, another GW company. But at Disney, we worked things differently. The Disney Channel could never pay as much to air a Disney animated movie as another cable channel, not owned by Disney, could. But we wanted to build the Disney Channel. So how do you deal with intercompany charges? How would the movie division be expected to take less from another Disney division than from an outside company? And what about our profit participants—were they expected to suffer? All conflicts, confusions, or compromises of this sort went to the VP of *mishegoss*. He simply decided what was fair and just and wise, and that was that. If nothing else, all that synergy was the basis for the construction of the Disney brand, and years later the ESPN and ABC brands. So, as everyone around him worked passionately to succeed, Frank Wells made sure their success didn't get in the way of the overall success of the company.

I suppose there are elements of this portrayal that might offer images of a calming, sage, King Solomon–like force in the executive suite. But I really think that's a disservice to Frank's legacy, and also misleading when trying to figure out why our partnership worked so well. First, as I've mentioned, Frank was creative, and also involved in creative decisions every day at the company. But second, and more critically, it suggests that we were a yin-and-yang pair, focusing on our differences, and I think that undercuts the most important element of our partnership: no one could get between us. How many companies have crumbled because of tension and weak relationships between people at the top of the company? At Disney, every meeting I was in, Frank heard about from me afterward. Every meeting he was in, he'd tell me about. Early on, people would certainly try to manipulate one of us against the other—in most cases not so much because of ill will as because they wanted to get closer to us. It was not the way to go. When it happened, I would tell people the same thing my father had told me years earlier, when I had told my mother something, and insisted to her, "You can't tell my father." He'd say, "Don't ever tell your mother something you think she's not going to tell me—because she'll tell me.

Remember, she's my wife, you're my son." As a kid, I may have felt betrayed, yet I was secure in knowing my parents were truly together; their marriage would eventually last fifty years. Now, as an adult, seeing a clear parallel in my job, I realized more than ever that it was a good sort of betrayal. Nothing should have come between my mother and father, and nothing should have come between Frank and me. Even if our titles were different, in the executive suite we operated as a single unit, keeping nothing from each other.

Earlier in my career, I'd had something similar with Barry Diller, but that had been developed in the boiler room of the entertainment industry when we were just in our mid-twenties, and as I recounted earlier, it was an alliance almost fostered by our own Darwinian competitiveness—by realizing we could best survive by working together. With Frank, of course, accepting the job at Disney was accepting the partnership, and all I had to do was follow his lead. Never was there a moment wasted on questioning motives, on fretting about who got credit for what, on worrying that in the future, he would be tired of standing in the public shadows. For Frank, the partnership always came first, and he was thrilled for it to be that way. Recently, I found a letter Frank wrote to Jane and me in 1989, five handwritten pages of appreciation for what we had done at Disney together, but as ever, deflecting the credit away from himself and noting, to both Jane and me, that he and his wife, Luanne, wanted to "acknowledge . . . our feelings about you both and what you've done for Disney and, derivatively, for our family as well."

■   ■   ■

It's eerie to go through the folder that I saved from April 11, 1994, a warm California spring afternoon that was the culmination of an awful two weeks I will never forget. That Easter Sunday, March 27, had been a rare day of relaxation for me; I had played a round of golf with my middle son, the last time, incidentally, I ever played golf. I had been getting ready to sit down for a family event hosted by my oldest son when the phone rang. It was my secretary Lucille Martin, which was strange because she almost never interrupted me during a family dinner.

"Michael," she said, "Frank is dead."

More than eleven years earlier, he had returned from his global climbing expedition, but he had never stopped looking for adventures outside the Disney lot. Climbing, hiking, skiing—you name it, Frank loved to do it. It made sense; after all, in the office, he was a guy who loved challenges, teamwork, and the satisfaction of succeeding at something truly difficult, and even dangerous. He had spent Easter weekend heli-skiing—taking helicopters to difficult peaks, and then hopping out and skiing down them—in Nevada. After a great day of skiing, on the way back, his helicopter had crashed. The pilot and all but one passenger had died. Another helicopter transporting the other skiers, on which were Frank's son, Kevin, as well as his old tennis and skiing partner, Clint Eastwood, had made it out.

Two weeks later, April 11, I found myself in the Disney lot, about to speak at the memorial service for the man who had become one of my closest friends, and who now, inexplicably, was gone. Just the Friday before he'd died, Frank, who was sixty-two, had told me he wanted to re-sign at Disney for another seven years, and that I should just tell him what deal I wanted him to have. He didn't need to try to climb Everest again, he said. "There are enough mountains ahead to have a great time scaling them at Disney." We had talked often, by the way, about how Frank should run for governor of California. He acknowledged to me that he would have loved being in office, but he didn't want to go through the negativity of running for it. He had never originally intended on staying at Disney more than five or ten years as president, but as he put it, he was just having too much fun. Looking through a copy of my speech at the memorial service that day, there are stories in there I'd forgotten, and others I could never forget. His son Kevin had shown me something he'd found in Frank's wallet, something he'd carried around for thirty years. It was a fortune from a fortune cookie, and it read, "Humility is the final achievement." There was so much more, but for Frank, that had always been paramount.

In the years following Frank's death, Disney continued to grow, most significantly through our acquisition of Capital Cities and ABC and ESPN. But it was never the same without Frank, and I was never able to find another partner quite like him. Frank Wells and I had ten great years together. I had smoothed the way for him to be successful, just as he smoothed the way for me. We strategized about how to keep our executives happy and our critics at bay. The years I worked with him were markedly different from the years I did not have Frank Wells as a partner. I'll never be as good politically inside a company or as effective at handling a sensitive personnel situation as Frank Wells and I were together. Frank was a much better corporate politician than I am. He handled Stanley Gold and Roy Disney the way the great Venezuelan conductor Gustavo Dudamel handles the Los Angeles Philharmonic. Alone, when Frank was not my partner, I stumbled politically several times. But when we were together, we kept the ship sailing even in rough waters.

Because Hollywood always loves a good story, the tales of the other partnerships I tried have been told before. Jeffrey Katzenberg, who had done terrific work alongside me for nearly two decades at both Paramount and Disney, left the company when he didn't get Frank's job and after Roy Disney demanded he be fired. A year later, we hired Michael Ovitz, the head of Creative Artists Agency, who had been a business friend of mine in Los Angeles for years, to be Frank's replacement. Fourteen months later, he was gone after the arrangement failed.

In the mid-1990s, Bob Iger became president of the company, and eventually my successor. Bob was the closest thing I had to Frank as a partner at Disney. As with Frank, there was roughly a ten-year age difference between Bob and me—except this time, I was older. He came to the company from ABC in the 1996 Capital Cities merger, with a background in television. Over the next nine years, he eagerly soaked up an education in the movie business, theme park business, consumer product business, and more. Often during our time together, we would trade phone calls and e-mails when no one else was awake. Just a few weeks ago, Bob sent me an e-mail that I noticed was written at four thirty in the morning. "I notice you're still up before the rest of the world," I wrote back to him. "I remember getting to work in New York and you were still up in L.A.," he responded. "That was almost fifteen years ago! How did that happen? Time flies."

Today at Disney, like Frank and me, he is carrying on Walt's legacy with style and grace. The workload at Disney is enormous—I hope he finds a partner as good as the one I had.

In many ways, that history and that success have their roots in that first meeting at Stanley Gold's house. In the ten years I worked with Frank Wells, I asked him about that afternoon many times. I asked him why he had been so agreeable to letting me be sole CEO. The answer he always gave me was almost too simple. He said any disagreement at that point would have kept us from getting off on the right foot. Like an amazing chess player, he was already looking ahead.

2

WARREN BUFFETT AND CHARLIE MUNGER

"Warren and I are kind of an historical accident. It's not a standard model."

Through all the deals, all the companies, all the money, all the stock, all the interviews, all the plainspoken advice, all the good spells, and even the few bad ones, there's one thing everyone should know about Warren Buffett.

The man is having fun.

At eighty years of age, Warren is the rare senior citizen who eats as much candy (chocolate is his fancy) and drinks as much Coke (cherry, not diet) as he wants. We met up for our conversation about this book in an airport, and as he greeted me—excited as ever—he went straight for a nearby ice cream sandwich. The economy was in shambles, his company, Berkshire Hathaway, was a few weeks away from announcing that it had had the worst year in its history, and flights were delayed hours because of snow, but to be with Warren, you wouldn't have known it. He talked excitedly about ways the economy could be fixed, and spoke with real concern about the millions of people who were hurting, and how they could be helped.

He also talked, as he often does, about his businesses. Something you can never forget about Warren is that he is a businessman in the most classic sense, and through Berkshire, he owns literally dozens of companies, from insurance companies (Geico) to underwear companies (Fruit of the Loom) to paint companies (Benjamin Moore) to restaurant chains (Dairy Queen) to airlines (NetJets) and furniture stores and jewelry shops and more. Berkshire also has major stakes in corporations like Coca-Cola, Wells Fargo, and the Washington Post Company. It was the middle of February that day in the airport, the day before Valentine's Day, and a day after I broke my foot walking in Washington, D.C., talking on the phone and to my wife at the same time while checking e-mails on my BlackBerry and not seeing the end of the sidewalk. Talk about a twenty-first-century injury! After the obligatory sympathy for my foot, Warren talked about See's Candy, his chocolate business, and how See's was having its biggest day of the year, with thousands, if not millions, of men all across the country scrambling to get their wives and girlfriends gifts at the last minute. Warren talked, and as always, I learned.

"The man just looks at the positive side of everything," I thought to myself, making a mental note to consider his example the next time I got frustrated at the office. It's a kind of fun that doesn't just come from having a lot (okay, a tremendous amount) of money; believe me, I've met plenty of people with more money than they could ever spend who are miserable. It's a different kind of fun, a fun that comes from being able to share success—and, just as important, failure—with someone else.

"You've got to enjoy it," Warren told me that day. "It's crazy. I would have had a lot of fun over the years, but not nearly as much fun without Charlie."

Charlie is Charles T. Munger, Warren Buffett's sidekick, confidant, intellectual kindred spirit, and best friend. Officially, Charlie is the vice chairman of Berkshire Hathaway. Unofficially, and more notably, Charlie has been Warren's partner in one way or another for pretty much everything he's done over the past fifty years. If you follow the business world, and Berkshire, closely, you know who Charlie is, but if you're just a casual observer, you may never have heard of the man, which is fine with him. Still, make no mistake: every business move Buffett makes comes after close consultation with Munger.

The partnership has added up to one of the most successful runs in business in American history. But just as significantly, as Warren says, "With Charlie, it's basically been nothing but a good time."

■　　■　　■

Officially, when you consider all of the businesses it controls, Berkshire Hathaway has thousands of employees scattered throughout the country and the world. But in Omaha, Nebraska, the company's headquarters is modest and nondescript, with just a few dozen employees, including, of course, Chairman Buffett.

"Take a look at this," Warren said to me recently, reaching into his back pocket and pulling out an old-fashioned pocket date book, the kind people used to carry when a blackberry was something you ate, not something you charged at night. "It's completely empty. I just sit in my office and read all day."

I tried to call his bluff. "C'mon, Warren, it's not completely empty," I said as I took the small book from his hand to thumb through. I found an appointment filled in after a few pages.

"That's one of my college days," he explained. "I have six business schools come in, limited to about thirty students each, and I do a daylong seminar thing. I do about half a dozen of them a year. Panel in the morning, question-and-answer, they take pictures with me, and so forth. I love it."

"Do you ever identify a kid who's clearly really talented, and hire him to come to Omaha to work for you after graduation?" I asked.

"I have, once or twice, but it really doesn't work out too well. There's just not that much to do. If I want to talk to somebody about something, I'll just talk to Charlie."

Charlie Munger and Warren Buffett grew up just a few miles from each other in Omaha, and as a teenager, Charlie actually worked for a short time at Warren's grandfather's grocery store, Buffett and Son. But because they were six years apart in age (Charlie is the older one), their paths never crossed as kids. Instead, the first time Warren heard the name Charlie Munger was in the mid-1950s, at a meeting with a physician named Eddie Davis, whom Warren was recruiting for his fledgling investment business. Warren was in Davis's house, giving a surely passionate sales pitch to convince the doctor to let the twenty-six-year-old future whiz kid invest his money. But as he gave Dr. Davis his best shot that day, the older man stood in the corner of his living room, seemingly barely paying attention, and leaving young Warren to address Mrs. Davis, his wife, who appeared much more engaged by the conversation. Finally, when Warren had just about exhausted himself, Mrs. Davis turned to her husband to get his thoughts.

"We'll give him a hundred thousand dollars," he said, suddenly looking up. "He reminds me of Charlie Munger."

Warren had no idea who Charlie Munger was, but it was an auspicious prologue to the relationship nonetheless.

The money did well (of course the investment would be worth billions today), and Dr. Davis would invest more with the young Nebraskan over the next few years, once even mistakenly writing a check to "Charles Munger" instead of "Warren Buffett." And in 1959, the Davises succeeded in bringing the two men together.

Munger had been living in Los Angeles, rising to prominence there as a young Harvard-trained lawyer, all the while spending time on side deals and outside work to augment his income and reach his candidly declared goal of becoming a very rich man. When his father passed away, he returned to Omaha to tend to the estate, and Neal Davis, the son of Dr. Davis and Charlie's childhood best friend, insisted on bringing together the two men who reminded so many people of each other. So a lunch was scheduled at the Omaha Club. Sure enough, the two men took to each other instantly; Warren once told me that as soon as he saw Charlie "rolling around on the floor laughing at his own jokes," he knew they'd get along great. A few nights later, before Charlie left town, the men got together again with their wives in tow, and for the second straight meal, stayed at the table talking long after the waiter had cleared the table.

It was 1959; the men stayed closely in touch through old-fashioned snail-mail letters. Charlie was the older man, but Warren was the one succeeding in a more substantial way, at least if substantial meant accumulating some wealth.

" 'Charlie,' I'd write," Buffett told me, " 'law is okay as a hobby, but a guy with your brains, you're wasting your time. You've got to manage money.' "

And gradually, Warren pulled his new best friend into the investment business.

"It made no difference if we weren't investing together in the same pot," says Warren. "If he was interested in something, and wanted to talk it over, I was as interested in it as if I had my whole net worth in it."

And over the next few decades, they'd talk over virtually all of their decisions and deals, and sometimes invest in the same companies, most substantially Blue Chip Stamps. They'd use that position to buy a series of other companies, including See's Candy, and in 1982 they finally officially joined together financially. Since then, Munger has been the vice chairman of Berkshire Hathaway, operating from his office in Los Angeles at the law firm he helped found, Munger, Tolles, & Olson. The pair's most well known public get-togethers have long been at Berkshire's annual meetings, gatherings in Omaha that shareholders and Buffett devotees attend with the zeal of a religious revival. Together, each year, Warren and Charlie hold court in front of thousands, offering a well-rehearsed and familiar brand of salt-of-the-earth midwestern ethos. Warren does most of the talking,

and when he's done making a point, he turns to Charlie for
an addendum. The response is always the same.

"I have nothing to add."

Nothing could be further from the truth.

■   ■   ■

The offices of Munger, Tolles, & Olson are located in downtown Los Angeles on Grand Street. Charlie Munger has not
actively practiced law there in several decades, but, in his
mid-eighties, he still dresses like a lawyer with his crisp suit
and tie. He has long had trouble with his eyes, and a few
decades ago, lost one of them. I bring this up only because
of the joy Warren took in telling me the story of Charlie pop-
ping out his glass right eye at the DMV in California for reasons that were lost amid my "You've got to be kidding me"
response. There are also Charlie's frequent appearances for
the Harvard Westlake School in Los Angeles, where he and
my wife share board seats. Some of the meetings are way up
at the top of the Los Angeles hills, along tiny windy roads.
And at the end of each one, close to midnight, Charlie exits
to his car and heads off into the night alone, eighty-six years
old, no driver, one eye, no request to be dropped off, and no
fear. The man in the thick glasses and pristine Brooks Brothers suit has a mind as sharp as it's ever been, and like his
partner, he favors simple and homespun over complicated
and pedantic.

"If you want to get a good partner, the way to do it is be a
good partner. Though Warren and I are kind of an historical
accident. It's not a standard model. It's a mental partnership,

an intellectual partnership. We don't even live in the same city, so we're not interfacing that much and so forth. This is like two academics who sort of stumble into the same ideas and like one another. It's quite peculiar."

So to hear him tell it, the conversation that began at the Omaha Club on that Friday afternoon in 1959 has just continued for half a century, with Charlie still in Los Angeles, and Warren back in Omaha. I've never been able to figure out exactly how often they talk—I imagine it varies somewhat—but apparently those conversations are the crux of the decision-making process of Berkshire Hathaway when it comes time to do a deal. Then again, the talks are also the culmination of what Warren and Charlie do when they're not on the phone with each other, which to hear them tell it, is very simple: they read.

"If Charlie and I were stranded together on a desert island," Warren says, "and we somehow had the Library of Congress available to us, we'd both be very happy for a long, long time."

"That's part of the secret," Munger says, a thousand miles away from his partner, but talking as if he's nodding along to what Buffett would say. "You could hardly find a partnership in which two people settle on reading more hours of the day than in ours."

"Look," Warren continues, "my job is essentially just corralling more and more and more facts and information, and occasionally seeing whether that leads to some action. And Charlie—his children call him a book with legs."

Maybe that's why both men agree it's better that they never lived in the same city, or worked in the same office. They would have wanted to talk all the time, leaving no time for the reading, which Munger describes as part of an essential continuing education program for the men who run one of the largest conglomerates in the world.

"I don't think any other twosome in business was better at continuous learning than we were," he says, talking in the past tense but not really meaning it. "And if we hadn't been continuous learners, the record wouldn't have been as good. And we were so extreme about it that we both spent the better part of our days reading, so we could learn more, which is not a common pattern in business."

It's not how you'd think it would work. You'd think Buffett and Munger would have the smartest young business school graduates locked to their desks, obsessing over figures and going blind in front of computer monitors, and then coming to them with proposals about which new companies and investments to look into.

"No," says Warren again. "We don't read other people's opinions. We want to think. We want to get the facts, and then think."

And when it gets to the thinking part, for Buffett and Munger, there's no one better to think with than their partners.

"Charlie can't encounter a problem without thinking of an answer," posits Warren. "He has the best thirty-second mind I've ever seen. I'll call him up, and within thirty seconds, he'll grasp it. He just sees things immediately."

But Charlie himself sees it as an acquired, rather than natural, genius, thanks to all the studying he does.

"Neither Warren nor I is smart enough to make the decisions with no time to think," Munger once told a reporter.

"We make actual decisions very rapidly, but that's because we've spent so much time preparing ourselves by quietly sitting and reading and thinking."

He added to that thought when I met with him in his office.

"Warren knows an amazing amount, and he thinks very rapidly, and he talks very persuasively. I'm very similar in many ways. You get two people like that who really like and trust one another, and have been together for a long time, you're going to learn a lot from each other, and you're going to advance faster. So the learning machine is working faster."

Any two businessmen, though, could talk over decisions on the phone, no matter how big, and not have the track record Buffett and Munger have. Yes, these two are damn smart, but there's more to this match than that. This pair may both be fans of campy jokes, and may say they think the same way, but their differences—or more specifically, their different roles in this partnership—are integral to their success.

■   ■   ■

We'll start here: Charlie isn't just a partner, he is a teacher. Early in his career, Buffett was a strict and passionate disciple of a Columbia economics professor named Ben Graham, whose theory of investing advocated buying stock in companies selling for less than their assets were worth, and then, when the market price of these companies improved, selling them. Professor Graham will always be one of the most important people in the Warren Buffett biography, but

Charlie Munger added another component to the Buffett, and Berkshire, strategy: buy and hold. Buy strong, well-run companies, and hold on to them for the long run.

For Charlie, that may have been common sense, and it also may have been because of the simple way he learned about money and investing: he taught himself. During World War II, which came in the middle of his time at the University of Michigan, he enlisted in the service, but attended the University of New Mexico and Cal Tech on the side, earning credits in meteorology. After the war, he found a way to get himself into Harvard Law School without technically ever getting his undergraduate degree. Then, once he was a lawyer, to hear Warren tell it, he got frustrated "because he thought he was smarter than everyone else he was working for. So he decided he was going to do something smart for his most important client—himself. He was going to sell himself what he deemed the best hour of the day to work—six to seven in the morning—and think about nothing else besides matters for this client—himself—during that time. And through those surely intense early-morning sessions with himself, he got himself into real estate, built some apartments, and expanded his moneymaking beyond the law." Soon after, in Omaha, he met Warren, one of the few people on earth who shared his rabid hunger for knowledge and unending desire to learn. And the self-taught Harvard graduate, if there is such a thing, convinced the hotshot young investor of the virtues of a new, if totally logical, investment strategy: buy companies that are well run and well conceived. Their value will hold up and, in times of prosperity, grow.

"Charlie didn't go to business school," continues his partner, "but he was a natural. As a young lawyer, he always wanted to know as much about the business of his clients as possible—and eventually, would feel he knew more than the client."

In the years since his salad days as an attorney, and since that early lesson in investing, Charlie has continued to learn, which fits perfectly into the structure of his partnership with Warren.

"He works harder," says Munger about Buffett, very matter-of-factly. "I have always wanted to improve what I do, even if it reduces my income in any given year. And I always set aside time so I can play my own self-amusement and improvement game."

That self-amusement and improvement game is chiefly about learning. Charlie's idol is Ben Franklin, perhaps the most celebrated Renaissance man in American history. Charlie's friends and family even cajoled him into publishing a book called *Poor Charlie's Almanack: The Wit and Wisdom of Charles T. Munger*, in the model of Franklin's classic *Poor Richard's Almanack*. It's been sold at Berkshire's annual meetings, a five-hundred-page coffee-table-size volume filled with various Mungerisms like "Take a simple idea and take it seriously," and "The way to win is to work, work, work, and hope to have a few insights." In following the example of Ben Franklin, Charlie has never stopped learning, even into his eighties. And all that knowledge means that when you ask Charlie about something, he's much more likely than not to know what he's talking about. And he uses that vast array of knowledge in his decision-making. Charlie has something he calls "The Lollapalooza Effect." No, it has nothing to do with rock music. In the *Almanack*, it's defined as "the critical mass obtained via a combination of concentration, curiosity, perseverance, and self-criticism, applied through a prism of multidisciplinary models." In other words, it's the process of coming to a decision after examining any number of factors in any number of areas. I have personal experience here, as my wife has for those fifteen years been with Charlie on the board of the Harvard Westlake school. Once, after Charlie made a very generous donation to build a science building, Jane asked me to loan Disney's head architectural planner to the school to offer some design choices. I did. Charlie was not very interested. He just went ahead and helped design the building himself. So yes: this is a guy who donates buildings to schools—and then helps in all aspects of the process. The school, incidentally, loves the building.

Some teachers nurture their pupils, encouraging them along the way. Charlie may not exactly be the nurturing type, but he is a teacher and a collaborator who is far from a superficial cheerleader. Quite frankly, the last thing Warren needs is someone encouraging him. Buffett has been quoted himself as saying, "CEOs get into trouble by surrounding themselves with sycophants. You're not going to get a lot of contrary thinking." Charlie is anything but that. You will get contrary thinking with Charlie.

"It's beneficial," he says, "to have a partner who will say, 'You're not thinking straight.' When I call Charlie with an idea, he has three reactions. One is, 'Warren, that's a dumb idea.' Then, we put one hundred percent of our net worth into the idea. If it's, 'Warren, that's one of the dumbest ideas I've ever heard,' we put half of our net worth into the idea. And if it's, 'You've gone out of your mind, and I'm going to have you committed,' then we pass."

He's laughing as he says it, but you get the sense there's a

lot of truth behind what he's saying. This is the partner serving as skeptic, hugely important in the business of investing. I got an up-close look at this aspect of their partnership
when Disney bought Capital Cities/ABC in 1996. I, of course,
was ecstatic about this great new property for Disney. Meanwhile, Berkshire Hathaway was the controlling shareholder
in Cap Cities, and in that we made half of the deal with Disney stock, I realized quickly Berkshire would become one of
our largest shareholders. That was great news for our company, but I knew Charlie hated the entertainment business.
I had heard many times in conversations with him over the
years in Los Angeles how he hated "the waste," "the lack of
stable management," "the insane fees paid to talent," and a
business run by "one's gut rather than one's mind." I was hoping—even praying—that Charlie knew that at Disney, and before that at Paramount, we tried to run things differently,
with intelligence in place of ego, but still I asked Warren the
day we closed the deal for his thoughts on the future of their
investment.

"Are you planning, Warren, to hold your Disney stock after
the deal closes?" I asked.

"Well," he quickly responded, "I never make a decision to
sell and buy the same asset on the same day." That was it. But
I knew it was only a matter of time until Charlie's influence
would prevail here. Berkshire reduced its holdings in Disney
stock several years later, quietly and with no negative publicity. I wasn't angry at Warren, or Charlie. Warren had slyly
hinted what would probably happen in a way that actually
made me like him more. What a great attribute—to like a
man when he gives you bad news as much as when he gives
you good news. It reminds me of Frank Wells.

In my conversation with Warren, he told me about one time when he called up Charlie with an idea, saying they should buy stock in the Pittsburgh and West Virginia Railway. The response was less than enthusiastic.

"Well, I don't like railroads," Charlie started. "I don't like businesses with a lot of labor content. I particularly don't like when they're unionized. I don't like capital-intense businesses. I particularly don't like eastern railroads. But if you are telling me that you've researched this thing from A to Z, that you'll follow it twenty times a week and you'll keep track of it and take full responsibility for it . . . then I'll just shut my eyes and say no."

In this instance, the chairman listened to his partner—though several months later, he did make a big railroad purchase, paying $26 billion for the Texas-based Burlington Northern Santa Fe.

But you get a sense of how these conversations go, always with a verbal twist at the end, almost as if a playwright had written the dialogue.

"You have to have someone who tells the truth," says Buffett. "There's just no way that Charlie would not tell me the truth."

Munger's role as the ombudsman fits him well; though both men admit they will exaggerate their differences for amusement from time to time, generally, Charlie is more pessimistic, and Warren more optimistic.

"Charlie thinks exactly like I do," says Warren, "but he puts things through a tougher filter than I do. There are only two things he's ever liked better than I liked that we've done. One was the tool company Iscar. I loved it—but when Charlie falls in love with something, forget about it. Also, there's a deal with a Chinese car company, BYD, we did recently. I wasn't so sure about it. Charlie tells me the Chinese guy running the company, Wang Chuanfu, is the Henry Ford of China. I'm still not jumping. Then he says he's the Thomas Edison of China. Still no. Then, the Bill Gates of China. Nope. Then, his trump card. He's the Warren Buffett of China!"

But usually it's Warren doing the selling and Charlie the listening—and the questioning, playing the role of gentle skeptic. In fact, Warren once told me with a laugh that a familiar refrain at the end of a Buffett-Munger conversation is Charlie saying to Warren, "Look, you'll end up agreeing with me because you're smart . . . and I'm right."

Still, often, Warren gets his way, and Berkshire Hathaway takes a risk that Buffett wants and Munger fears.

■   ■   ■

Warren told me another story when we chatted. Several years ago, Charlie Munger was testifying at an arbitration hearing, and getting grilled about a recent board meeting. He claimed he didn't recall what the lawyer was asking him about. "Mr. Munger," the lawyer said, "you are reputed to have a very good memory. Are you really telling me you don't remember it?"

"Well," Charlie is said to have responded, "I only listen when I'm the one talking."

Indeed, Munger is not the standard model for the kind of partner who prefers to lie low and fade into the background. Everywhere else in his life, Charlie Munger plays the alpha role—with his family, in board meetings for the variety of companies and charities with which he's involved, with me when I visited him at his office. I usually don't have trouble getting a word into a conversation. Talking to Charlie Munger is different—I did a lot more listening than talking.

"That's one of the beauties of the partnership," says Charlie. "I am in so many activities where I am the dominant personality. Most people do not 'fit into' that mode—they can *only operate* in that mode. Yet I am particularly willing to play the secondary role. Warren's a more able man in doing what we're doing, so it's the appropriate response. There are some times you should be first, some times you should be second, and some times you should be third."

"In fifty years," says Warren, "the guy has never second-guessed me in any way, shape, or form. There's never any 'I told you so,' or anything like that. He has absolutely no problem being number two with me. And if we disagree, we probably won't do a deal, but if I decide to do it, that's fine. He is behind me one hundred percent."

Even if something doesn't work?

"Absolutely. And it doesn't work sometimes. He just is *with* me, basically."

Which means they'd pretty much do anything for each other.

"It's a little like something he told me one time about his dad," says Warren. "Charlie said if he came home when he was a kid, at midnight, woke up his dad, and said, 'Dad, I need your help on something, I've got this body in the basement, help me dig a hole to bury it in,' he said that his dad would go down there and help him bury the thing. And just go back to bed afterwards. [Please note that the previous sentence used the word *if.*] And that's the way Charlie is with me.

And incidentally I feel the same way about him, too." (Fortunately Charlie's interactions with associates have never called for him to literally or figuratively kill anybody!)

"Years ago, I bought into US Air, and it was in trouble as the ink was drying on the check," Warren remembers about a deal that he's called his worst mistake. His partner had not supported it.

"But Charlie went on the board with me, flew back and forth to Washington—he worked harder on that deal than any other."

Through it all, both men claim they've never had an argument that escalated to anything more than an intellectual disagreement. Amazingly, you'll find most of the partnerships in this book say the same thing. It's eye-opening, but to me, having seen dozens of these types of partnerships fail in Hollywood and beyond, I have long focused on the unlikely scenario of such a classic "number one" in Charlie willingly playing the clear "number two" role. Especially considering that Charlie has been happily quoted by many friends as saying, "Humility is a trait I admire greatly—even if I am deprived of it."

"It's not letting ego or jealousy or your own personality take over," he says. "Intelligence takes over."

But is it about intelligence, or is it about the qualities of successful people that don't so much have to do with brainpower as moral power?

At the annual meeting, one of the many routines these partners use as a teaching tool for the shareholders has been a review of the seven deadly sins. Gluttony? Not something you want, but there's an upside to it, at least in the short term. Lust? There's some real upside to that, the two men chuckle.

The list goes on . . . each sin, at least in the short term, has some enjoyment attached to it. Except one: envy, which just makes you sick. It's a complete waste—there's not even any short-term benefit that would come back to haunt you.

"I have never in fifty years observed any action of Charlie's that would indicate he possesses the ability to be jealous or envious," says Warren. "He just doesn't have it."

Let's go back to those workshops Warren runs for students a few times a year. The focus isn't on the secrets of investing, it's on something more important: the ethics of business. He plays a game: each student is asked to pick a classmate—and they will get 10 percent of that classmate's earnings the rest of their life. Which classmate will they pick, and why?

"Are you going to pick the one with the highest IQ?" asks Buffett. "Are you going to pick the guy who can throw a football the farthest? The one with the highest grades? What qualities will cause you to pick them?"

Next, the stakes change: the students can sell short (i.e., bet against the prospects for success), changing the stakes of the game completely; the students now basically have to choose who would do the worst. Will they choose the student with the lowest IQ, the lowest grades? The qualities of the people they pick for each scenario are written down in separate columns—the positive qualities on the left, the negative ones on the right. Inevitably, the most useful of them have nothing to do with IQ and grades; the attributes people write down have to do with generosity and kindness and integrity. The question is then asked: Which qualities on the left-hand side are you incapable of having, and which on the right-hand side are you incapable of exorcising from yourself?

To Buffett, the answer is none. These qualities are choices

people make. People decide whether or not to be generous, they decide whether or not to take credit for things they didn't do, whether or not to keep score in life, whether or not to be envious. And when you look at it, all of these types of qualities are achievable, and much more important than whether you know modern portfolio theory. In the end, the qualities you want from the person you're buying 10 percent of are the qualities you want to develop in yourself.

And, of course, the qualities you want in a partner.

"You're looking for three things, generally, in a person," says Buffett. "Intelligence, energy, and integrity. And if they don't have the last one, don't even bother with the first two. I tell them, 'Everyone here has the intelligence and energy— you wouldn't be here otherwise. But the integrity is up to you. You weren't born with it, you can't learn it in school.'"

Warren was fortunate to be able to get early lessons in integrity from his father, a U.S. congressman for several years when Warren was growing up. Being able to get that kind of ethical education from one's family can be paramount in any personal journey. Years ago, my high school headmaster, Bruce McClellan, wrote my father an all-encompassing letter about my progress as a fifteen-year-old that contained the following: "Mike was not always cooperative in the necessary discipline of group living. He far too frequently tries to play the angles to get away with what he can. He has been rather loose about smoking rules. His excuse when confronted is that 'others do it,' which is a weasel defense. It would be out of character for me not to mention Mike's throwing a cherry bomb (prohibited) out of a third-floor window, but also out of character for Mike not to have thrown it." It's enough to say, the day after that letter arrived was the worst conversation I ever had with my father. But when I went to bed, I found the letter on my pillow, with a sentence underlined by my father. "He is delightfully full of life and unofficially I regard such incidents . . . within reason . . . as symptoms of good health rather than original sin."

I still have that letter and remember it word for word. And it was with that letter that I began my journey of learning the value of integrity, the different kind of missteps you can make as a young person, the mistakes that hurt people and those that are harmless and take a backseat to the kind of integrity that's really important. And that kind of integrity is at the center of why Charlie Munger and Warren Buffett are such perfect partners. They have complete trust, complete faith, and complete belief in each other. And that reverberates through every phone call they have, every deal they discuss, and every decision they make.

"You cannot keep score," says Warren. "It just doesn't work with the best of human relationships. It shouldn't be even suppressed—it should be something that doesn't even exist."

And to compare them to the students, both Buffett and Munger were born very smart, and born with a lot of energy. The integrity, however, they say they chose.

"You decide to be dishonest, stingy, uncharitable, egotistical, all the things people don't like in other people," argues Warren. "They are all choices. Some people think there's a limited little pot of admiration to go around, and anything the other guy takes out of the pot, there's less left for you. But it's just the opposite."

Buffett and Munger do not claim that their partnership is even—they don't have to. As Warren says, one guy has to let the other guy do the dance, but with these two dancers, that's the way it should be. After my great experience with Frank Wells, with Frank happy to cede much of the spotlight, you'd think I would have always known this, but I didn't. Warren tried to tell me years ago, soon after Frank died, when I asked him if he thought a partnership between me and Michael Ovitz, the head of Creative Artists Agency and the media-anointed most powerful man in the entertainment business at that time, would work. He shocked me by saying no (everyone else was telling me it was a great idea).

"Both of you want the spotlight," I remember him saying bluntly. "Take Charlie and me: I want the spotlight, but he doesn't. So it works. And Charlie has integrity, which further ensures that it works. You will be in conflict with Ovitz from day one, and you will never trust him. Don't do it."

I did. And Warren was right—the partnership lasted barely a year.

"Warren and I think the same way," says Charlie. "It's very peculiar for two people this old to be doing something this long. But Warren likes doing it. And I like doing it. It's much more fun, two than one. When something good happens, everybody wants to call somebody. It's a human need—we're social animals. Even Einstein wouldn't have been successful if there weren't other people he didn't talk to all the time. Total isolation does not work. You need interaction, putting your own thoughts into expression; you learn things just from doing it."

Two of the smartest men you'll ever meet were born by historical accident just a few miles apart in the middle of America. They join forces, one up front, the other quietly but confidently in back, and set out to make more money, and better business, than anyone in the world. And they succeed, in part because of their intelligence, in part because of their energy, but really because of their shared integrity. They read, they study, they talk, and most important, they learn from and teach each other. With every decision they come to, and every deal they make, they see, as Michelangelo saw, "an angel in the marble and carve until they set her free."

"One plus one with Charlie and me certainly adds up to more than two," says Warren.

You've certainly heard many times that Warren Buffett is America's most respected businessman. Now, in case you didn't know, there's something else to learn from him.

He didn't get there by himself.

3

BILL AND MELINDA GATES

"Be smarter faster."

She says that for the first three minutes, they always think the same thing. But only for three minutes.

Melinda Gates, cochairwoman of the largest private foundation of the world, walks into a room in a country somewhere with a roster of ministers and high-ranking officials, sits down at a table across from them, and they all give her a look that says the same thing: "I guess we got the wife."

They assume that because her husband, Bill Gates, grew one of the greatest fortunes in the history of business, the foundation that bears both their names is really just his. They assume that she is merely along for the ride, sent by the real boss in his stead to make an appearance, shake a few hands, pose for a few pictures, and return to her hotel. They assume that in the ultra-high-stakes, ultra-complicated world of global health, she is at the table only as a surrogate for her husband.

But as I said, she knows all those assumptions will last only about three minutes.

Because in those three minutes, Melinda Gates shows them—in the nicest way possible—something else. Melinda was the valedictorian at her high school, Ursuline Academy in Dallas. She got her bachelor's and MBA at Duke in five years, and was a fast-rising star at Microsoft before she happened to meet and marry the founder of the company in 1994. And since then, in addition to raising the couple's three children alongside her husband, she's become an expert on improving education in America, and one of the world's experts on solving problems of global health.

What they don't know, they learn: that Melinda Gates is an equal partner. They did not just "get the wife."

"When we enter any room, it's clear, people want to hear from Bill," Melinda told me recently, seated next to her husband at the Sun Valley Resort in Sun Valley, Idaho, where I've spent five days with them and a couple hundred other people at Allen and Company's annual media and business conference, held each summer for the last several years.

"They think he's doing it all, and that's okay. That is just the state of affairs. But I think as soon as they start to hear me talk about the issues and talk about what's real and why we're doing it, they start to realize, 'Oh, okay, we get it. This is a partnership.' "

And it's a partnership at the heart of some of the most important work being done in the world today. With an asset value of well over $30 billion, the foundation donates over $3 billion a year to a variety of very carefully selected causes across the United States and the world. Bill and Melinda Gates are incredibly rational thinkers and givers, and have approached the phenomenal opportunity to make a profound difference with their money in a deliberate and purposeful way. The CEO of their foundation is a former high-ranking Microsoft executive, Jeff Raikes, and like Bill and Melinda, he works as if he's running a business—except here the goal is not to turn a profit, but to save and improve lives.

What they've already accomplished is eye-opening. They've funded research for a malaria vaccine that Gates has said can be successfully achieved within the next eight to fifteen years, and research for drugs to drastically reduce the risk of getting AIDS that he hopes could be available in several years as well. They have also fought other diseases that have largely been eradicated in the United States but still kill millions of children in Africa every year, like polio and measles, and ailments that are treated or even shrugged off here but kill there, like pneumonia and diarrhea. Also in Africa, they have invested money in agriculture, helping families farm, which helps them feed and support themselves, which in turn leads to better opportunities for children to get educated and lead better lives. Here in the United States, using similar logic, they've determined they can make the biggest impact—that is, improve the most lives—by bettering education. So they've distributed over $2 billion in grants to create better and smaller high schools all across the country, schools where students have tested better, and attended college in greater numbers.

Taking a cue from their friend Warren Buffett (whose role in the foundation cannot be understated, from his huge pledge in 2006 to his mentorship of both Bill and Melinda—more on what he's done later), Bill wrote his first annual letter to the public at the end of 2008. The letter expanded on all the achievements and progress the foundation had made, and yet was also realistic and candid about setbacks and disappointments. It also made clear that the man who per-sonified the computer revolution has found satisfaction in the next phase of his life, through the intellectual challenges of determining the most effective and efficient ways to help the world, and also through the opportunity to partner with his wife. For most American couples, the best products of the partnership of marriage are children. And nothing in a married partnership is more important. But Bill and Melinda Gates have two important products: their family, and their philanthropy.

"A special addition for me at the foundation is getting to work with Melinda," he wrote. "She and I enjoy sharing ideas and talking about what we are learning. When one of us is being very optimistic, the other takes on the role of making sure we're thinking through all the tough issues."

And after I spent an afternoon with both of them, asking them about their collaboration at the foundation and listen-ing to them constantly finish each other's sentences, it was clear to me just how complete their partnership is, and how important it is to the success of their work. They've been married since 1994, but the success of their partnership can actually be traced back much further, to childhoods that taught both of them the value of a close family, and to one of the most storied career ascents in the history of business.

For Bill Gates, a legend of the computer age, success in business, and his monumental rise, has consistently been based—always for the better, no matter the emotions, the deviations, the conflicts—on partnership. But it wasn't until recently that Gates realized that partnerships don't always have to take on the same shape.

■   ■   ■

Gates was nineteen years old when he decided that it was no longer a good use of his time to be a student at Harvard, and that he would be better served starting his own computer software company. This decision may sound like a sharp turn for the average college sophomore, but for Bill, it was a culmination of years of rabid devotion to the field that had become his passion. And something else is relevant, too: Gates wasn't operating alone.

In the late 1960s in Seattle, at the private Lakeside School in the northern part of the city, a group of strong math and science students had become interested in the rapidly growing study of computer science. Back then, of course, computers didn't resemble anything like the ultra-portable, ultra-personal machines we use today; they were huge machines available for use only in special labs. (When I met my wife—around this same time—she was a programmer at the second biggest computer installation in the world, the Metropolitan Life Insurance Company. She and twenty other programmers maintained and wrote the English-language program that the two hundred other programmers used to run the vast insurance company, where four 64K machines stretched from Twenty-third Street to Twenty-fourth Street on Madison Avenue in New York City.) Meanwhile, back in Seattle, to meet the growing interest of its students, the Lakeside

School soon began a relationship with a local enterprise that sold time on its computer to private companies. The business agreed to let the students "test" their machine for free. Soon a small group of kids were spending nearly all their free time there, including an eighth-grader named Bill Gates, whose brashness and brilliance ensured he'd have no problem fitting in with the upperclassmen. He quickly found kindred spirits in older students like Paul Allen, a guy two years older than him. Eventually, when the company decided there had been enough "testing" done, it began charging the students for the time they spent on the computer—which became no problem when the group broke the security code and found a way to work for free. They were soon caught and had to pay up, but it didn't make much of a difference; the company soon went out of business anyway.

Still, Gates, Allen, and their friends had caught the computer bug, and would not be stopped. The original group was four: Bill and Paul, and then Kent Evans, a classmate of Bill's, and Ric Weiland, another upperclassman. When Allen graduated from Lakeside and went to college at Washington State, Gates grew especially close to Evans, and the pair began working on a project commissioned by their school to create a computer program that designed student schedules. The two spent day and night working on the project for months, until tragedy struck: Kent Evans was killed in a hiking accident.

"I had never thought of people dying," Gates told *Time* magazine years later. "At the service, I was supposed to speak, but I couldn't get up. For two weeks, I couldn't do anything at all." Gates would never forget his friend, and years later, he'd return to Lakeside with Allen to donate a new math-science building to the school, dedicated to the memory of their "classmate, friend, and fellow-explorer, Kent Hood Evans."

When he regrouped, the prodigy returned to his incredibly prodigious work, collaborating with Allen away at college, long-distance. Gates was such a capable student in high school that he was allowed to pursue his own independent projects, and he and Allen spent several weeks during Gates's senior year working for a company that hired them to do work in Vancouver, Washington. The following fall, after being accepted into the Ivy League's three most prestigious schools, he enrolled at Harvard and quickly became the leader of a new group of computer whizzes there. His sophomore year, he met an unlikely match—a phenomenal math student and large, social personality who did everything on campus from manage the football team to publish the school paper. The guy's name was Steve Ballmer, and he quickly established a bond with Gates.*

For now, though, Paul Allen remained Gates's closest friend and collaborator. The pair discussed finding a job somewhere together, with Gates willing to take a leave of absence from Harvard. Instead, Allen ended up taking a job at Honeywell in Boston, and driving cross-country to live near his pal at school. Allen soon became a regular sight at the Harvard computer lab, and after reading an article in *Popular Electronics*, the pair became transfixed with the holy grail of computing: the personal "mini-computer." They read about a

---

* Ric Weiland, the fourth member of the original group, was one of the first employees of Microsoft. He left the company in 1988, mostly devoting himself to philanthropy, before committing suicide in 2006. He had bequeathed $65 million to gay rights and HIV organizations.

company based in New Mexico that was developing a model, and after writing a letter to the CEO, Paul found himself in Albuquerque making a presentation. (They had agreed that Paul would go, because he was more mature-looking, but Bill actually made the first phone call using Paul's name.) A few months later, Bill Gates took a leave from Harvard, and the two Seattle boys moved to New Mexico to continue working on the "holy grail" project. Soon, they'd branch out on their own to start the company that would become Microsoft.

■   ■   ■

"I've never done anything solo," Bill Gates told me in our conversation. "Except take tests. But with the exception of that, I would always seek someone out." It's clear from the early part of Bill's life that partnerships were integral to all that he did at warp speed. However, it could be debated whether he sought out those partnerships or they sought him out. Consider the mere nature of the work in those early days: there was just one big computer to work on, with all sorts of code to write, and thus a team effort required. In computer science, there was always someone—or more likely several people—to collaborate with, to teach, and to learn from. Even though he was younger than his partners at Lakeside, he was the one who emerged as the ringleader. No one was as intense as Gates, and often the toughest and most formidable personality wins, particularly at younger ages. He was two years younger than Allen, but clearly not intimidated. Friends like Ballmer were similarly taken by his strength of mind; when Gates returned to Harvard for a semester in his

junior year before dropping out for good, Ballmer successfully lobbied for his friend to gain entrance into his social
club, the Fox, hardly a joint populated by so-called computer
nerds. Gates wasn't shy about proclaiming his goals—among
them, to be successful, intellectually adventurous, and of
course rich—to those around him, and as if he were a jet
taking off at sonic speed, everyone seemed to want to come
along for the ride.

Not that the ride was so easy.

"I had to be the dominant partner," Gates admitted to me,
and he had to do it in more ways than one. When he and
Allen formalized their partnership agreement in 1977, they
settled on Gates getting a 64 percent share and Allen getting 36 percent. Originally, when they were just informally
aligned, Gates had had a bigger share, since Paul had been
working on several projects at once in Albuquerque, making his commitment to Microsoft technically part-time, but
when they signed a deal, Gates took an even bigger stake, on
the logic that he was dropping out of college and Allen was
already receiving a salary. They had known each other since
they were barely teenagers, but the tenacious and younger
Gates "had to be dominant."

Still, even if he had to be the senior partner, by his twenties, Gates did understand the value of having someone at
his side. He was attacking complex challenges in uncharted
engineering territory, and the simple bonus of having several
minds attack a problem at once would have been clear. And
then, once Microsoft grew and moved to Seattle from New
Mexico with more employees, narrowing that collaboration
down to one person whom you trusted, and who knew you
better than anyone, served a very useful managerial pur-

pose. Through those early years of Microsoft, into the 1980s, Paul Allen remained that partner for Bill Gates. But again, it wasn't easy. As much as any executive in the last several decades, Gates—particularly in his earlier days at Microsoft—was known for being demanding, and his personal interactions were famously marked by that attitude. For years, "That's the stupidest thing I've ever heard" was one of the most quoted Gates lines you'd hear coming out of Microsoft, although my guess is that he didn't say it often. If he didn't agree with you, he would let you know, and if he was disappointed with what you were doing, he'd let you know with certainty. I never saw that competitiveness in person, or that temper; never anything other than a gentlemanly seriousness, until a Disney meeting we had with Bill and a small group from his company in the 1990s. I innocently asked why Microsoft was not being a team player with an industry-standard project that seemed so obviously in everybody's interest. Bill was sitting silently in the meeting—actually testing out his new writable tablet notebook computer—when suddenly he jumped in, angrily, his voice at a higher decibel, proclaiming that they would never cooperate unless a Microsoft operating system was at the center of the technology. It hadn't occurred to me he would care, considering how small a deal this was.

It was at that moment I understood how competitive Bill Gates was. I wasn't upset; frankly, I was impressed. I remember thinking that the success of Microsoft now made total sense to me, and thinking of a Paul H. Dunn quote I'd always loved, that successful people don't fall to the top of a mountain. I can still hear that fierce competitiveness in Gates's voice.

Meanwhile, during those years, the person who no doubt had to deal with Gates the most intimately was Allen, his closest collaborator, the number two person at the company and his longtime partner. As Microsoft grew, Paul became known for his brainstorms and ability to imagine new products. As Gates put it at the time, "I guess you could call me the doer and Paul the idea man. I'm more aggressive and crazily competitive, the front man in running the business day-to-day, while Paul keeps us out in front in research and development."

In an interview with Gates biographers Stephen Mane and Paul Andrews, one Microsoft employee summed it up by saying, "Paul had an incredible amount of the initial vision of the company, and kept kind of pushing Bill around . . . by daring him into things and kind of goading him. And then Bill would come back, and they used to have these incredible fights all the time, just tantrums, and a lot of the tantrums and arguments resulted in very good decisions." This was one perception; my own suspicion is that this employee saw one "fight" and assumed this was what governed their working style. And my guess is this employee was not in the inner circle, and therefore didn't really get it. In any partnership, a "battle" can go only so far before it becomes a war. And Bill Gates and Paul Allen were never at war. There may have been yelling and disagreement, but it was effective because at the heart of the relationship was an understanding that this was how they communicated. And that understanding led to progress, and of course success.

Still, life frequently offers its own agenda. By 1982, as Microsoft continued to push forward at breakneck speed, Gates, Allen, and the rest of the Microsoft team were still pulling hundred-plus-hour weeks, weeks filled with those intense and emotional debates about ideas and products and everything in between. In September of that year, Allen felt some lumps in his neck and went to see a doctor. He had Hodgkin's disease, a treatable form of cancer. After weeks of grueling radiation therapy, he was cured, but had lost his taste for the pace of the Microsoft life. He resigned in March 1983, leaving Bill Gates without the partner with whom he'd started working on computers fifteen years earlier. Allen would remain a major shareholder, and would of course go on to invest billions of dollars in a variety of businesses, but never as successfully as with Bill Gates at his side.

Gates, meanwhile, did the only thing natural to him. He found another partner.

■   ■   ■

Steve Ballmer had originally joined Microsoft in 1980. After graduating from Harvard, he tried out a few different industries, including the movie business, which he decided wasn't worth starting in from the ground up. He was unsure of his next step when he visited his old college friend Bill Gates in Seattle. Gates was only twenty-four, but Microsoft was on its way, and it needed the help of someone like Ballmer, who might not have had any real computer experience but had the same mind for math and business as his friend, and also had his implicit trust. He came on as the assistant to the president, without any specifically defined role, which is typically a recipe for trouble. That said, he quickly made himself at home with an intense style that echoed Gates's.

By the time Paul Allen left the company three years later, Ballmer was running several different units, and he quickly stepped into the void as his old college buddy's new partner. He remained in a similar role until 2000, when he took over the CEO title, while Gates maintained his status as chairman and chief software architect.

There is a term you'll hear at Microsoft—bandwidth—that is used to refer to the amount of information transferred in someone's head or between two people having a conversation. Gates used it in our conversation to describe his relationship with Ballmer over the years.

"You just get so high-bandwidth," he said. "Steve and I would just be going from talking to meeting to talking to meeting, and then I'd stay up late at night, and write him five e-mails. He'd get up early in the morning and maybe not necessarily respond to them, but start thinking about them. And the minute I see him, he's [up at the office whiteboard], saying we could move this guy over here and do this thing here."

In the beginning of his computer career, Gates valued partners because they made him smarter—by putting two (or more) brains on a problem, you were more likely to solve it. Then, when it came to running a company, things got more complicated—but still, having a partner, trustworthy and as smart as him, was paramount. And through Gates's two partnerships—first Paul Allen, then Steve Ballmer—Microsoft may have had a few problems through its incredible success, but stability at the top was never an issue.

"The notion that anybody would actually think they could get between you when you have that kind of partnership [is preposterous]," Gates told me. "Your fun is actually coming from working with that other guy. Because we were living together, we were growing up together, we were feeling good together, and we were feeling bad together. There's some magic to that when you can find it. Nobody was confused— there was no number three."

Just as, at Disney, no one could get between Frank Wells and me, and no one could get between me and Barry Diller at Paramount, and no one could ever get between Warren Buffett and Charlie Munger, no one could ever get between Steve and Bill. They may not have agreed on everything, but in the end, there was that trust—which originated on the other side of the country over dining-hall dinners and late-night conversations at Harvard—that never disappeared. Of course, also significant was Steve's long-term understanding that while he was a partner, it was still Gates's company.

"Steve had accepted that he wasn't going to get the visibility, the glory, and the final decision on anything," Bill told me with frankness. "And I was good at saying, Steve, do you want to say anything more [while making decisions]? But I had to make the final decision."

When Ballmer took the CEO title, things changed somewhat, but Gates was still the senior partner. No matter how great any title sounds, Bill was still the founder. However, Bill was mellowing, and preparing ever so gradually for his departure from day-to-day operations. Like everything at Microsoft, the transition to make Ballmer the "A" partner and Gates the "B" partner was thought out and meticulously planned. But for a long time, it didn't quite work as they hoped.

"We learned more about how many rules we had been living by when we tried to flip it around after a couple of years,"

Bill continues. "Because I had gotten super-good at giving Steve last looks on everything, and then when Steve was put in charge, he didn't have any instinct to make me feel like, okay, I gave you that last chance." From my own experience at Disney, Paramount, and ABC, that lack of instinct is not surprising. My guess is, Steve did not forget to check with Bill for that "last look"; he simply wanted to be his own force. Sometimes a desire to appear to be the boss convinces people you really are not. Moving into control takes control.

A revealing *Wall Street Journal* article published in 2008, and featuring interviews with both men, illuminated the extent of the struggles in the year or so after Steve was named CEO. There was a meeting that ended with a shouting match and Gates storming out of the room after Ballmer defended some colleagues his longtime partner had criticized. There were also projects that suffered because the two executives couldn't figure out how to divide power. Eventually the Microsoft board got involved, with other executives confronting both Bill and Steve to let them know their struggles were affecting the company's performance. One of the longest and most successful partnerships in the history of modern business was on the verge of imploding.

Finally, in 2001, Gates and Ballmer had a long dinner at a restaurant in Seattle where they finally began in earnest the process of figuring out how this was going to work. Surely their modus operandi of pushing for territorial space through some confrontation had contributed to a serious breach, but the long trust they had cultivated won out. At the end of their dinner, they turned a corner, and the real road to shifting their relationship to a place where Steve would be a controlling partner, and Bill a supporting partner, began. In June

2008 Bill stepped away from day-to-day involvement with the company, leaving Steve to lead Microsoft, and perhaps find his own partner to help him. To hear Bill talk, it would be great for their company if he found one. In the end, Bill Gates will always be the founder of Microsoft, and will probably remain the largest shareholder for a long time. And that seems to now be enough for him.

"With technology companies, the CEO jobs are completely overspecified jobs," he says, sounding happy not to be one anymore. "You've got to have somebody—one person who you can really open up with, and be weak with, and be afraid with, and be out of control with, or screwed with. It helps to go through that together. Because you're the leader, and any weakness that comes from you, not to have that one other person to talk that stuff through with is very tough."

Bill, meanwhile, has a new partner in his new job, who told me with a grin that she's happy to join her husband at the office at this point in his life.

"I joke with Steve that he kind of got Bill ready for this partnership."

She might be right.

■   ■   ■

Melinda French was twenty-three years old when she first met Bill Gates at a Microsoft event. She was working for the company and soon found herself dating the boss. If this had its awkward moments, it was nothing Melinda couldn't handle. She had been a standout in high school and college, and was moving up the ranks at Microsoft in the division that handled information products like Encarta and Expedia when she decided to quit the company to begin a family with her new husband. Family was important to her; she had grown up in a close-knit middle-class household in Dallas, where her father was an engineer who took on a second job to make sure he could afford college tuition for all four of his children.

The notion of a close-knit family was also not unfamiliar to Bill Gates. All that time he was progressing as a computer prodigy in Seattle, he was closely supported by his family. Bill had two sisters, and parents who were well respected in the community; his mother sat on several civic boards, and his father was a partner at a prominent law firm. It wasn't easy for him, raising a boy genius as brash as his son. Among the most memorable tales that the Gateses have recounted is one when Bill mouthed off to his mother at the dinner table, and his father doused him with a glass of water. (Young "Trey," as he was called around the house, apparently snapped back, "Thanks for the shower.") Soon Trey was sent to therapy, where the thirteen-year-old apparently told the counselor, "I'm at war with my parents over who is in control."

Soon, though, the parents eased the reins on their son, even when the mess in his room from all the computer tape he brought home got excessive. (They just adopted a policy whereby he always left his door closed, convenient for later in high school when he would quietly pull all-nighters at those computer labs, and his parents would be tricked into thinking the closed door meant their son was sleeping.) Though reluctant, they were supportive when he dropped out of Harvard to begin his career, and that support was key a few years later when he and Paul Allen decided to move from

New Mexico back to the Seattle area. When Bill returned, he would still have weekly dinners at his parents' house.

Bill's father would go on to help his son find Seattle businesspeople to serve on the Microsoft board. He also played a role helping to convince Steve Ballmer to move to Seattle and join Microsoft when Bill brought his father along to a major recruiting dinner. Yes, Bill Gates could be very hard to work for, demanding and impatient; but underneath the confidence and strength was a kid who had grown up in the embrace of supportive parents. Ever so occasionally, employees remember, that soulfulness would come through. Maybe he didn't have the understated ways of his parents, particularly his father, but the values he had learned from them were there.

In so many ways, in marrying a billionaire, you'd think Melinda was entering another world when she and Bill were wed on New Year's Day, 1994. But in fact, she was just marrying into another close-knit family.

"Our relationship with respect to the equality is based on my parents," Bill acknowledged to me.

"And my parents had a small business that they were running together," continues Melinda, "so we both come from places where the husband and wife were working things out all the time and there was that mutual respect, and that mutual view of, I want to make sure that I'm doing the best, I'm on my path—but that my partner is also on my path. It's no fun if one is advancing and the other is stale, and I think if you always have that as the guiding principle, it's this unbelievable respect, and it's about how can I help the other person be the best, or see this thing, and a lot of honesty, if one of us isn't at our best, or to say it to the other person.

"There aren't a lot of people who are going to give us feedback, where we are now. So I think having that in our backgrounds helps a lot."

The foundation itself started very much as a family affair. Sadly, just six months after the wedding, Bill's mom, Mary, died of a rare form of breast cancer. For years, she had been urging her son to get more serious about philanthropy, but the ever-preoccupied "Trey" was all about computers, figuring he could commit to giving away his money when he was much older. Suddenly, though, things were different. Six months later, his seventy-year-old father had an idea: with his free time, how about he start going through some requests and give some money away? Soon after, Bill set aside $100 million, and Bill Sr. began doling out grant money. I remember seeing Gates at Sun Valley around that time, discussing his entrance into the philanthropic world, and mentioning to him how amazing it was that in a short moment of history, he had gone from anonymous computer programmer to someone the United States government deemed an antitrust threat. He was on his way from famous inventor, modern-day Edison, black-hat industrialist to white-hat philanthropist in just twenty years.

In any event, gradually, the foundation got bigger, with employees, and a former Microsoft executive named Patti Stonesifer was brought in to help the elder Mr. Gates handle day-to-day operations. All the while, Bill and Melinda were increasing their involvement, and preparing for the day when philanthropy would become their full-time occupation, a day that's now arrived. Still, William Gates Sr. remains healthy, and a significant support for the couple as they've taken their partnership to the foundation.

Today, thanks to their good friend Warren Buffett, the Gateses are giving away more money than they ever could have hoped. In June 2006 Buffett decided that he would begin giving his own fortune away through the Gates Foundation. He essentially donated more than $30 billion worth of Berkshire Hathaway stock to the foundation, practically doubling the endowment; though in typical Buffett form, he did it in a distinctive and clever way, with annual gifts that ensure an increase in foundation giving every year. There's also something else worth noting: Buffett has made clear that the partnership between Bill and Melinda is a huge reason he made the gift.

"Bill really needs her," Buffett told a reporter soon after the announcement of his donation. "He's smart as hell, but in terms of seeing the whole picture, she's smarter."

"He's been around both of us a lot together," Melinda told me. "He's been around Bill a lot, and me alone, but he's seen us together and I think he sees that we play really nice counterbalancing roles for each other together. I think he understands that in a good marriage or partnership, that is what you do for one another, and I think he senses that we have a huge amount of respect for each other. And that neither of us would let the other get off track very far. And I think there's a certain amount of beauty in that, which he certainly saw. I also think he believes in a lot of the causes we believe in, and that's the beauty of it."

Until Bill really left Microsoft, Melinda was much more the couple's link to the day-to-day affairs of the foundation as their partnership there developed. But that didn't mean he wasn't paying attention.

"It's not fair to say that I was dominant," Melinda clarified to me. "One of the things you have to understand is that from the very beginning, this has been the two of us. So even while I had a lot more time to spend on the foundation, we've been in partnership every step of the way. So while I would sit and do a one-and-a-half, two-hour meeting with Patti Stone-sifer every couple weeks, believe me, I was coming back with the twenty things we discussed, and knowing the three that Bill's got to know about, and that we have to decide on and give Patti feedback on. So one of the things we've made sure is to keep it a partnership all the way through, and I think that's been really important so that neither of us, even now, have gotten out in front or ahead of the other one."

Bill Gates, not trying to be the dominant partner?

"The foundation is the most equal of my partnerships," he says, looking back. And if it's logical to think that might be because the partner is his wife, Gates thinks another element is relevant: age and maturity.

"One thing that was satisfying for me," he told me, "is that in going to this most equal partnership I've ever had, you know, if you've kind of proven yourself and gotten through your twenties and thirties—it helps to be done with that. The idea of jealousy creeping in goes away, and you become much more of a long-term thinker. You're less prone to panic or starting to have ego coming into play. I'm a better equal partner now, and if you go through my partnerships over time, they've become more equal.

"I think with Steve it was unusual, in that I ran it for most of the time, and then in the year 2000, he stepped up and we had a couple years where there was some ambiguity, and then he was clearly the lead partner. That was the idea in 2000, but it took a while before that was reality. And that was an interesting transition, where I got good advice from Melinda as we went through that."

That transition was followed by another one—from Microsoft to the foundation in 2008. Very quickly, the cofounders found themselves with a small test of equality: picking a new CEO. How they dealt with that challenge is illustrative of how their partnership works.

"It was a case where our perspectives could have diverged," says Bill, "because one of the candidates was somebody who had worked with me, and for me, Jeff Raikes, who was a super-important person at Microsoft. And Jeff had molded himself to work for me, and had a great deal of respect for me, and had grown up in the Microsoft system, which Melinda had a little bit, but she didn't have that same history with Jeff. We had a few other candidates who got to a very serious level, and that was a conversation over a four- or five-month period that was very interesting."

"That's one of the key things to understand about how we work," says Melinda. "We force the up-front discussion. I needed to know when we were going to hire the next CEO, whomever we picked, it absolutely had to be somebody who we both wanted. I wasn't going to go along with somebody he wanted, and he wasn't going to go along with somebody I wanted. There was one candidate in the pool who I was actually a bit more in favor of, who I had also worked with. And Bill was skeptical about that person, just like I was skeptical about Jeff. I knew Jeff outside work, and had a huge respect for him, but I knew they had a deep partnership, and wondered if I'd ever be able to form a deep partnership with Jeff. If I needed to discuss something difficult about him with Bill, or something difficult in the organization, would I be able to do that? So we established the principle up front: whoever it was, we had to both be one hundred percent sure we wanted them.

"Warren gave us great advice," she continues. "He said, whoever you choose, it has to be somebody who gets the best out of both of you—not the best out of Melinda, or the best out of Bill, or the best out of the organization—but the best out of both of you. And when you find that person, you've found the right person. And I think we used that principle all the way through. And I went to some people who I knew at Microsoft, who I knew would tell me the truth, several levels down— not just the peer relationships—and asked them, What's been hard with Jeff? Where does he work well with Bill? Where does he work well with Steve? Where does he not work well with these guys? When doesn't it work? And that was actually incredibly helpful."

In the end, they hired Raikes. He has now worked two years at the foundation, and when we spoke, both Gateses seemed ecstatic at how working together was working out.

"We're still in sort of an early honeymoon stage," acknowledged Bill. "We'll have all kinds of crises that I can't predict up ahead. But it's been great in the way that the partnership helps you brainstorm about those things. How it helps you be smarter faster."

Be smarter faster—what a concise way of summing up the benefits of partnership. As equal partners with complete trust in one another, Bill and Melinda are able to essentially take one mission and divide it up among two brilliant, focused minds. It may take three minutes in the meetings Melinda goes to for everyone to realize they have a real partner in the room, but once they do, things get rolling.

"We've talked about that behind the scenes," Melinda says. "Because quite honestly, there are only so many stages we can take, so much opportunity to get the message out, which is what we need to do—to convince governments to do the work we want to do. And if we can make sure it's clear that we have equal roles, we'll get a lot more bang for our buck by the two of us traveling separately, and giving different speeches.

"I used to get Bill's itineraries when he would go off on these Microsoft trips," she adds, "and I would look to see what hotel he was in, what time I could call him, and toss the rest of it. Well, now, I get his itinerary, when he's going on a foundation trip, and I'm reading a lot of the background to make sure they're not out ahead of me, because I didn't get to go on this trip about agriculture, but also so I know what key meetings he's going to. When he comes back, I can say, 'Okay, what were the outtakes? What did you really think of this meeting with this prime minister, etc.?' So we've always run this thing as coequals. And now he has a lot more time, in fact, some weeks, more time than me at the foundation."

With their kids still young, Melinda surely balances being a mom with being at the foundation. But when she's at the office, Bill says, having Melinda alongside him has huge benefits.

"The partnership thing is the ability to, as you go through success and failure, as you go through mood swings, as you want to be fanatical about something, to have one of you say, without getting rid of your fanaticism, 'Hey, you said you want to fire somebody'—but in twenty-four hours, you might want to think about it again. Or, if you go into a meeting and something is not pleasing, I can look over at Melinda during the meeting, I can talk to Melinda afterward, I can talk beforehand.

"When your partner surprises you with insights into the area that you're supposedly the expert in, that's fun. Or when you're kind of explaining something and it doesn't make sense to them—maybe it doesn't make sense. But there are highs and lows in terms of how these things go. Right now I'm particularly impatient about a few things. Do we have the right people? Are we pushing them in the right way? Why haven't they done it quite as quickly as we would have liked? How do I [deal with] the impatience? It's a fun thing to talk through with Melinda."

■   ■   ■

While Warren Buffett and Valentino might vie for the prize for the longest partnership in this book, Bill Gates wins for the number of successful partnerships. All of them have been scrutinized by biographers and the media, but the desire of writers to simplify them can be frustrating.

"People who attempt to capture in one paragraph the 'Bill's a scientist, Melinda loves babies' story line—it's got to be [too simple]," Bill said. It's much more nuanced than that; maybe Melinda is a bit softer around the edges, but in the end, there's way more crossover than that stereotypical division of labor gives them credit for.

"We've picked things that we're both deeply interested and engaged in," says Melinda. "If he wants to learn about fertilizer, he will have read two books on fertilizer that I am never going to read. But I'm interested to know what his outtakes are on fertilizer, and how it relates to the work, and how it's going to change the work in his view that we might do, or what scientists we both need to go to to make sure we both understand the area."

There is one thing they do completely together, though, and that's setting the strategy of giving—the foundation of the foundation, if you will.

"We would be making a mistake if we weren't doing that together," says Melinda. "In fact, there was a group inside the foundation, going a while back, and they kind of recommended to me at one point after one of our children was born—because I took a three-month hiatus—they kind of came up with this memo that said, Why don't you, Melinda, do education, and let Bill do the science piece of global health, and you can split it up that way. And we talked about it and said to them, You've got to be crazy! Then we really would be running two separate foundations—you might as well just split one of them apart, and let one of us do one thing and one of us do another. Both of us care deeply that we can figure out that we're doing the strategy of the whole thing together, and we can figure out the places where one person wanted to lead a little bit more, and the other one would maybe not lead quite so much."

As a kid, Bill Gates first entered partnerships while working on computer projects at school, his intensity, intelligence, and sheer force of will making him a leader in everything

he did. As his company made a transcendent rise from upstart start-up to global brand, he remained, as he readily acknowledged to me, a dominant partner. But in the decades
since, he gradually learned that he could also find success,
and satisfaction, through more balanced, equal partnership.
That couldn't have been easy; after all, Gates had been phe-
nomenally successful his way for so long. Part of the evolu-
tion came from hard work adapting to a new role at Microsoft
alongside Steve Ballmer. And the rest came at his foundation, with his wife, where he's begun conquering problems
much bigger than operating systems and word processing,
problems that require him and Melinda, more than ever, to
be smarter faster. Even Bill himself would admit that at one
time, he would have been one of the last people on earth
to engage in a partnership marked by equality. What Gates
learned is also the lasting lesson to me of his experience with
partnership: he doesn't have to dominate to find success.

That all said, on a more personal level, I remain fascinated
by his working relationship with his wife. They are among a
rare group of married couples where the husband and wife
are both in the public spotlight—along with the marriage. Although very different from the Gateses, perhaps the most
famous of the last few decades has been Bill and Hillary Clinton. It seems entire libraries have been filled analyzing conflicts in their marriage. But when I've spent time with them,
I found exactly the opposite to be true. In 2001, we tried to
entice the president to work for ABC News when his second
term ended. Following a spur-of-the-moment 4:00 p.m. Tues-
day call to set up a meeting, Jane and I found ourselves at dinner with both Clintons four hours later in Chappaqua. Late

into that evening, after the restaurant had cleared out, we found ourselves in a somewhat personal conversation. Hillary was now the new star, a recently elected New York senator, and the president was coming off harsh criticism while leaving office. But her achievements were never discussed. Instead we were watching them together, with Hillary telling us how many people Bill had spoken to in Tokyo, and how many publishing companies wanted his book, and how Bill had done this and that. He was the injured quarterback, she the fawning cheerleader. But then the roles reversed, and the president began to talk, and became her agent, her admirer, his pride. He told us how none of it—his governorship, his presidency—would have been possible without Hillary, her brains, her instincts, her strategy. Then he asked me why ABC wanted him.

"Because you are so goddamn interesting," I said.

Hillary jumped in.

"That's why I married him."

He touched her. He held her hand. I suddenly felt like I was in high school with an affectionate couple in the backseat at a drive-in. I saw real affection, real support, and real intellectual closeness. It wasn't phony—I'm too cynical to be fooled by phony, and where I come from, phony is sport.

Partnerships are generally public affairs, while marriages usually remain private. But both the Gateses and Clintons have been forced into the spotlight everywhere. They are a team not only in marriage but also in business. They work together, and they've raised their families together, publicly. I've been married over four decades, and consider my partnership with my wife, and the three wonderful sons we've produced, to be one of the great successes of my life. We don't work together, but we do all grow together. I don't know if I could have ever been totally comfortable working in business with my wife. At Disney, I usually called her three times a day, twice to make sure the sun was really still shining, and the third occasion to find out what time was dinner. Of course, on occasion, I'd call to report on a success or a failure, or to seek her advice, or check my instincts—or more important, her instincts. And we were definitely partners as well on many things, including our own charitable foundation, minuscule by comparison to the Gates Foundation. But then I'd come home, and she'd ask me how my day was. I would simply stare back at her, unable to even bring myself to respond. After talking to actors, directors, board members, investment bankers, agents, sports executives, cable operators, theme park performers, managers, union representatives, lawyers, doctors, and heads of state in a variety of different time zones and languages, I just couldn't rehash it all again. But bring up an issue with our kids? That was like throwing kerosene on my ever-present curiosity and affection toward them. So that kind of conversation ignited the moment. I'd be happy to change the subject anytime and deal with that—our joint project, our family. Just not the office. Eventually, after hearing about the kids and their latest ups and downs, I would start to open up about the day at work, and my wife's advice was always helpful and wise.

For their part, Bill and Melinda have found a way to juggle both partnerships—personal and professional—constantly, all day long, and neither suffers. Marriages can clearly be successful in any number of guises. I guess it's no surprise that business partnerships are hardly any different.

"Well," Melinda says referring to their two "businesses,"

"it doesn't mean every single day you talk about the foundation. There are definitely days when you've both been at the foundation and you just don't want to talk about it that night. But so you wait a couple days, and you talk about it then. We know when we go for a walk, it's not going to be just about the kids. There's going to be a lot of time to talk about it."

Those walks are a huge part of their marriage, and their partnership at the foundation. It lets them get away, whether it's a walk around the neighborhood, or in an unfamiliar city or country during one of their trips. (And don't worry about Bill's BlackBerry going off—he doesn't carry one. He carries a cell phone only because it has a clock, and says he's "the least interruptible person on the planet.") And beyond those walks, it's clear from spending time with them—they really are intellectual soul mates. Even on vacations, Melinda told me, they've chosen to read the same books at the same time so they can compare them. Or, when they read different books, they're practically reading the same book, because at every meal, they're telling each other about whatever they've read.

To hear Melinda talk, nothing could be more engaging—in a marriage, or beyond—than doing what she and her husband are doing.

"It deepens your relationship," she says. "I absolutely loved when we were in the phase when I was raising the kids and Bill was working at Microsoft. But as I've said to some of my friends, there's a whole deepening that happens when you're working on issues together, and when you're really talking about mothers losing children, or getting a kid through high school and successfully through college, and you're working at a really deep level on societal problems that you really feel deeply about. Working on problems where there's really huge intellectual rigor to what you're doing, and all the scientific pieces of it are deeply rewarding.

"At least twice a year, when we take time off when it's just the two of us, you'd be amazed how much of that time is spent talking just about foundation issues, because we care so deeply about them."

The world is better off for it—for their marriage, and for their partnership.

4

BRIAN GRAZER AND RON HOWARD

"We view the world differently,
but we arrive at the same conclusions."

For maybe a billion movie fans around the world watching the Academy Awards, the surreal night at the Kodak Theatre (and before that, the Los Angeles Music Center) is the absolute height of Hollywood magic: female movie stars in borrowed couture dresses and jewelry; male stars in all sorts of formal tuxedos; producers; directors; composers; cinematographers—so many famous faces in entertainment coming together to celebrate the previous year's work. And let me tell you—that's barely half of it. There are also the executives and studio owners—and wannabe executives and wannabe studio owners—plus of course their hangers-on, joining the scene. Inside the auditorium, network executives mingle alongside their lighting people and cameramen and -women. And then of course, just as formally attired as anyone: the extra audience sitters, who hide empty seats when someone needs a break from the soaring lights or the long show, or simply a restroom. Oh, wait—don't forget about the movie fanatics yelling and screaming outside. All in all, it's high stakes for the many companies that made the nominated movies—the Paramounts and Warner Bros. and Foxes and Disneys—and even higher stakes for the talent, along with pure promotion and adulation around the world for this fantastic industry.

Anyone who's ever seen the broadcast on television knows what it must be like to win an Oscar. The winners bound up the stairs to the stage, excitedly grab the award from the beautiful woman or handsome man holding it, get the obligatory osculation, thank the Academy, and sometimes a hundred other people, and go on their way. Like most awards in any industry, they are mostly justified, and all participants (getters, watchers, givers, even competitors) walk away satisfied, as well as emotionally drained.

Few at home, however, ever bother to think about what comes next—just as few people in a movie theater think about the process that went into the making of the movie. The winners are ushered offstage and basically told to stand there and wait until they are taken to a place called the interview room, where the media will ask a thousand questions and snap a million photos. Yes, after that, it's on to a night of partying and celebrating, but first comes an odd purgatory, where you're left alone without anybody—not even the stage manager, who has gone to retrieve the next award to give out, or the Hollywood star award-giver, who's gone back to his or her seat. It's just you and the Oscar.

And so it was that Brian Grazer and Ron Howard found themselves sitting on a cold, uncomfortable bench just behind the stage in the brand-new Kodak Theatre in March of 2002, just seconds after the highlight of their careers thus far, an Oscar for best picture for their film *A Beautiful Mind*. As partners on the project—Grazer as producer, Howard as director—they had each other. But Howard's back was aching, and his stomach was absolutely killing him.

"I never have stomach problems," he told me recently, looking back on that night, "but I was pretty uncomfortable. I didn't even realize that I had just spent the last four hours in total physical anguish."

It was the best movie he had made in an already terrific career. But after coming up short a few years earlier for another great film, *Apollo 13*, Howard—and his intestines— had taken nothing for granted, though *A Beautiful Mind* was heavily favored for the award.

The child television star (Opie Turner) turned teen star (Richie Cunningham) turned A-list director groaned a bit, turning to his friend and partner of nearly twenty years to let him know about his sudden turn from ecstasy to agony. And on cue, Grazer reached into his tuxedo pocket and pulled out a Tums.

"It was like a commercial for middle-aged men in show business," joked Howard. "We're sitting here with our Oscars, and we're also sitting here with stomachaches."

The Tums did the trick. Both men made it to the media room and all the parties successfully. The pair sometimes called "Hollywood's Odd Couple" had pulled off the ultimate triumph in a career full of successes—spearheaded by a partnership just as remarkable, and enjoyable, as anything in the long and wild history of the movie business.

■ ■ ■

From the earliest days of moviemaking, the entertainment industry has been stocked with partnerships and alliances. Some of the most legendary names in the business—Metro-Goldwyn-Mayer, Warner Bros., Disney (originally Disney Brothers)—began as partnerships between friends, or siblings, or business acquaintances. Along the way, some unique and talented teams have taken control of companies and worked together to achieve great runs of success. While I was enjoying a wonderful decade with Frank Wells at Disney, at the same time at Warner Bros., Robert Daly and Terry Semel were stringing together sixteen straight years of record earnings, including thirteen best picture nominations and three wins. And during that same time the Weinstein brothers, Harvey and Bob, revolutionized independent filmmaking at Miramax. Then of course there are the many purely creative partnerships—years ago, Dean Martin and Jerry Lewis, one of the most popular and skilled comedy teams of all time; and today, behind the camera, the Coen brothers, Joel and Ethan, directing and writing so many original and terrific films.

But more often than not, these Hollywood partnerships tend, at some point, to ultimately end. In an industry town where ambition and ego are in high supply, like every town in the world, many producers and executives can easily fail to see that not as much success will come from working alone as from working together. The mirror of envy generally does not provide a reflection that instructs members of a team to control it. On the creative side, collaborations can stall artistically, and partners may determine (often, it turns out, correctly) that it is necessary to work with new blood to find more success. Such breakups occasionally come tumultuously, but just as frequently the partings are amicable, and the decisions to move on mutual. The commonplace nature of the comings and goings make a partnership that stands the true test of time all the more amazing—particularly in the case of Imagine Entertainment and Brian Grazer and Ron Howard, whose union combines the business and creative elements of producing content, and has thrived for nearly a quarter century and counting.

It's a union that began when making big Hollywood movies was, for these two, merely a dream, and it has continued through their ascent to creating one of the most recognizable and respected brands in entertainment. Recent Imagine movies done by Howard and Grazer have included *Frost/Nixon*, *Cinderella Man*, *The Da Vinci Code*, and *Angels and Demons*. On the television side, the company has overseen the success of *24*, *Friday Night Lights*, *Arrested Development*, and *Parenthood*, among others. The partnership has been informal and then formal; based in a small private firm, then atop a public company, and then again private. It is a match of opposites who appear to have little in common, but also a pairing of close friends who share everything.

"We view the world differently," Howard once said, "but we arrive at the same conclusions."

■   ■   ■

Charlie Munger once was quoted, surely in his usual dare-
to-disagree-with-me way, as saying, "Opposites don't attract.
Psychological experiments prove that it's people who are
alike who are attracted to each other." Charlie is both right
and wrong—it all depends how you define *alike*. My wife and
I are religiously different, historically from different planets,
and emotionally the opposite, besides the fact that she is a
redheaded, left-handed computer programmer, all of which
I am not. Of course we basically think alike about important
things, the exception being which television show to watch.

Alas, if Charlie ever met Brian Grazer and Ron Howard,
he might be—at first—rendered speechless. At first glance,
few people appear more different from each other than Brian
and Ron. Brian is quintessential Hollywood, a creature of
Tinseltown, a smooth operator at the center of the pulse of
the entertainment world, while Howard lives three thousand
miles away in suburban New York. Then there are the appearances. Grazer is rarely seen in anything but a black suit,
white shirt, and thin black tie. And he may be best known to
the general public for his hair, which stands up straight atop
his slight frame. Now, back in the days when I had hair, mine
may have been known for heading off into often unplanned
directions—but this is different: Brian actually styles his to
go straight up. (For sports fans looking for a comparison,
Chris "The Birdman" Anderson of the Denver Nuggets has
a similar style.) Meanwhile, Howard's signature look is perhaps quite contentedly no look at all: he is most often seen in
a pair of jeans and a baseball cap.

Charlie Munger, though, is a smart man, and if you were to tell him about all the differences between Brian and Ron, he'd probably ask you to take a closer look. Doing that, you might notice that the two talk in a similar way—enthusiastically and quickly, with the words tumbling over each other as they come flying out. You'd also notice that as they talk, they shift often in their seats, crossing and uncrossing their legs, sitting forward and then leaning back. I'm not exactly sure what that means. I'm tempted to say it's a sign of their enthusiasm for life, and for creating content that entertains people; just as they're always looking for the next great project, they're also always searching for the next interesting thought. Then again, maybe it's just a coincidence—but I stand by the central point: Brian and Ron are a lot more similar than they appear.

"Our lives are so different," Howard once said. "That's one of the interesting things about the partnership. It's built upon this shared sense of what we want to accomplish together, and what we have in common."

They came to that point from starkly different places. Howard, of course, was the child star, born into an acting family, with his first television roles coming as a five-year-old in 1959. Then came Opie Taylor on *The Andy Griffith Show*, followed by a show that ended up defining not only his early career, but mine as well. In 1970, while waiting for a plane in Newark Airport with my wife and infant son during a snowstorm, I had written an outline for a television series called *New Family in Town*. As an ABC executive in charge of programming, I sent it to Paramount as an idea for a television series. Soon it was incorporated into an episode of a program called *Love, American Style*, costarring Ronnie Howard. Alas, the ABC research department confirmed through their studies that the 1950s setting on television in the 1970s wouldn't work. Then George Lucas cast Howard in *American Graffiti* (while *Grease* was playing in a small theater in Chicago). So maybe the 1950s would work. We shot another pilot as *Happy Days*, and Ronnie Howard, playing the character of Richie Cunningham, became a teen idol.

For nearly his entire childhood, adolescence, and even postadolescence, then, Howard had two lives—one as a normal-as-could-be kid in Los Angeles, and the other as the star of two top-rated television shows, one of the most familiar faces in America. When he played high school basketball, opposing fans would chant "O-pie, O-pie" as he shot free throws. All the while, Howard remained grounded in real life as well, even as he began harboring dreams of a life behind the camera, rather than in front of it. He went to film school at USC, and afterward directed a few small TV movies. But he had trouble taking the next step, to feature films. No one took Richie Cunningham seriously when he came in their office as a director to pitch a movie. (For what it's worth, I hope I would have, had he come to my office. I had many negotiations with his lawyer Harry Sloan, who was tough and smart and fair, and in those types of negotiations, you always know that the client is the real voice. I knew in 1973 that Ron Howard was the real thing, in talent, in business, in life.)

Meanwhile, a few miles away from Howard, Brian Grazer had enjoyed perhaps a more ordinary life in the valley, though the doctor's son had entered into adulthood no less ambitious. Grazer went to law school, where he became interested in the film industry. No stunt was too big for Grazer—as a law student he bought a Porsche to appear rich; while working as a law clerk, he convinced his bosses to let him move from a cubicle into an empty office meant for a vice president; and when he got a job working at Warner Bros., he had a unique ritual. Every day, he'd try and meet a new person.

"I would start every day by making a call," he recalled to me recently on a couch in his office in Beverly Hills. " 'Hi, my name is Brian Grazer, I work in Warner Bros., this is not associated with studio business, I do not want a job, but I know your work and I want to meet you for five minutes.' It could be Richard Brooks [the director of *Blackboard Jungle* and *Cat on a Hot Tin Roof*], it could be Mel Brooks, David Picker [the studio head of United Artists], it could be Jules Stein, Lew Wasserman, who brought in Sid Scheinberg [all three atop Universal Pictures]. So I met every principal in the business, basically."

Eventually Grazer transitioned to Paramount, where he had a corner office on the lot, and says he used to see me and Barry Diller talking every Friday out on the sidewalk.

"I saw Ron Howard walking by one day," says Brian, "and thought, 'Okay, this is who I'll meet today.' I called the operator and asked for Ron Howard. 'Ron Howard? Hi, Brian Grazer, I'd really like to meet you.' "

For his part, Ron actually says he remembers meeting Brian briefly before that, as they crossed paths leaving the office of an NBC executive named Deanne Barkley a few years earlier.

"I was coming in, Brian was coming out," he remembers, "and she was like, 'Wait, wait, you guys have to meet each other, you guys are sort of going to run the business some-day. And we met sort of in passing."

Now at Paramount, they had finally really met, thanks to Grazer's daily ritual, and the ambitious young producer sug-gested to the former child star that they have lunch. It was, surprisingly, an unfamiliar experience for the twenty-four-year-old Ronnie.

"Having grown up in the Hollywood business, I still had never had a Hollywood lunch," he says. "It had just never happened. I would have an annual pep-talk lunch with Garry Marshall [the writer and producer of *Happy Days*], but that was as close as I came. So Brian and I had a bona fide Hol-lywood lunch, my first ever."

"He was really shy—like, really, shy," remembers Grazer, "and he said, 'I'd like to be a movie director.' Basically what he really said was, 'I want to be a mainstream movie director, and I'm not getting anything done. I don't feel like the movie executives respect me.' Still, he just had this aura about him, and all I thought was, Whatever this guy tries to do, it will work out real well for him. But I had no evidence at this point that would occur, other than that he had been an actor on *Happy Days* and *Andy Griffith*. And so we pitched a few ideas back and forth."

The idea that seemed to set off a spark was one that Grazer had, about a pair of guys who start a brothel out of a morgue in New York City.

"It was dark to him," says Brian, "and I think that was im-portant to Ron because it would destigmatize him" as a fam-ily star.

The movie was made, called *Night Shift*, starring Henry

Winkler—popular at the time as Howard's old costar on *Happy Days*—and a little-known but talented actor named Michael Keaton. Originally, though, the studio heads who were interested in Ron and Brian's pitch wanted the hottest comedy team in Hollywood at the time, Dan Aykroyd and John Belushi, to star. But in the mixed-up world of the movie business, that meant Howard and Grazer would have to get the script to them—and if Aykroyd and Belushi liked it, maybe then a deal would be struck.

Well, talking to Aykroyd was one thing, but in the early 1980s, it wasn't exactly the easiest thing to get John Belushi's attention. For weeks, getting the script to the brilliant if, um, addictive personality became a crusade for the two aspiring filmmakers. All around Los Angeles, and then New York, and then again L.A., they tried to get him. And today, when they tell the stories of those days, the enthusiasm, passion, and, most important, fun they had comes through. A studio interested in the movie had given them an office to share. ("It wasn't really an office—it was just this room. There wasn't any furniture in it.") At one point, weeks after they had actually gotten the script to Belushi, they still couldn't get a response, but then found out that he was filming a movie called *Neighbors* on a nearby lot.

"So Brian gives me a script," Howard recalls, "and says I have to go over there and crash the set. 'You're Ron Howard, they'll let you on the set. You go up, and you give the script to John, tell him he must have lost the other one, but here it is.' "

The plan actually worked—Howard bumped into Aykroyd, who took him to Belushi, who kept him in his trailer hanging out and cracking jokes for a few hours, and was apologetic about not having read the script. As he walked back from the lot, Howard decided he'd have some fun with his new partner.

"I'm not usually this mischievous, but I had to get him," he remembers. "So I walked in, and he asked me how it went, and I said, 'I had to hit him!' And he said 'What!' And I said, 'I had to hit him, my dignity was at stake. I tried to give the script to him, but he had hot coffee in his hand, and he threw it at me, and took a step toward me, and I had to hit him.' And he said, 'Oh my God, Ron, I'm so sorry,' and he put his face in his hands and curled up in the fetal position. But he wasn't pissed that I had blown it. He was saying, 'I'm so sorry I put you in that position.' And when he said that, I had to say, 'Brian, I'm sorry, I'm yanking your chain, I gave him the script, I have no idea if he'll read it, but I had a pleasant two hours with him, we'll see . . . ,' and he took the joke well."

Eventually, after Belushi and Aykroyd declined, the studio did agree to make the film with Winkler and Keaton, and it was a minor hit but well respected around Hollywood. Howard directed and Grazer produced. The film's plot also paralleled the partnership that had begun—Keaton's character and Grazer sharing the role of the street-savvy deal-maker, Winkler's character and Howard more uptight and risk-averse. The pair had found a way to get a movie made, whether it took working in an unfurnished room in a forgotten corner of a studio lot, or chasing down John Belushi on both coasts, or relying on an old friend, Henry Winkler, the Fonz, to star in it. Yes, Howard had his connections, but really, they were two rookies who found a way to get the job done, no matter what it took.

"We were walking down the street in New York after the rough cut was done," says Howard, "and the studio didn't like Michael Keaton's performance. And we thought, Oh my God, we have a problem, and then we just started laughing. And we said, 'We feel like we're in one of those old-fashioned commodes, floating in a toilet bowl, and the studio executives are looking down, holding the chain, yelling 'We might pull it!' "

I wonder if on nights like the Oscars in 2002, Grazer and Howard look at each other and think back to those days, when they were worried that their futures were going to be flushed down the toilet.

I get the sense they do.

■　　■　　■

In the momentum of making *Night Shift*, Brian was able to convince the talented comedy writing team of Lowell Ganz and Babaloo Mandel (another partnership) to draft a script based on an idea he'd had in his office drawer for a long time, about a mermaid who washes ashore in present-day New York City. Howard remained involved, first in the development process and then ultimately as the director of *Splash*, the pair's first major hit, starring Tom Hanks and Daryl Hannah. It was also an important film for Disney, the first to be released under the new Touchstone label.

"Brian was just so dogged about getting *Splash* made," Ron remembers. His friend's passion—and the fact that another

mermaid film was rumored to be in the works across town—
stoked his competitive juices.

"If you want to get in a race with them," Grazer told the
Disney executives, "there is no way their movie will get to
the market before ours does. I will live here if I have to—we
have a great script, and we will do it."

They did, and of course the movie was a great success.
And from there, the Howard-Grazer partnership took off,
right? Not exactly.

"On *Splash*, I also wrote the story, and I felt I was the au-
thor of *Splash*," says Grazer candidly. "When it came out, I
didn't get nearly as much credit as I wanted to, or as he did.
And it was very hard for me to get credit—it just didn't work
that way because Ron Howard was a national treasure. So as
hard as Ron tried to make me feel good, and get me attention, it just doesn't go that way. And I just didn't feel as if I
could live with that, because I just felt like he's going to get
too much credit for stuff. My ego wouldn't feel comfortable."

Again, I know what you're expecting. That Grazer's ego
learned to live with the presence of Howard, that the thrill
of working with his new partner outweighed the sacrifices
of losing a lot of the credit that went into moviemaking. And
like Frank Wells and Charlie Munger, he stayed in the wings
as the partnership thrived. That would be the happy ending
Hollywood would often want you to believe happened, but
it is not the happy ending that actually happened in Hollywood.

What actually occurred next was that Grazer and Howard
went their own separate ways, Grazer to produce films like
Real Genius and *Spies Like Us*, Howard to direct *Cocoon* and
Gung-Ho. There was no fight, no conflict, no disagreement—

just two people who were going to check out the alternative for a while.

"I still don't think it was a stupid ego thing," Grazer says today. And he's right. I can assure you, Brian Grazer is not some crazy movie executive egomaniac. He's just an honest human being. As anyone who's ever created anything knows, what comes from the imagination, from inside someone's brain, their heart, and their soul, is very personal. The most modest of creative types still want a bit of recognition.

"We were both sort of looking around and exploring things," recalls Howard about what came next. "But we were still talking on the phone every day anyway, and seeing each other regularly, and talking about what we should do. We spent a lot of time talking about how it was tough to service each of our deals, and we started saying, 'Wouldn't it be great if we had a place we could focus all our creative energies, and the business side would sort of take care of itself?' "

From a deal Grazer had at Tri-Star Films, a co-venture of Columbia Pictures and Time, Inc., that arrangement soon became a possibility, with some seed money to start their own official production company, which the pair called Imagine Films Entertainment. At the time, production companies were hot in Hollywood, and they were able to capitalize on the momentum of their growing careers to sell shares in the new company and take it public, making a deal with Universal Studios to market and distribute their films. Within a few years, though, forget about ego—the young filmmakers had bigger problems: the headaches of running a public company, the rising costs of moviemaking, the difficulties of the obligatory dealings with Universal. The business side wasn't, in fact, taking care of itself.

So they did one of the smartest things they've ever done: they took their company private in 1993. And despite various opportunities over the years to merge with other big players in entertainment, that's exactly how they've kept it, churning out movies with a continued relationship with Universal, as well as television shows thanks to a deal with Fox.

But whatever happened to Brian's ego?

"Two things happened for me," he explains. "Look, I do have to get attention—I mean, I have this hairdo. So first, Ron is like the only person I can do this for because I have this unconditional love for him—almost like a wife. I think he's the kindest, most outstanding human being I've ever met in my entire life. So I love him like a child almost."

It makes sense—Brian says he views the world in absolutes, and you won't meet a much more likable guy than Ron Howard. Anyone who works with him loves him, so it makes sense that Brian Grazer would be first in line. That said, that love is not, in a candid analysis of the partnership, as crucial as what the producer says is the second key to why it works.

"When we formed our actual partnership," Grazer remembers, "I said, 'You made *Cocoon*, you get a lot of money to direct, I get a lot—but not as much—to produce. We should have a sixty-forty partnership.' He said yes after me selling it to him, but then he called back five minutes later and said, 'I just talked to Sheryl [Howard's wife], she will not allow it. We have to be fifty-fifty.' And so they insisted on fifty-fifty—that he should not be ahead of me, and that's what's kept it together for twenty-five years."

To this day—no matter what Imagine does, no matter who

works on what, no matter who gets credit for what—Grazer and Howard split every penny of profit down the middle. Every movie, every television show, anything and everything goes fifty-fifty. And in an industry where the creativity involved makes business personal, that's huge. It makes a very complicated part of the business tremendously simple.

"Financially, there have been three phases of our relationship," says Brian. "In the first phase, he did make a lot more money than me—in the pot of money, he made more. In the middle stage, it became equal. And now in the third stage, I'm making *American Gangster*, I'm making a lot of movies, *Inside Man* or *Eight Mile* or *Liar Liar* or *The Nutty Professor*, movies that he's had nothing to do with. So the third stage, my income has been far greater. And if it weren't fifty-fifty, I know my personality, I'd say, once I started to get ahead, I'd say this isn't cool."

So Brian and Ron share it all, as a real team, with no edges. Granted, this is pretty unheard of in Hollywood. Directors always get a financial edge. Their lawyers and agents and managers know movie directors are among the chosen few. In television, the opposite is true. The producer is the sovereign, and the agents and lawyers and managers know that. But the notion of putting aside the envy and pettiness, and instead going fifty-fifty, is not a decision to be made by those lawyers and agents and managers. It's decided by the principals: honest people acting decent and smart. The possibility of gaining an edge at various points of time is just put aside by both Brian and Ron. And that is truly unusual.

So then, what is the single, most substantive thing that has created a noncompetitive balance between Ron and

Brian? The thing that takes away the unconscious drives of two men competing together for a trophy? The single thing that removes a need to win independently, to be the leader of the pride, to "father" the future? Certainly, in this case, being totally equal financially, and therefore always being a cheerleader for the other, even in a field where the drivers of profit change over time, is the answer. The field is level, equality is assured. Exhale—there are no tensions, just relax and create. It was their solution to the ego and credit battle that has doomed so many other partnerships—in Hollywood and, surely, so many other places.

It's an even more particularly quirky arrangement when you consider how the company is run. You can kind of think of it like a baseball team owned by two guys, with one co-owner, Grazer, managing the team, and the other one, Howard, serving as its ace pitcher. At Imagine's offices in Beverly Hills, Brian is the one you'll find in the office every day, involved in every project that the company does. Meanwhile, though they talk every day, Ron is only occasionally in L.A.; he's either at home in New York or working on one of his films. Those films, of course, are the flagship of the company, but now represent only one part of the business. Sure, Howard will weigh in on rough cuts and ideas on all sort of things, but primarily, the "ace pitcher" focuses on his movies.

"I've never wanted other directors to feel like they're working for me at Imagine," says Howard. "I read scripts, I see cuts, I'll talk to Brian, I'll go to previews, but I don't want the directors to feel like they're working for me, and I don't think Brian does either. I always feel like I'm a very active and available consultant on everything else we do, but my main job is to develop stuff I believe in, stuff either I can direct, or hand off and we can get made."

"We talk every day—at least every day," says Brian, "about company business, projects, whatever. So even though his involvement is very limited in television, I'll ask him taste questions, and he has really good taste."

And when a show like *24*, or a movie like *American Gangster*, which was directed by Ridley Scott, does well, Howard still benefits as much as his partner. On the other hand, when a movie like *The Da Vinci Code*, which Howard spent more than a year of his life planning, shooting, and editing, becomes the second-highest-grossing movie of 2006, Grazer reaps the rewards as much as his partner.

"There's this kind of assumption that in the end," says Howard, "whatever kind of limitations there might be, whatever years one guy might be generating more earnings than the other—it's all going to come out in the wash. And there's a value in the partnership, there's a value in the structure of that, sort of beyond monetary definition. It takes the score-keeping out of it, that's the big thing."

And in a business partnership, no scorekeeping—no worrying about who gets what—typically means that together, the team ends up scoring a lot more.

■　■　■

Now a quarter-century old, Imagine Entertainment continues to thrive, with one partner ensconced in the Hollywood establishment and the other, quite contentedly, three thousand miles away from it.

"He's a complete Hollywood animal in a lot of ways," says Howard. "He's brilliant with the system. I was always traveling around working on the different movies, but I also moved back east, so we weren't in each other's face every second. When we were in the same offices, we spent a lot of time together, did a tremendous amount of problem-solving, and the communication was always there. And that was the thing we understood making those first couple of movies—even though our sensibilities were quite different, and our problem-solving styles were quite different, in the end, our tastes were similar and our sense of right and wrong was similar. Our sort of ultimate code of what we ought to do and what we ought not to do was more or less the same."

Projects can come from either partner. With *A Beautiful Mind*, Grazer first heard the story from *Vanity Fair* editor Graydon Carter, who had published a story about Princeton professor John Nash. With *Frost/Nixon*, Howard saw the play in London, called Grazer immediately afterward, and excitedly told him he had to see it and they had to make the movie.

"Early on," says Howard, "we both agreed that we don't have to agree on everything. If I love something, let me know what you think, but back me up. And if you love something and I don't, I will be dead honest with you, but only with you. And that has really worked and never even been challenged."

It certainly doesn't hurt that they are so close personally, that so many years together have bonded them. Having that kind of relationship means that when failure inevitably comes, it only drives them harder.

"We talk it through, it becomes therapy," says Howard. "We are both competitive enough, and passionate enough, and care enough that it hurts like hell, and we talk it through. There's never any blame, like you should learn this lesson, and we should both take this from this. No blame. Dark humor, yes, and anger, but no blame."

But it's rare that their projects don't succeed either critically or commercially, which is a result of this terrific combination of talent. And while there's no doubt in my mind that Brian Grazer and Ron Howard each would have been successful even if they had never crossed paths, they also make each other better, each in distinct ways. Working together improves each of their work, and the valence of the pair creates a whole new combination.

For Ron, that means Brian is the guy who does the dirty work.

"With agents, lawyers, business managers," Grazer once told a reporter, "I'm the bad cop. It means I have to say no to people and be kind of combative, be a warrior, and fight for all the things I think Ron and I are entitled to and our company is entitled to, and try not to get screwed on the deals."

And as someone with a bit of Hollywood experience, I can assure you—despite all the satires and send-ups you've seen— ultimately, it's not about being mean. It is, however, about being strong, and having the willingness and the ability to negotiate in the boardrooms, and do it with the right kind of toughness. Yes, Ron Howard is one of the nicest guys you'll ever meet, but he has that reputation even in the shark's tank of Hollywood, in no small part because of Brian Grazer, who not only protects him from the occasional ugliness of the process but does his job in such a successful, fair way that Ron's own reputation isn't just harmed—it's raised.

"Brian functions as Ron's id" was the way one actor put it.

"It's the one thing I was missing," says Howard. "Even though I was on a number-one-rated television show, and had been in the business all my life, and could even produce television movies and all of that, I didn't have that sort of vision, or that chutzpah, that Brian had."

Meanwhile, you read earlier about Brian's love for Ron, how he feels like his partner "defines goodness." It's important to realize that this admiration doesn't happen in a bubble. One of the reasons Brian loves Ron so much is that, much like a good marriage, being with him makes him better.

"I'll stir a lot of things up," Grazer once said. "But not all those things are good or productive or useful. Ron has an amazing amount of wisdom and a really strong creative vision. He always has a smart answer to everything I ask him."

And along the way, Brian has become as admired as anyone in entertainment, for a versatile range of skills spanning all through both the creative and business sides of the industry.

Tom Hanks, who first worked with the pair on *Splash*, and most recently on *Angels and Demons*, has said that "they do complement each other. Ron likes to tinker on movies, and Brian is a SoCal classic dealmaker kind of dude. And there's some gestalt Vulcan language that only Ron and Brian speak to each other."

And somewhere in that language is a deep bond, with roots

sown in that empty room in a bare corner of a studio lot, in edit rooms for *Night Shift*, and everywhere since. Like every partnership profiled in this book, Ron and Brian really like each other, and that personal relationship matters as much to the two men as the professional alliance.

"If once in a while," says Ron, "he says something or takes a position that bugs me or vice versa, we're pretty good about talking about it directly. Over the years, you can read the nuances of someone's voice. He could be on the phone, go- ing, 'Yeah,' but you kind of know there is something bugging him."

But it has to get a little tricky when Brian watches a rough cut of Ron's movies for the first time, and has some, um, thoughts.

"I do it very delicately, even to this day," says Brian. "We have a very 'Catholic' kind of relationship. No yelling, no finger-pointing, it's not dynamic like that. Even though that's my nature, I will conform to his nature. In terms of com- municating, I conform to his basic nature. I know that his nature is the right nature."

In the entertainment industry, this kind of creative part- nership lasting for decades is rare, even if short-term part- nerships are not. I've had hundreds of partnerships with producers or directors or executives. The give-and-take on a project, with two minds adding value to an idea, is not only helpful, it's fun. Whether in the script stage with television or movies or on the theatrical stage producing *The Lion King*, give-and-take with the creative head and an executive is very productive. In my career, I have served as an editor to people much more talented than I am, but with tactful advice and good relationships, I like to think that following this kind of partnership, the end product has been better. The ultimate American example is Nathaniel Hawthorne and Herman Melville, who over a period of time in the prime of their careers corresponded as they wrote *The Scarlet Letter* and *Moby-Dick*, respectively. Years later in the creative world, being able to forge many partnerships is essential; here again one plus one usually adds up to more than two. And Brian and Ron have been successfully doing it together for decades.

If Charlie Munger spent enough time with Ron Howard and Brian Grazer, he'd certainly conclude that while this is a pair who might appear to have very different skill sets and nothing in common, in fact they have the most important thing in common: their moral code. They are two people who do things the right way, and do it all together. They know that taking the high road leads to self and universal esteem and higher profits, and that the low road, the path traveled by far too many, leads only to the abyss of failure. That road leads them to treat each other well, treat others well, and make the decision to handle the financials the right way. As is the case for every other partnership in this book, that way of operating is a huge key to their success.

Long ago, Brian Grazer wanted to meet a different person every day as he climbed the Hollywood ladder. It may sound a bit unusual, but the exercise had a real purpose. Grazer just didn't realize its biggest impact would come from meeting Ron Howard.

"In a business that is so crazy," says Howard, "to actually

know that there is somebody who is really smart, who you care about, who has your interests, and who is rowing in the same direction, is something of immense value."

And as Ron Howard and Brian Grazer keep happily rowing together for years to come, everyone who enjoys their entertainment will continue to benefit from the greatest partnership working in Hollywood today.

5

VALENTINO AND GIANCARLO GIAMMETTI

"This isn't a story about money or fashion or power. It's a story about love."

There are plenty to choose from, but to me, the pivotal scene of the documentary film *Valentino: The Last Emperor* occurs in Paris, when the legendary designer receives the Légion d'honneur award, the most prestigious honor that the French government can bestow. The scene takes place in 2007, as Valentino nears retirement after decades atop the fashion world, and represents a crowning achievement for the Italian native who began his career in Paris more than half a century earlier. It occurs about halfway through the movie, after the viewer has met Valentino, learned about his rise to the top of the high-fashion world, and watched him behind the scenes overseeing two fashion shows. All the while, though, the audience has just one eye on Valentino, and the other on another man, Giancarlo Giammetti.

Giancarlo is the man who has been Valentino's business manager, co-owner, confidant, and above all, partner for the last half century. Since July 31, 1960 (the date is seminal in each man's personal and professional history), he has been at the side of the iconic designer, and at the heart of all of his success, fame, and riches. And on this day, in the summer of '07, as the cameras show, Giancarlo was, as always, at Valentino's side as he got out of his car outside the president's mansion to receive the award.

"In your speech," he instructs his old friend, "you should thank everyone who came today." The comment comes as the paparazzi and crowds begin to descend, and it's unclear how much of the advice registers. In an earlier scene in the film, showing Valentino joking with a pair of women, one of them asks him if he'll mention Giammetti in his speech. "Just a little at the end" is the response, but he is smiling, and the viewer wonders what will really happen.

To this point, the film has spent an enthralling forty-five minutes introducing us to both men, and illustrating their powerful bond. But along the way, what's also evident is that the partnership has worked with Giancarlo content to live completely in the shadows, willing to solve any and all problems that arise, able to maintain the bubble in which Valentino lives and works, and seemingly at peace with Valentino getting all the plaudits. And so, after seeing Giancarlo—behind the scenes—at the center of every decision made, when Valentino receives the Légion d'honneur, we are anxious to see his partner get a bit of credit for once—from someone who relies on him so much, and a friend who, even if he can only joke about it with a few women, loves him very much.

"He will never tell you—or tell me, specifically—how much he cares," Giancarlo tells the camera just before the ceremony is shown. "Or how much he is grateful, or how much he understands how much I did for him."

And so there is a tension in the film as Valentino receives the award. The honoree is clearly emotional during the ceremony, and the camera pans to Giancarlo, as ever in the shadows, sitting near the back of the room. The speech begins, as the designer lists a series of individuals who have helped him throughout his career. He finishes the list by noting he could continue to name "many others . . . if I had more time." There is a pause, as the camera flips between Giancarlo and Valentino, and the designer continues.

"But my gratitude . . ." And he has to stop to gather his emotions. "But my gratitude goes especially to Giancarlo Giammetti. My partner from the very beginning, who stayed by my side all these years. I want to thank him personally from the bottom of my heart."

Perhaps the most glamorous, decorated, and admired designer in the twentieth-century history of high fashion is, by now, crying. His partner, so long invisible in their amazing relationship, is frozen by emotion, biting his lip and joining in the applause. He is applauding Valentino, and applauding their partnership. And we, the audience, are applauding alongside them.

■   ■   ■

This is in many ways the deepest, most intense partnership explored in this book. Warren Buffett and Charlie Munger met a year before Valentino met Giancarlo, but considering that the investors have never lived in the same city, while the designers spend nearly all their time together, it's safe to say that they have spent more cumulative time together than any pair we've profiled so far.

"They travel together, they eat together," actress Gwyneth Paltrow said a few years ago. "I'd say they eat ten meals together a week, at least. They're like family. You don't know where one stops and the other begins, sometimes."

But until the 2009 release of *The Last Emperor*—and before that, to a lesser extent, a 2004 profile in *Vanity Fair*—the partnership was only known to an elite group of fashion cognoscenti. Now, thanks to the film, and the subsequent burst of publicity that followed, Valentino and Giancarlo are known to the mainstream—and known, to their initial alarm, not just as a fashion icon and his business partner, but as two very human men. At first, the portrayal and its exposure frightened them terribly, but as they quickly learned, it actually served as the perfect culmination of their story.

That story begins on July 31, 1960. Valentino Garavani was a small but growing celebrity in the small fashion scene in Rome. He was in his late twenties, a native of a northern Italian town in the Lombardy region who, ever since he could remember, had wanted to design women's dresses. In *The Last Emperor*, Valentino reflects romantically on watching movie stars like Ava Gardner and Rita Hayworth, and dreaming about someday making dresses like the ones they wore so glamorously in their movies. When he was seventeen, Valentino moved to Paris to study couture, or dressmaking. Today,

Paris of course is a capital of fashion and style; half a century ago, it was *the* capital, and thousands of bourgeois women were served by the haute couture, or high-dressmaking, industry. Through shows and personal viewings, the fashion houses dressed the wealthy and privileged women of European culture in expensive custom-made garb. There were no department stores or even ready-to-wear clothing stores; anything and everything fashionable was made just for the very rich, in these small houses. Valentino spent several years apprenticing in these shops, and then decided in 1959 to return to Italy and set up his own fashion house in Rome.

"At that time, Rome was very small in fashion, and Italy was nonexistent in fashion," Giancarlo told me. "Valentino brought a French glamour to it—he was young, very good-looking, and was all over the papers. People were talking about him."

Giancarlo was six years younger, in his second year of architecture school and living with his parents in Rome. And on the last night of July 1960, he was having a drink on Via Veneto, the famous street in Rome made famous that very year by Fellini's *La Dolce Vita*, when Valentino walked into a crowded bar, spotted Giancarlo sitting alone at a hard-to-come-by table, and asked if his party could join him. Giancarlo recognized him, and the two began to talk. By coincidence, fate, or instant planning, they were both headed on vacation to Capri the following day, and the conversation continued there. Soon enough, a romantic relationship followed, which meant Giancarlo was spending time at Valentino's new fashion house in Rome, which he had opened with financial support from his father and a family friend. The press may have been fawning over Valentino's designing talents, but Giancarlo, even though he was young and hardly experienced in business, quickly found out something else: the new house was going bankrupt.

"I would go to his office," Giancarlo remembers. "And I saw there was no one there who could make a decision. Valentino didn't know what he was doing."

So Giancarlo quit school and took over managing his new boyfriend's business, actually determining that the best strategy was to close the original, failing company and start fresh with a new one. Things began to turn around quickly. In 1961, Valentino dressed Elizabeth Taylor for the premiere of *Spartacus* in Rome. And then that year at a fashion show in Florence, his collection was a huge success, keeping Giancarlo up all night writing orders. Soon, big names in the international world of haute couture were wearing Valentino, no one bigger than Jacqueline Kennedy, who bought six black-and-white Valentino dresses to wear in mourning after her husband's assassination. Earlier, Kennedy had been at an event and was impressed by a friend's dress. When the friend told her Valentino had made it, she soon made an appointment to see some more of his dresses and ordered several of them on the spot. There may not have been a more desirable, glamorous client in the world at that point, and Valentino cried while telling *Vanity Fair* about his long friendship with Mrs. Kennedy (later Onassis).

In just a few years, Valentino's star had taken off. He was one of the most famous designers in the world, a king of high fashion doing what he had always dreamed. He had the talent, no doubt, but it all would have been impossible without someone else quietly in the background, enabling his genius by ensuring that he could create undisturbed by any outside concerns.

■   ■   ■

About a half hour outside of Paris sits the Château de Wideville, a castle on a 120-acre estate more than four hundred years old. Claude de Bullion, the finance minister for Louis XIII, once lived here, as did one of the mistresses of Louis XIV. Valentino bought the mansion in 1998, and had it restored impeccably. Not including his 157-foot yacht, the Paris residence is one of his five homes, and he proudly gave me a tour of the downstairs when I visited him and Giancarlo there on a cloudy spring day. Giancarlo doesn't live with Valentino—he has his own apartment residence in downtown Paris—but they are otherwise virtually joined at the hip, as friends and business associates. Giancarlo says in the film that over half a century of knowing Valentino, he estimated that all the days they haven't seen each other would add up to no more than a couple of months. He had told me they'd prefer to be interviewed separately, so I spent time with Giancarlo first before Valentino made a dramatic entrance into the parlor, with one of his trademark pugs in tow. Both men, in their seventies (though they looked at least a decade younger), were impeccably dressed (of course), wonderful hosts, and seemed happy to look back on half a century spent together accumulating the wealth and success that allowed them to enjoy ultra-luxuries like a seventeenth-century French castle.

"We used to work in the same sixty-square-meter office,"

Valentino said to me. "He realized then that I was very concerned about my creations, my clothes, and I think I formed
my name [in the fashion industry] because I was always tran-
quil, I was always calm, and I didn't have any interference."

"It was not a very brilliant operation at first, let me tell
you," Giancarlo told me with a smile. "He probably doesn't
even remember we were in bankruptcy. I would do everything. I would make calculations on how many meters of fabric we had to send to the tailor."

I had dealt totally with Giancarlo when setting up the interview via e-mail, just as for the past fifty years, everyone—
tailors, press agents, public relations people—had always
dealt with Giancarlo when looking to get to his partner.

"Valentino essentially hasn't changed since the mid-1950s,"
Matt Tyrnauer, the director of *The Last Emperor* and *Vanity
Fair* writer, said over lunch in New York a few months after
I met with the pair in Paris. "He's a man of the twentieth
century. Valentino is backward-looking; he's always looking
to the romantic past. And Giancarlo is basically the part of
him that is in the present. That's one of the keys to the partnership."

It was, then and now, a bubble: Giancarlo was there to let
Valentino focus entirely on the creation of his masterpieces,
and Giancarlo would deal with everything else. And in the
1970s, everything else became even bigger with the introduction of licensing and ready-to-wear into the Valentino
brand arsenal. Licensing had actually originally become a
big business far from the luxury goods sector. In the 1930s
and '40s, Roy Disney convinced his brother and partner Walt
to let other manufacturers produce items featuring Mickey
Mouse and company. Luxury houses like Christian Dior and

Pierre Cardin and others were paying attention, and soon began licensing their names—and essentially the prestige that went along with them—to things other than dresses, like sunglasses and umbrellas and handbags. Ready-to-wear was a similar economic model: couture houses began mass-producing their designs to sell in department stores, largely in the United States, to women who would never in their wildest dreams have been able to afford couture clothing. As the 1970s dawned, Jackie Kennedy and others had made Valentino's name one of the most desirable in the world. And Giancarlo was there to make sure that the man behind the name could benefit from it.

"A woman came to me," Giancarlo remembers, "and said she was from this big, super-luxurious store called Bloomingdale's. I had never been to America at the time. And she asked me, 'Can you make thirty of this coat [Valentino had designed]?' I remember it was a red coat. And I shipped it for a good price—things cost very little in Italy, and the workmanship was nothing. And then I never heard anything. And then a friend of mine came to me and said, 'You're crazy—do you know that your suit coats are downstairs in the basement of Bloomingdale's?' And I didn't know anything about it. And that's how it started—Lord and Taylor, Saks, and Alexander's. They would come, and they would order the couture dresses, ready-to-wear, and money started to flow in for us. America was very important for us with Jackie Kennedy, and Valentino became a big star."

Ready-to-wear may have been big, but for their bottom line, licensing was even bigger. Belts, bags, sunglasses, perfume, jeans, pretty much anything you could think of. At one point in the 1980s in Japan, the most lucrative licensing market for the company, you could buy an entire Valentino bathroom. It all brought in millions and millions of dollars a year in royalties, eventually dwarfing the earnings from the couture business and making the two men extremely wealthy.

"I had an enormous advantage that other houses didn't have when I did licensing," Giancarlo told me. That advantage was Valentino. "We had a great designer with the most glamorous and luxurious couture collection. And that was the umbrella for everything I was doing. Nobody ever judged Valentino [for permitting licensing], because everyone just looked at the top of the pyramid."

For his part, Valentino was happy to have the money pouring in, and was also well fit to play a public role in marketing the growing empire his partner was building for him.

"Valentino is not just a good designer, but he is also the best at public relations for his company," Giancarlo continued. "The moment he arrives, he has that kind of star quality, that charisma. And he was born for the spotlight."

Licensing continued to support the couture business, which had gradually been shrinking since its mid-century height. Then, in 1998, Giancarlo made the pair even richer when he sold the company to a conglomerate headed in part by Gianni Agnelli, the head of Fiat. Four years after that, Valentino S.p.A., earning revenues of nearly $200 million, was sold again to another Italian company, Marzotto Apparel. *The Last Emperor* details the dynamics between Valentino and Giancarlo and their corporate owners—not always a perfect relationship, but one that didn't impede the designer from continuing to spin out glamorous dresses for couture shows every year. Again, if there were any problems, they were dealt with by Giancarlo, allowing Valentino to stay in his bubble, and focus on his work.

"Valentino was such an asset for them—whatever he said, they had to shut up," he said, adding that "nothing changed— we were still the boss."

From those early days of sharing a small office to the more recent years of conglomerate ownership, the way the company did business remained pretty much the same. Valentino designed, and Giancarlo did everything else, with a small and intimate support team around them.

"I was the one designing the advertisement, designing the show, choosing the models, choosing the licensing items," Giancarlo told me, "and it was a lot of work. I was very bad at delegating, because I don't trust many people, and I'm used to doing things myself, dating back from early days—I started out low, not like these young people now who come out of business school and become COOs and CFOs. So I know all parts of the business—I know details about fabric, and so forth. I know how to do it, and I can do it faster than others."

The fashion world is filled with all kinds of success stories, many of them of the individual nature. I have known Diane von Furstenberg for thirty-five years, and know that she is involved in every detail of her iconic business. James Perse, a friend of my sons growing up in Los Angeles, has his own successful fashion company, and lives, breathes, and sleeps all aspects of his growing concern. My daughter-in-law, Stacey Bendet Eisner, founded Alice + Olivia, and I know well that she somehow balances sixteen-hour workdays with being a wife and a mother. But Valentino and Giancarlo's partnership is also not uncommon in the world of fashion. The partnership to which they are most frequently compared is

Yves Saint Laurent and Pierre Bergé, who themselves met in the late 1950s, and remained business partners until their haute couture house closed in 2002. Giancarlo insisted to me that the designers themselves were very different artists, noting, "Valentino would sketch drawings to explain to the dress production team what to do, while Saint Laurent was drawing for himself, for the beauty of the drawing. As artists, they were very different." There's also another difference, at least in the minds of some.

"Everybody always said, 'Pierre Bergé, Pierre Bergé,'" Diane von Furstenberg told *Vanity Fair.* "But the truth is, Giancarlo is much smarter. Of all the businesspeople in the fashion world, Giancarlo should get more credit than he's getting, and he never takes credit. As opposed to Pierre Bergé, who *demands* the credit."

Bergé and Giancarlo also apparently didn't have any love lost between them, with Bergé once telling *Women's Wear Daily* about his Italian counterparts, "I know they hope to be like Mr. Bergé and St. Laurent . . . but it's all just wishful thinking."

In the end, there's little doubt that Bergé sought the spotlight much more than Giancarlo, and, specifically, looked to market himself as "the partner of the genius."

"I've never tried, really, to show off about what my position is," Giancarlo told Matt Tyrnauer. "Here, there is so much glory, and only one should have the glory—and not share—you know? Also, I don't think I deserve the same glory. And I don't give a damn. That's what it is. I never gave a damn. Because his glory, his success, and his problems have all been mine."

As the film details, citing age and the end of an era in high fashion, Valentino and Giancarlo decided to retire in 2008. Haute couture was essentially a relic of the past at this point, with only a very, very small group of people able to afford that kind of clothing. Economically, it was largely a symbol for the company, and inevitably, even if the desires of the partners did hold serious sway with their corporate owners, the operation—and the budget—was getting smaller and smaller.

"I think fashion today is really for Target, Zara, H&M, Top Shop, and a slew of other discount or middle-priced store brands," Giancarlo says. "There are a lot of women who still dress attractively, but the moment when the designer was alone in deciding fashion, and then the company followed him in his strategy is not anymore there. The strategy comes first, and then the designers follow. We were the last ones— that's why the movie's called *The Last Emperor*."

I note that he doesn't say that with any hint of jealousy that the movie wasn't called *The Last Emperors*.

■ ■ ■

In a tribute book published around the time of Valentino's retirement, called *Valentino: A Grand Italian Epic*, written in concert with the filmmakers, their friends from the fashion and art worlds fawn over the partnership that's been behind the success.

"I cannot imagine Valentino without Giancarlo, Giancarlo without Valentino," says the artist Robert Bruno. "When we talk about Valentino, we are thinking about Giancarlo, and when we talk about Giancarlo, we are thinking about Valentino. It's a very strong duo. It is like a machine."

"Valentino and Giancarlo Giammetti have a perfect partnership," says Amy Fine Collins, an editor at *Vanity Fair*. "It is a dynamically balanced union of talents, temperaments, and tastes. Their dedication to each other—and to what they have created—is so civilized, romantic, and extravagant, it should be the subject of an opera. Imagine the costumes!"

"The whole world knows Valentino the designer, Valentino the brand, Valentino the name," says Tommaso Ziffer, a friend of the pair. "But everyone who knows them for real, either professionally or personally, knows Valentino *and* Giancarlo."

It's impressive, but why does it work? In this incredibly close and passionate partnership, why is Giancarlo—clearly taken by the glamour and fame of the fashion world—so content to be behind Valentino? Charlie Munger, though he clearly thinks highly of his own intelligence, doesn't like press, and is happy to live in the shadows of Warren Buffett. It took Brian Grazer a long time to come to terms with Ron Howard's fame, and a unique financial arrangement also helped maintain their partnership. They are each remarkable partnerships; how did it come to be that Giancarlo Giammetti joined their ranks?

At the beginning of *The Last Emperor*, Giancarlo is being interviewed by the fashion press at a show. "How would you define, in one word, your choice to live in another man's shadow, even a significant one?" is the question that comes from the reporter.

"Happiness" is the answer that comes from Giancarlo.

He elaborated upon it to me.

"I never felt that my position was not in the spotlight. When I started working with Valentino, I was twenty, and I always thought that I had my spotlight through him. Maybe I'm different than other people. On the other side, I don't think that Valentino ever felt the need to give me more light. I think we were happy in this way."

It calls to mind the great line by the writer Edith Wharton: "There are two ways of spreading light: to be the candle or the mirror that reflects it."

Giancarlo continued.

"I agree also that some people say that the businessman is always strong, and the artist always weak—in my case, it is completely the opposite. Valentino is a rock, and in the movie, you can understand that better than following our partnership from afar. My strength, in most cases, was to work in the back, and then in the end, do what I want. But this has been terribly difficult with someone so strong and so convinced that what he's doing is best, and convinced that there is just one way to judge things—his way."

When you meet him, it's clear Giancarlo is just as stylish as Valentino, and certainly one of the smartest people to come along in the fashion world in the last fifty years, but he is also a much more accessible personality. He carries an iPhone, he has a Facebook page. He's also accessible in the sense that he's so surprisingly normal in so many ways, which I couldn't stop thinking about as we sat near a crackling fireplace in the Paris castle, and he recalled all those years of shows and reviews.

"Valentino never read one review of his work, never," he told me, still incredulous. "I'd wake up at five a.m., very nervous—until the last show, even after forty-five years of work, and read the papers, go on the Internet, and everything. He would wake up at eleven, twelve, and say, 'So, what are we doing today?' and I would respond, 'Don't you want to know the reviews?' And he'd say, 'Oh right, what were they?' and I'd tell him, and he'd say, 'Oh, that's stupid.' And that was it—*finito*."

Geniuses tend not to care what other people think or write; the rest of us suffer with Giancarlo, getting up at 5:00 a.m. to find out. Alas, countless geniuses have passed through the world without making an impact; Valentino made his because of the hard work of Giancarlo.

"My work has always been to bring to Valentino new possibility to enlarge his vision," he told me. "Valentino never knew how much work was behind everything. He never went to a meeting for a store, even for a show. He was working in his studio, with his clothes."

This is, again, all said cheerfully, without any hint of frustration or envy. If Valentino follows Coco Chanel's mantra, "It's amazing how many cares disappear when you decide not to be something, but to be someone," for Giancarlo, it is about being effective to someone else's causes and success.

Tyrnauer, whose many visits to Europe to shoot the film were the equivalent of spending months and months with the partners, says one reason the partnership worked so well is that Giancarlo could easily distinguish between fame and something else.

"I think Giancarlo likes power in a lot of ways more than he likes fame," he says. "And he has a lot of power. Valentino is nominally in charge—his name is on the company, he's the famous one—but Giancarlo is an enormously powerful person in the relationship, because he's the gatekeeper.

No one gets to Valentino without going through Giancarlo first."

That power, incidentally, came not from just his access to Valentino, but because of his superb business acumen.

"Mr. Giammetti's ability in both the business side and the communication and image side is legendary," Veronika Simon, the director of model casting for Valentino, has said. "He is the most up-to-date on all aspects of fashion, photography, cinema, and literature, and always very much ahead of the times with all his ideas."

Still, something more than the power and the money has made this partnership so remarkable.

"This isn't a story about money or fashion or power," Giancarlo told Matt Tyrnauer. "It's a story about love."

And it's a love story that has persisted despite the fact that sometime in the early 1970s, Valentino and Giancarlo ceased their romantic relationship while maintaining their close bond and partnership. They've had other boyfriends and romantic partners since, but in their unique world, there apparently are no rules that say that when the love affair ends, the love does, too. And through the 1960s, '70s, '80s, and '90s and up to today, they have always spent the same amount of time together—virtually all of their time.

"That's the secret ingredient here," says Tyrnauer. "And it's just very interesting to see people surviving this long, and figuring out a way to make it work. Because a lot of love affairs end, and a lot of business partnerships end, and people fall out of love, and businesses run their course. But this is one that stayed together, and I think that Giancarlo made a great deal of sacrifice through the years to keep the family together. And I think he saw it for the greater good, not only for the general welfare—meaning the literal wealth—but also I think there's something very special between the two men that they were able to create early on, and continue, a life-long partnership that has been as fruitful as any one I can think of. It's one of the great, if you want to call it, love affairs of all time."

Tyrnauer couldn't take his eye off the love story in making the film, and the result is a portrait of a business marriage rarely seen in such detail. But when Valentino and Giancarlo themselves saw the level of that detail, they were not happy at all.

■ ▓ ■

Despite being among ultra-high-profile characters in the high-profile world of fashion, Valentino and Giancarlo are actually very private men. When their company began to grow in the 1960s, both men's mothers moved in with them, but Giammetti told *Vanity Fair* he never told his mother he was gay. She knew, yes, but for two Catholic men of Rome, it just wasn't something that was talked about. Really, the *Vanity Fair* article in 2004 was the first time they addressed their twelve-year romantic relationship publicly. It was an open secret, of course, but the acknowledgment nonetheless made huge headlines in the Italian press.

The magazine article was a glowing biography of their partnership, and led the men to agree to let Tyrnauer work on a follow-up project, the documentary. For over two years, the writer, with a small crew, would visit for periods of several days at a time and film the goings-on at the company, trying to capture the essence of the partnership that had captivated him while he wrote the article.

"I tried to tell them what kind of movie I was making," he says, "but they weren't really focused on that. I think they were expecting something much more conventional, about glamour and celebrities and style, so it didn't really matter. I had never really made a film before, so I don't think they were even holding much stock in it, and they weren't involved at all in the funding of it, so they didn't have to worry."

At least until the first-time filmmaker needed to get their signatures on a very important document, one that would allow him to have total final cut approval. It took a year—while filming was going on—to negotiate this, but thanks to some good lawyering, it eventually got done.

"I kept telling them I need final cut because this needs to be my movie," he explains. "It's not a viable commercial project if it's your movie, and they were responding, We don't understand that, why not? And I was saying, You don't understand, clearly, and we're just going to have to agree to disagree, and I can't do the movie if we don't have this, and eventually they relented and signed it."

The result is an extraordinarily entertaining—and honest—movie, less a documentary than a feature film, with a completely improvised script, about the final years of Valentino and Giancarlo at their company. Yes, there is plenty of charm in the images of the seamstresses poring over ornate dresses, and scenes of the models donning the finished products as Valentino looks on, calling for alterations here and there. But even more memorable are the scenes that feature the partners working—and squabbling—together. One memorable example: when Giancarlo plans what turns out to be Valentino's final show in Paris, Valentino shows up—and immediately begins criticizing the desert theme, which his partner planned as a tribute to a show forty years earlier that had the same motif. Perhaps because they were so used to the cameras, or perhaps because they thought they were a safe distance from the lens (always be wary of the capabilities of a powerful zoom), Valentino and Giancarlo argue freely, in a free-form combination of English, French, and Italian (subtitled when necessary). Like an experienced married spouse, Valentino starts by gently questioning the idea, but soon works himself into a small fit, concluding by saying, "This sand idea is ridiculous." Giancarlo, knowing it's too late to change, responds with bemusement and a joke. "Your belly is showing," he tells his partner, to try and get his mind off the disagreement. The argument fades with both men smiling, but in the next scene, Giancarlo is shown as the desert set is loaded onto the stage, and he appears nervous. (The show is a complete success.)

Other scenes show similarly unguarded moments, such as a particularly memorable one in a car, when Giancarlo mocks his longtime friend for being too tan. There are many points when Valentino loses his cool and expresses frustration, and others when his vanity and extravagance are gently mocked. All this is why Matt Tyrnauer put off showing Giancarlo and Valentino the film for as long as he could. But eventually he had to, and in a screening room in London after several months of editing, they watched it.

"It was Valentino, Giancarlo, a couple of their friends, myself, and the two editors of the film," Tyrnauer remembers. "And they completely freaked out when the lights came up at the end. They were devastated by the film, and I think they were disoriented by it. They thought all the story lines were wrong."

After five decades, their amazing partnership was on display thirty feet high for ninety minutes. But for these two men, it was tough to stomach.

"I had a lot of phone calls from Giancarlo," says Tyrnauer, "when I was, you know, holding the phone several feet away from my ear as he screamed. They were very upset, and not prepared to go out [and promote] the movie, but they couldn't do anything about it because they didn't have any right to stop it."

In life, we know that even the best marriages have their moments of difficulty. But Valentino and Giancarlo, even if they knew that better than most, had managed their life so meticulously before the film that they didn't realize that people would appreciate an honest movie more than one that hid all the imperfections. The imperfections are what make it so perfect.

"I think they were being hypersensitive," says Tyrnauer, "but when you have the mirror held up to you, it's very difficult. I am sympathetic to that. A magazine article that talks about your relationship is one thing, but to have a movie about basically your love story, which is what this movie is—when you are these two gentlemen who are in their seventies, live in Rome, are just frankly Catholic guys from a different generation, it's really hard to deal with. Valentino was highly uncomfortable with it, and it was Giancarlo's job, as ever, to fix the situation. But unfortunately for Giancarlo, there was nothing he could really do to stop the film."

But a few months later, the film was accepted into the glamorous Venice Film Festival, and despite their state of dismay, they probably knew that boycotting would exacerbate any negative press; plus, the allure of this glittering Italian event was too much to pass up. Tyrnauer says the tension at the festival was still high, but was countered by the excitement of the Italian press and fashion paparazzi. Valentino had instantly become the biggest star at the festival, and the red carpet before the premiere was packed with cameras.

There were 1,600 people in the audience in Venice, and at the end of the film, all 1,600 stood and cheered. Everyone turned to the balcony, where Valentino was seated, and he offered a regal wave, "shades of Evita," as Tyrnauer remembers it. After years of people applauding his dresses, at long last, they were applauding him. And suddenly, after months of shunning a film that he feared would reveal too much, Valentino was ready for the revelation.

"There were many things in this movie," he said the next day at a press conference, "that I would have preferred not to have seen. And if I had known what the movie was going to be about, I would have known how to avoid them. But you see me as I am, and I have to accept that."

But several months later, when Valentino made a grand entrance into the living room of his castle in Paris to greet me, I was still curious if he really did. I would soon find out.

■   ■   ■

After the movie was released in the United States, Valentino and Giancarlo became able public relations forces for Tyrnauer. There was a bevy of newspaper and magazine interviews with the pair, and I had seen them with Charlie

Rose talking about the film and their partnership, and even caught Valentino on ABC's daytime talk show *The View* chatting with Barbara Walters and company. After fifty years of promoting their brand, the men were no fools. Particularly after the reaction in Venice, there was no sense in giving the film the stigma of "the movie Valentino doesn't want you to see." Going along with the momentum of the reviews and acclimations was the smart thing to do, even if they remained a bit uncomfortable at first with the candor of the film. All the praise, I think, eventually put them more at ease, and they cooperated with Tyrnauer on the book I mentioned, which is a huge coffee-table-size celebration of Valentino's work. When I sat with Giancarlo, he talked with a smile about his Facebook page, and all the friend requests he was getting from fans of the film. He was also willing to acknowledge that the film showed how such a great partnership works.

"There are some examples in the movie that might seem superficial or stupid," he said, "and there are more important things that are not in the movie that are about this kind of a relationship. But in the movie, there is a very funny part, of deciding the theme of a show, and the stage."

He was talking about the desert theme for the fashion show I mentioned earlier.

"In the end, he arrived there [on show day], and he liked it," he said. "Because I know what is good for Valentino, and I know what is beautiful in his own version of beauty. So I will never do things on my own that I am sure that I won't have his approval at the end."

We talked for a little over an hour, and then, suddenly but dramatically, Valentino came around the corner. He was wearing a light-colored suit, which accentuated his permanent tan. There wasn't a hair out of place, even as he moved energetically to introduce himself and the dog he was carrying. Some people—movie stars, athletes, even businessmen and businesswomen—are born with an air of charisma that immediately makes them the center of attention in a room. Valentino, I was sure after about three seconds, is one of those people.

He talked freely and openly about the movie, by now surely rehearsed in repeating its themes of partnership and love.

"I trust Giammetti to the point that I don't know how much money I earn," he told me. "Numbers, anything—because he does everything. The confidence and security I have in him is tremendous."

Incidentally, though I didn't ask, and though Valentino may not even know himself, I've heard that Giancarlo gives Valentino 51 percent, and takes only 49 percent himself, another example of his deference to the designer. Meanwhile, when I asked him about the long success of the company, he attributed it to the closeness they shared not only with each other, but everyone else they had brought into Valentino S.p.A.

"We made our decisions very much in a family way," he said. "We succeeded because we had fantastic people with us. Look, for instance, at the seamstresses—they came when they were sixteen years old, and now they are sixty, and grandmothers. All the fashion houses around us envied us, because of our relationship, because of our group of people, because we are all very close."

I then brought up a scene in the movie when Giancarlo questions a decision Valentino made about the design of a dress. It featured white, sequined strips all around, and Valentino had decided to leave out a few strips in certain places. When Giancarlo saw this, he wondered where the strips were, which appeared to annoy Valentino no end. So I asked him what happens in those situations.

"If he came into the office, and said he didn't like the dress, I will do three the same," he said with a defiant smile. "I scream at him when he says something about my collection. I never want anyone to interfere. Of course, I ask, do you like, because you are so close, and you talk. But he was always a great, great admirer of what I did."

As Valentino continued to talk about his partner, he sought at once to sing Giammetti's praises but also keep himself in the forefront.

"Let's not now make Mr. Giammetti out to be in a bad position, like he was the slave of the situation. Not at all, not at all. He chose himself—because he was not a designer—to be the organizer. But when we were—not fighting, but having discussion—I say to him, 'My dear, you can have all the publicity in the world, but if the good dresses are not there, nothing happens.' "

He was correct, but it was still a bit jarring to hear it said out loud—after seeing the movie, and reading so many tributes to the partnership. In a sense, Valentino's honesty—his insistence on putting on the record that his contribution was most important—was as telling about the success of the partnership as anything I had read about or seen on screen. Every other pair of partners I had spoken to had taken care to point out the value of their counterpart. But there was no hiding Valentino's ego. The joyful and romantic tone of the movie, I realized, had masked some of the difficulty of being

Valentino's partner—and just how remarkable the endurance of the partnership was. Perhaps the designer was right—the company would not have succeeded without his creative genius. But at the same time, it wouldn't have had a chance without Giancarlo Giammetti doing everything else.

We talked for another hour, and then joined Giancarlo—and my wife, who had joined me on the trip—for a brief tour of the castle and then an exquisite lunch with a few other guests. They were retired now, with a noncompete clause that prevents them from starting up another company while the one still named Valentino goes on without them. They had both talked about having more time now to enjoy life, to see the flowers bloom at the castle, and to pursue other small projects. The movie, unexpectedly, had given their professional lives a wonderful exclamation point. Meanwhile, watching the two longtime partners interact at the dining room table was like having hopped inside the movie screen. They poked fun at each other, most memorably when Giancarlo chided Valentino about always lying about his age—even to his own doctor during a recent physical. They charmed everyone.

Valentino was at the head of the table, Giancarlo on the side.

6

STEVE RUBELL AND IAN SCHRAGER

Two guys from Brooklyn

I t is an unusually cool spring night in May of 1977. A few months before the Son of Sam serial killer wreaks havoc all across New York City. About half a year before a film Barry Diller and I will bring forth from Paramount, *Saturday Night Fever*, cements disco as a worldwide cultural movement of the 1970s. Let's say it's a Wednesday—between ten and eleven in the evening, right around the time most working people are starting to get ready for bed. But in the heart of the world's most exciting city, where there's always action, seemingly all of it is pointing to one block: West Fifty-fourth Street between Broadway and Eighth Avenue. All the limos and taxis head that way, if not to stop, then just to cruise by to check out the scene on the sidewalk. There they'll view seemingly every piece of what makes New York the most diverse place on the planet all coming together. Wealthy partiers in mink coats and not . . . next to blue-collar kids from the Bronx and Queens . . . next to professional socialites whose days are about getting ready for nights . . . next to anyone else who just wandered up because they were curious. All converging on 254 West Fifty-fourth Street, and forming a half line, half amorphous mass of people outside the front door. There are literally hundreds of people cramming toward the entrance, as one man—who would never be confused with any of the well-built, good-looking types making up most of the crowd—ushers them in, or more likely sends them away, one by one.

"You—you're in. You—go home. You too—no way. Maybe I'll let you back when you wear something nicer. You two, come here. No, no, not you. I don't care if the three of you are together—I'm only letting these two in."

Those accepted saunter in; those rejected slump backward. It is, to the uninitiated, a very curious scene.

It is also the signature snapshot of perhaps the biggest social phenomenon in New York City, or even elsewhere, ever: Studio 54. That may sound like an exaggeration, but think about it: exaggeration is what Studio 54 was about. When else has there been one setting—one place, one club, one disco—known by so many people all over the world? Studio 54 was, above all, a destination, for people from London and Los Angeles and Jackson Heights and the Grand Concourse and Bruckner Boulevard to Paris and Rome. It was a phenomenon that raked in thousands of dollars a night, and millions of dollars a month. It may have lasted only a little over a year, but for those who were there orchestrating the mania, it was the ride of a lifetime. And at the core of it all was a partnership between two men who at once shared so much and differed so dramatically.

Eventually, of course, the ride got too intoxicating, and Studio 54 became a victim of its own wild success. But despite the ensuing disaster, as the ethical compass went awry, the partnership between Steve Rubell and Ian Schrager survived—even through the year-plus-long jail sentence that was the result of their improprieties. And had heartbreak not struck in the years to come, Rubell and Schrager might still be on top of the list of the business world's premier duos today. Instead, the one surviving member continues on his own, having learned from the mistakes of greed and ethical gaps, and insisting that not a day goes by that he doesn't think of his partner. Then again, Steve Rubell was a tough guy to forget.

■　■　■

Today, Ian Schrager looks a lot younger than his age—sixty-four—might suggest, especially given the fact that his life has included an extended stint in the nightclub business. Schrager's office today is about fifty blocks south of the old Studio 54, in the heart of Manhattan's West Village. It's in what looks like the garage of a renovated brownstone, intricately designed and ultra-hip. There is a large bulletin board that runs the length of one of the walls, with a variety of clippings about things that it appears Schrager likes or has interest in, mixed in with advertisements and announcements related to his successful hotel business. The Ian Schrager Company owns and operates forty boutique hotels around the world, ranging from the Royalton in Miami to the Hudson Hotel and Gramercy Park Hotel in New York. In the past few years, he's also started a new joint venture with Marriott to begin a new chain of one hundred boutique hotels around the world, as well as some residential ventures. The hotels bring in millions of dollars a year. In other words, life is pretty good for Ian Schrager. Just don't try and tell him how much you admire his success.

"You know, I've sort of plodded along, I've done my hotels, I did my deals with Marriott, nobody has to feel sorry for me," he says. "But if Steve were there networking with me—I think, in the hotel business, I think we would have had a business more commensurate with the impact we had on the nightclub industry."

It's strange to hear that, especially since Ian Schrager hotels have in fact had a major impact on the hotel business. If you've ever been to one of his ultra-chic spots, you'd agree—the dimmed lighting in the hallways, the small but stylish rooms, the always bustling action in the lobby. They are, in their own ways, the smaller, less famous children of Studio 54—their own mini-destinations and mini–status symbols of luxury, coolness, and fun. Schrager, though, would be the first to remind you that Rubell was a cofounder of his hotel business, and at the heart of what went into making the brand so distinctive.

Always, until the day he died at the much-too-young age of forty-five, Steve Rubell knew how to bring people together around something fun and enticing. And Ian Schrager was the person who managed him and fostered his creativity, the person he trusted, the person he respected, the person who understood what Steve's genius was, and what he needed to make his dreams reality. And picking up where we left off in the last chapter with Valentino and Giancarlo Giammetti, there is, unmistakably, a particular sort of genius in that kind of ability to manage.

They first met in the mid-1960s, as undergraduates at Syracuse University. Steve was a senior and Ian a freshman, but they were from adjacent neighborhoods in Brooklyn. Brooklyn guys always have a bond, and theirs was surely helped by the masses of suburban kids at the school, whose experiences growing up and worldviews set them apart from city kids.

"The kids from Brooklyn sort of gravitated toward each other," says Ian today. "We were the anti-Westchester, the anti–Long Island group, and probably looked with disdain on the 'Stepford Wives' kids."

Also, there was the small significance of Ian's father, who worked in the garment district, but was long rumored to have been a major player in mobster Meyer Lansky's numbers racket. If you ever knew Steve Rubell at all, you'd know something like that would have gotten his attention.

Steve, the son of a postal worker, had always striven to stand out. He had been a star tennis player as a teenager, and when he got to Syracuse, became one of the most well-known faces on campus, a social gadfly who moved between crowds and seemed to know everyone. He hung out with a variety of different fraternities, was elected to an honor society that recognized school service achievements, and even played tennis with the chancellor. When he helped a friend get elected student-body president, he received in return an important job: handing out student tickets to varsity football games on Saturdays. Though Steve never attended the games himself, the ability to decide who did gave him a lot of power on campus, and impelled others to befriend, if not respect, him (an auspicious sign of what was to come).

The story Schrager always tells is that the two guys from Brooklyn actually met when they both found themselves dating the same girl. She eventually went by the wayside, but the friendship did not, and it continued when Rubell—enjoying his life at Syracuse, and also looking for a legal way to avoid the draft—stayed at the school to take graduate courses in business. He was an unofficial mayor of the student community, and along with the somewhat quieter but cool Schrager, the guys from Brooklyn had a good time with university life in the late 1960s.

"We just became friends," says Ian. "We had a similar approach, similar values. We just had a lot of commonality in a lot of different ways."

Steve was theatrical, alive, a star from the city transplanted to central New York State, the kind of guy who would know where the best party was on a Saturday night, the kind of guy who would know which classes to take and not to take, and the kind of guy who could even get you a favor from the chancellor's office. Who as an undergraduate at a university of 16,000 students plays tennis with the chancellor? And here was Steve Rubell at a university founded in 1870 by the Methodist Episcopal Church, a closeted gay Jewish student from an urban center, doing just that. By the way, Ian says he did not know that Steve was gay at the time, and in fact he figures he was probably the last to know.

"He may have thought I didn't approve or something, even though I didn't care," he says. "It didn't happen until we got out, and we were in the nightclub business years later, a girl he was going out with actually saw him kiss a guy at a club. Then people came up to me to tell me about it, and he still didn't say anything to me, until eventually I approached him and said, 'Look, I don't really care, by the way,' and that was that. It just didn't matter."

When Ian graduated in 1968 and returned to the city to attend law school at St. John's, Steve remained in Syracuse. They stayed in touch, and then became close again a few years later when Steve, finally back in New York, had happened upon his first business project: the steak-and-brew restaurant type that was popular then—all you could eat and drink for $5.95.

Ian, though, wanted nothing to do with the restaurant business ("There's no money in it," he says today), and once he got wind of his friend's plans, he wasn't too confident of success.

"He completely undercapitalized," he remembers. "He couldn't pay his bills. So I was acting as his lawyer, and making the deals to keep the creditors off his back. And he became my first client—he paid me a thousand dollars a month retainer. But he was already in too deep—he had overextended himself."

As Ian did his best to bail his friend out from his overzealousness, Steve saw the potential for a more permanent and equal partnership.

"He didn't understand why I wanted to be an adviser, and not a principal," remembers Ian. "He didn't see me in an advisory role. He didn't understand why I wouldn't want to be in business for myself. Why would I want to be advising other people, and telling them what to do?"

Steve was lost without someone to rein him in. Ian wanted

no permanent part of his friend's business. But as the two guys from Brooklyn made their way into the world, they came upon something else that appealed to them both much more than a steak-and-brew. Something they would take to a bit more naturally.

■   ■   ■

On weekends, they had been getting together with old Syracuse friends to explore the nightclub scene. Rubell took to it like a natural, the perfect new setting for the campus mayor to make new connections. For Schrager, meanwhile, the exposure to the scene was a window into a world of opportunity.

"You didn't even really need to know anything to go into the nightclub business," he says. "You didn't even really need to have capital. You just have to be able to work at it. There was something about the lack of structure or discipline, and being able to do whatever it was you wanted to do with a nightclub. Anything: music, dancing, theater, video, whatever."

Plus, their timing was perfect.

"It was a phenomenon," he says of the dance club craze. "It was just beginning in 1973, '74, '75, it was just emerging." Steve and Ian took advantage of it in May of 1977. Seven months later, it was *Saturday Night Fever and* John Travolta. But even before Studio 54 opened, the heat was there, as chronicled in a 1976 *New York Magazine* article called "Tribal Rites of the New Saturday Night," from which we adapted the movie. Culturally, it had all emerged from a dark place. Even though the Vietnam War had ended in 1975, the damage it had wreaked on young America lingered, along with memories of the draft lottery, body bags on network television, cultural anxiety and assassinations, and memories of riots in a hundred cities, most notably at the Democratic convention in August 1968. In Ohio, sixty-seven shots by the National Guard in thirteen seconds had killed four unarmed students at Kent State. Demonstrations, drugs and more drugs, and the first decade of birth control pills opened up a venting spirit that permeated the country, a hell-be-damned spirit in dramatic contrast to the spiritless Richard Nixon. Nixon was the faithful, dutiful husband while unchecked sexual freedom raced across America, especially in 1977 in New York City, and perhaps most infamously at Plato's Retreat, a swingers' club with men and women "coupling" in every room. The desire to party was effusive, exuberant, and sad. But Ian Schrager looked at it as a business opportunity.

"You'd drive by a place, and there would be people standing on line, waiting to take abuse to get into the nightclub," Ian told me. "And I was thinking to myself, 'There's something going on here.' And Steve lost his steak business—but for him, it was like, Okay, let's try something else. And that's what we were going to do."

Thanks to Steve's incessant networking, and Ian's curiosity, they had met some players in the New York City club scene, including a man named John Addison, who agreed to partner up with them on a new venture: opening two clubs, one in Boston, and one in Queens. But pretty quickly, that three-way partnership broke down.

"Steve and I weren't really willing to take a backseat," says Schrager. "It wasn't so much about being out in front—it was just that we had our own ideas about how it should be done. And I was there when John was building it, so I learned what went into it all."

Soon after the clubs opened, they split up from Addison—letting him take the Boston club while they grabbed the Queens establishment, which was actually on the site of an old golf club. They called it the Enchanted Garden. Now the two kids from Brooklyn were in business on their own. They took to it comfortably.

"When we first opened up, in those first nights," Schrager remembers, "I would go up to the DJ booth and play with the lights, and he would go to the bar and hang out with the kids from Queens. It was sort of a warm-up run for us."

But almost immediately, Steve was thinking of bigger things, namely Manhattan. While the Enchanted Garden was out in Queens, some of the nightclub elite had been making their way to the club and connecting with Rubell. And one night, someone told him about a space in the middle of Manhattan that had opened up.

"I think a broker told him about it," says Ian. "And I was afraid, because it was big, and big is not good in the nightclub business. Small is good."

A pattern was developing in the growing partnership: Steve pushing forward, Ian cautiously clinging to what was safe. At Syracuse, Rubell's charisma had been enough to gain him popularity all over campus and get him on the tennis court with the chancellor and in with favors from professor after professor. But in the business world, charm can be fleeting—certainly in the restaurant business, but even more so in the über-social nightclub world. That, though, is where his friend came in, the lawyer who knew how to get things done, and who understood the importance of process alongside result.

"I remember people making a joke," Schrager says. "I'd be by the door, where we were taking the money, and he'd be by the bar, hanging out with the people having drinks. It was a business for me. But he loved it—he would have done it for no money."

There was also something else: trust. Like Warren Buffett and Charlie Munger, Steve Rubell and Ian Schrager were from the same place, and had become fast friends in large part because of those shared origins. Like Ron Howard and Brian Grazer, Rubell and Schrager had struggled together side by side to gain a foothold in the professional world. And like Valentino and Giancarlo Giammetti, one of them was a charismatic, creative genius, the other, a steady and business-focused presence. But now, on the precipice of instant, wild success, they would deviate from those other partnerships. Things were about to get out of hand.

■ ■ ■

Studio 54 opened on April 24, 1977. Schrager had supervised the renovations of the club, while Rubell had worked every contact he had made in the previous five years—promoters, power players, partiers—to generate as much buzz as possible. It worked.

"I've had some [ventures] that were not naturals," Schrager says, his eyes lighting up. "This was a natural."

Thanks to an invitation list put together by a friend they had made in the promoting ranks, Carmen D'Alessio, as well as tireless work by the two men, four thousand people showed up that first night—though only half were let in. Andy Warhol, Liza Minnelli, Cher, Truman Capote—it was a who's who of celebrities. And that was just the start.

"I remember getting a phone call from Steve in the morning," Schrager remembers. "We were on the front page of the *New York Post.*"

The money was pouring in for the two kids from Brooklyn—Studio 54 had a $20 cover (unless you were a VIP, in which case you were just ushered in for free). It was open every night, filling itself to capacity with 1,500 partiers . . . and every night was the party of your life.

The days for Schrager started at around nine in the morning, when he'd come into the office and begin troubleshooting and dealing with the day's business. He shared an office with Steve, who would make his way in around noon and make calls as he sat opposite his partner. Around five or six, the duo would go out to dinner—sometimes together, sometimes separately—and then Schrager would come back around ten or so, just as the club was opening up. But there was a reason Ian earned the moniker "the Ghost"—he would just go right to the back offices, and continue to monitor what was going on from there, leaving the actual management of the club to an employee. He would typically leave at midnight, just as Steve was returning from his extended dinner, usually with a handful of celebrities in tow.

"He wasn't really there to run the place," Ian remembers, "more just to get people in and take care of them."

Still, he was a familiar face out in front, where hundreds of people every night were willing to do just about anything to get in the door. And to hear Ian remember it, Rubell wasn't a vindictive emperor of the velvet rope.

"He was just unbelievable at the door," he says. "Steve didn't do it in a mean-spirited way—it was a more spontaneous thing, with an innocence about it. 'I'm not letting you in until you shave.' 'I'm letting you in, but not your wife.' Sometimes we had a doorman there who would do it in a mean-spirited way. But Steve didn't do it in a mean-spirited way. We were just trying to make a great party that night. It was almost like casting a movie."

Steve would stay until four in the morning, when liquor sales stopped, and sometimes as late as five, because at that time of night, people weren't going to clear out too quickly. And then the day would start again the next morning when Ian showed up. All the while, though, the press all centered on his more colorful partner. Many of the articles published that profiled Studio 54 didn't even mention Rubell's partner. Ian says he didn't care.

"I only cared about the success," he says. "I let him take the credit and take the bows. If he would have taken all the credit away from me, I might not have liked it. He was good at it. It more just kind of came to him."

It's an important distinction. The average observer would be unable to separate Steve Rubell's need to socialize and be at the center of the party from the fact that all the credit for Studio 54, at least in 1977, went to him. But for the freshman who had been befriended by the senior at Syracuse, it was never like that. The press just gravitated toward his friend's charisma and colorfulness—if that story worked for Studio 54, it worked for Ian Schrager. Plus, Ian knew that his partner made him better, and that the wild success of the club was due to the work of both of them.

"It wasn't as simple as front man and behind-the-scenes

guy," Ian says. "Steve was also smart about the business side of things. So it was more spheres of influence—he was out front, but it wasn't as simple as he was the front man and I was the back man. And that responsibility, that division, happened totally naturally. It was what he liked doing. I would do the door when he wasn't there, but to me, it was hard. He enjoyed it."

Rubell took pride in his role as front man, but he occasionally bristled at the idea of being just a figurehead, with Schrager the brains behind the operation. When one article about the pair portrayed the partnership that way, Ian remembers Steve being upset.

"It didn't create any friction between us, but he didn't want to read it," he remembers. "People were coming up and saying things to me, and I think he didn't like his role being minimized or trivialized. Because he wasn't just a front man. He was more than that. You don't share fifty percent of the profits with just the front man."

So once again in a partnership, there was one character happy for the limelight, and another who had no desire for it. Matt Tyrnauer's appraisal of Giancarlo Giammetti being more interested in power than fame comes to mind in the case of Ian Schrager. And like Valentino, Steve Rubell was a true character, whose charm and aura was a part of his art.

In their roles, the two guys from Brooklyn couldn't do anything to hurt their super-club. A few weeks into the club's existence, the city took away their liquor license. Studio 54 stayed packed even when they just served seltzer and lime. The club just had perfect timing. It was the waning days of the pre-AIDS world packaged in Ortho-Novum. In the words of Schrager, "It was the last time you could go out and do anything you wanted, and the next morning, walk away from it completely."

Unless, of course, what you were walking away from was money you owed the government. In its first year, Studio 54 made, by some estimates, $7 million—1977 dollars. Only Schrager probably heard any advice the pair was getting, and even he wasn't immune to the allure of surely rich power brokers telling them ways to skirt the system. It's too bad the club DJ never played any Waylon Jennings, who famously sang that "honesty never wears out." When we met, Schrager told me, somewhat sheepishly, but not without a hint of a smile, that in late 1977 he was driving around with a million dollars cash in the trunk of his car. The infamous Roy Cohn had done some defense work for the Studio 54 boys, but he wasn't exactly a model of legality on any level. Plus, it didn't help that by creating an environment where cocaine was clearly almost as easy to get as Coca-Cola, Studio 54 was enraging authorities (who also weren't thrilled that if the tables were turned, they wouldn't have a chance of getting in themselves as guests).

"We got so many people pissed off," Ian reflects. "I find that that kind of resentment finds an institutional outlet in some kind of way. And there were so many big-shot people pissed off at us because they couldn't get into Studio 54. They thought there was something elitist, something undemocratic, about it."

But they let the big-shot people in, right?

"Not all the big shots," he says with a laugh. "If I opened up a nightclub today, I'd let the bankers in. Then, it was the fashion designers, not the bankers. And it got really big-shot people pissed off."

In the words of Milton Friedman, the Nobel Prize–winning American economist, "Hell hath no fury like a bureaucrat scorned."

On December 14, 1978, less than twenty months after the club had opened, Studio 54 was raided by government agents, and Rubell and Schrager were arrested. Depending on who you believe, a disgruntled employee may have tipped off the feds, or the officials may have just been determined to break up what was going on inside. In any event, the partners were charged with tax evasion, obstruction of justice, and conspiracy for skimming $2.5 million in unreported income from the club's receipts. Schrager told me that the government offered him a deal to turn against Rubell, testify against him, and pin everything on the face of Studio 54. He had no interest in taking it, and they went to jail.

"Reinforcement worked in a positive way and in a negative way," Schrager remembers. "And so when we were spiraling out of control, we reinforced it in each other. And if things were channeled correctly, they were reinforced as well. It's almost like when you have a character trait. For example, if you're an obsessive person in business, it works well. But you can't stop being obsessive in your personal life, and can't cut it off."

Hard work and luck had led to wild success, which in turn had led to complete loss of reality and restraint. It showed that as much as a partnership can accelerate success, it can also quicken disaster. It's nothing more than simple physics. The momentum of two is much greater than the momentum of one. Yes, often partners can serve as counterbalances to one another—skeptics who stop each other from making the wrong decision. But surrounded by instant, wild success,

Steve Rubell and Ian Schrager weren't able to do that. And so, less than two years after their amazing rise, they fell off the cliff. The partners served thirteen months in prison. Over the years, Ian has talked about that time in prison pretty openly and at times colorfully. (The question: How did Steve do in prison? The answer: There were people in prison—he's always great with people.) But when we chatted, he made clear that those thirteen months were the worst of his life.

"If I told you that you couldn't leave your apartment for thirty days, with your television and all your food, you'd still go crazy. Having gone through it, I would never wish that on anybody."

They did, however, stay together, first in the Metropolitan Correction Center in New York, and then in federal prison in Montgomery, Alabama, where they were housed in a big dormitory. Being together under the worst of circumstances only strengthened the friendship. And they began figuring out what would come next.

"In the beginning, both of us were down, and very timid. But then, the hunger and ambition came back. If they took that away, though, then we really would have lost. That adversity either destroys or strengthens. In our case, it strengthened. If we had been separated, then we might have drifted apart. You're sitting in jail, your mind wanders, and all you have to think about is, 'Oh, Steve did this, and I never should have gotten in trouble.' But it didn't happen. We were there for each other."

They are the only two partners in this book who went to jail as part of their partnership. That should be a negative piece of trivia. But in fact, the only thing worse than going to jail together would have been going to jail alone. Behind bars, they stayed together, and returned to New York hungrier than ever.

■   ■   ■

When they got out, they began to rebuild. Almost to show the world that they could pick up where they had left off, they opened another nightclub, the Palladium, downtown, that did well. But the pair had their eyes on another business, the hotel industry.

"I wanted to get into hotels," says Schrager, "because it was an adjunct to the nightclub business." You could pamper the rich with creative luxury, and make money with a quality product. Steve was right beside him.

"It was this complementary thing," he says. "And Steve was a foil for it. We talked about it. He was a one-man sample. I always tell a story, when we were building the Palladium, he would turn to me and say things like, 'You think people still want to dance?' He would think about culture and things like that. He was smart."

They put enough capital together to buy the Executive Hotel on Madison Avenue, a down-and-out place they renovated and renamed Morgan's. And it was there that the pair began to put their own stamp on the hotel business, with creative and cool flourishes that set the property apart and made it, as much as a hotel to stay at, a place to go to. Steve continued to play a role only he could: part president of the company, part public relations czar, part liaison to the stars, while Ian, who had spent his time in prison reading about real estate and hotels, mastered the business. As with Studio

54, they made Morgan's into a theater set, leaving the hallways dark, putting the highly stylized photographs of Robert Mapplethorpe on the walls, making duvet covers out of unique striped oxford cloth, and hiring beautiful models and actors to work as the staff. Everything else was so intriguing that seemingly no one noticed—or at least cared—that the rooms were tiny.

"I liked design, I liked creating environments," says Schrager today. "I think hotels are more about that than anything else, because you have really no product but the environment you create."

That attitude had brought them amazing success in the nightclub business, and now good things were quickly happening at Morgan's. After a few years, Schrager and Rubell bought another neglected hotel property, the Royalton, near Grand Central Station, in 1988, and began the process of refurbishment there as well, to turn it into one of "their" hotels. But quietly, something else was going on. Steve was sick—with a bad cough, eventually diagnosed as tuberculosis. And then came hepatitis. The signs of what was going on were unavoidable.

Over the years, Ian Schrager has been quiet when he's spoken about his partner's death, despite the widely reported cause, AIDS. At first, citing loyalty to a friend, he would say that if Steve never told him about having the disease, then he had to assume he didn't have it, and go only by what he was told—that Steve died of toxic shock. But it's been two decades now that his friend has been gone, and a lot has changed in society, and in attitudes toward HIV and AIDS. That may be the reason Schrager felt comfortable opening up the day we met in his office.

"I never talked about this because he didn't want anyone to know he had AIDS. But I went to take the AIDS test with him, because it was the only way he would take it. So I went with him. He had tuberculosis, and there were statistics about TB—that something like twenty-four out of twenty-six people who get it also have AIDS. They didn't automatically test for it in those days. Steve's brother was a doctor, and wanted him to take the test, but he wouldn't go, so I said, We'll both go take the test."

It took a few weeks for the results to come back, and they didn't talk about it for those few weeks. But then, one of the few times Ian could remember him doing this, Steve came in to the office early one morning. And that morning, Steve's brother called Ian to tell him that yes, Steve was sick. After the shock had worn off, Ian remembered to confirm another small detail, that he himself didn't have it.

"You never forget that. And then, when you get sick like that, it's a fight. T-cell counts, doctors, back and forth. But he went fast. Steve was sick like a year before he passed. And it was an unlucky type thing, because if he had gotten sick a few years later, he might have had a better shot."

Steve Rubell died on July 25, 1989. He was forty-five years old.

■   ■   ■

There may never be another Studio 54, in New York or any-where else. There may never be that *one* place that everyone knows is *the* most exclusive spot to go to, and be seen at. That said, the influence of Studio 54, and that brand of ultra-chic, does still permeate society. There are still—and will always be—places that are populated only by the elite people in social circles, not to mention places populated only by the ultra-elite people. And Ian Schrager remains no stranger to these locales.

There's the Delano Hotel in Miami and the Mondrian on Sunset Boulevard in Los Angeles, as well as St. Martin's Lane in London, all opened by Morgans Hotel Group, the company begun by the Studio 54 boys. In New York, Schrager's home base, the Hudson Hotel near Columbus Circle, was opened in 2000. Eventually Schrager was bought out by another company, and in 2005 he left the company just before it went public to start another venture on his own, the Ian Schrager Company. His new focus has shifted somewhat—the new company does residential properties as well as hotels. In New York, one of his first projects was 50 Gramercy Park North, a luxury residence next door to the Gramercy Park Hotel, which Schrager had bought and renovated.

Along the way, he's also had his share of new partners. Some have been financiers, others real estate tycoons he's joined up with. For the kid from Brooklyn, however, nothing has come anywhere close to the depth of the relationship he had with Rubell, a relationship he's described more than once as "the perfect marriage." And as he himself has candidly lamented, his business—as successful as it has been— has suffered without someone like Steve to be constantly pushing forward, forcing his way into the spotlight by sheer charm and will. Hotel brands like Starwood's W chain have copied the Rubell-Schrager model successfully in a host of cities, and Schrager has admitted that that bothers him.

But a recent new project—and an unlikely new partner—

has thrust him back into the spotlight. The Ian Schrager Company and Marriott have joined forces to create a new line of approximately a hundred boutique hotels around the world, a chain known as Edition. The press conference in 2008 was certainly a striking sight, with one of the godfathers of Studio 54 at the dais next to Bill Marriott, the head of the venerable family-owned Mormon company. When we met, Ian told me the partnership is going terrifically.

"The Marriott people are the best and brightest in the business," he says. "The real, real successful people do play by the rules. The medium-successful, maybe they don't. But the really successful people are really as straight as can be, and really follow the rules."

If you push toward the edge, you must make sure not to go over it—a fine but important distinction. That, of course, was the one massive lesson learned the hard way through the partnership that defined Schrager. You can be born with basic intelligence and a basic personality. But, as Warren Buffett says, you can learn ethics. Many don't, but Ian Schrager did.

"When I do a project right now," he says, "I don't really care about the credit. When I work with a bunch of architects and designers, and you start the parochial fights about the credits, I say, if you're sharing in something really successful, what do you care about the credit?"

In their entire relationship, Steve Rubell and Ian Schrager had only one fight. It came while Rubell was fighting for his life, and Schrager wanted something they had always overlooked. Since their very first project in the mid-1970s, they had never had a partnership agreement, and now, with his best friend dying, he was concerned that without anything in writing, the aftermath with the Rubell family would be complicated and difficult. It was too late, though—Steve was in no condition to deal with the details, and Ian didn't push any further. And sure enough, a difficult separation ensued after Steve's death.

Like other strong and successful partnerships—Ron Howard and Brian Grazer come to mind—Rubell and Schrager simply divided everything up fifty-fifty. In part, they didn't have to write anything down; though also to be fair, figuring out all the details of buyouts and rights and permissions and so forth was probably tougher than simply dividing it up and shaking hands on it. In the end, they were just two guys from Brooklyn who went to the top together, fell to the bottom together, and—on their way back to the top—had their partnership sadly cut short.

Ian Schrager will never forget Steve Rubell. Anyone who ever went to Studio 54 will never forget what they did together.

7

ARTHUR BLANK AND BERNIE MARCUS

"It was always about the business. Whenever we did anything, the question was, Is it good for the business?"

Bernie Marcus and Arthur Blank had a problem. It had already been a rough few months for the two businessmen. They had spent years at the top of the executive ladder of one of the most successful regional retail operations in the country, Handy Dan Home Improvement Centers. Then, suddenly, they were finished, fired abruptly on April 14, 1978. Plenty of their close friends and family actually thought the firing was a good thing, because their boss, a man named Sandy Sigoloff, had been gunning for them for a long time and making their lives miserable. Bernie and Arthur have told me stories about Sigoloff, providing evidence that he in fact was the "worst boss in America," a title that

Marty Davis, the CEO of Gulf & Western, Paramount's parent company, and successor to Charles Blühdorn, could, at least in *Fortune* magazine's opinion, wrestle from him.

In any event, getting fired for any reason is never fun, especially for being too successful—which actually seemed to be Bernie and Arthur's problem. For years, Bernie had been one of the country's foremost experts at home improvement retailing, and over those years he had developed ideas on how, given the chance, he'd start an operation fresh, with a whole new set of rules that would turn the industry on its head. He had convinced Arthur, whom he had taken in as his sidekick and financial guru at Handy Dan, to come along with him in this new venture. And so here they were, in the old Hyatt coffee shop in the City of Commerce, a few miles up the freeway from Disneyland, going over the plans for a new kind of store, based on a new model of revenue. But as Arthur discovered, there was a problem.

The numbers didn't work.

Based on the projections that Bernie and Arthur had made on things like gross margins and per-store volumes and payroll costs, it was going to cost more to operate the store than what they thought they'd make back, even in a dream scenario. The math just didn't hold.

Bernie was unfazed.

"Okay, then," he said to his partner. "What do we need?"

"More sales," Arthur replied.

"Well, that's easy. Let's write in more sales."

It sounded simple, but to Arthur, it was heresy. You couldn't just change the numbers on a financial plan.

"Arthur, just do it," Bernie said, as recounted in a book the pair later wrote about the company. "Just raise the sales.

Look, this whole thing is not a fact; it's a product of my imagination. A business plan is just a creation. Just raise the sales."

Eventually Arthur gave in, and fixed the numbers in the business plan. Now, at least on paper, the partners' still unnamed company was profitable. That and a dollar could get you a cup of coffee at the diner where they were brainstorming. But this was no ordinary business plan, and these were not two ordinary entrepreneurs. And within two years their new store, the Home Depot, was making a profit that dwarfed even the pie-in-the-sky hopes put to paper that day in the diner.

Individually, one was a brilliant, visionary salesman and the other, a savvy, entrepreneurial accountant and former drugstore CEO. Together, they built the second-largest retailer in the United States, thanks to a partnership whose impact continues to flow through the arteries and veins of the company today.

But their path to the present was far from smooth and easy.

■   ■   ■

There is really no such thing as a "conventional" business. But if you're looking for one in this book, perhaps the closest you'll get is the Home Depot—a store with employees and products and margins and other familiar, old-fashioned business terms and parameters. Then again, this is a store that was built on a completely original set of ideas, and built by managers and executives who embraced novel strategies to grow their business. It succeeded by doing the unconventional, the unexpected, and at times, the unthinkable.

Today, nearly a decade after the departure of the two men who founded and led the company from one store in Atlanta, Georgia, to thousands all across North America, the Home Depot remains entrenched as one of the most recognizable brands in American business. Even in retirement, that brand is still close to the hearts of Bernie Marcus and Arthur Blank, long after they began pursuing new passions with the fortunes they made running the company. These days, if you visit Marcus in his spacious office in the Buckhead district of Atlanta, he'll cheerfully mesmerize you with descriptions of the downtown Georgia Aquarium, which he nearly single-handedly funded and built. Blank, meanwhile, can be a hard guy to track down in the fall, when he's on the road following his NFL team, the Atlanta Falcons, which he bought in 2002. Both men are also huge presences in Atlanta philanthropy, and are proud to tell you all about the work that each of their foundations does. But ask them about the Home Depot, and it's clear that orange is still their favorite color, and the franchise, their first love.

"Look back at the success of the company," Arthur Blank told me recently, "and people will say a lot about the numbers, the stock, and the earnings. But you know what? They'll also talk about the stories, building the company, the successes, the failures, how we overcame adversity, and what we dealt with. Those were really the great joys."

They met in California in the early 1970s, the age of the conglomerate in American business. They had both grown up as ambitious young men on the other side of the country. In New Jersey, Bernie Marcus had harbored aspirations of becoming a doctor, but when, he says, quotas on Jews in medical school halted his plans, he turned disappointedly to pharmaceutical school. A life dispensing drugs was not meant to be, however, and soon Bernie found that he was a natural at selling things—first cosmetics, then sporting goods, then major appliances. He had found his calling, and by the time he was twenty-eight, he was overseeing a billion dollars' worth of business for a discount chain called Two Guys.

"I'm a merchant," he told me when we chatted in his office. He pointed to a napkin. "You look at this white napkin and you see a white napkin. I look at that napkin, and see multiple ways to turn that into money. I can sell the product, I can sell advertising on the product, I can sell a new use for that product. In other words, a real merchant understands that."

Eventually, Marcus moved to the Daylin Corporation, a company that ran several regional chains in various parts of the country, including Handy Dan Home Improvement Centers, based in California. There he met another fellow about a decade younger from the East Coast. The man's name was Arthur Blank. Arthur had grown up in Queens, the son of a pharmacist who had died young. Arthur put himself through Babson College in Boston to get a bachelor's degree in accounting, and then handled the financial side of his family business before it was bought by Daylin in 1968. Blank stayed on at the conglomerate, eventually working his way up to chief executive officer at a chain based in Atlanta called Elliott's Drug Stores/Stripe Discount Stores. When the parent company stopped the expansion of Elliott's/Stripe, Arthur began making plans to leave. But he had gotten to know Bernie Marcus at Daylin corporate events, and Marcus brought him in to work as the controller at Handy Dan, and later the vice president of finance.

"We had a tremendous amount of chemistry," says Blank. "We had a lot of shared philosophies, and our backgrounds were similar in many ways. Not only religiously, but we both came from a very middle-class background, we shared a lot of the same kinds of values, and our philosophies about life and business were very similar. Our styles were very different, which ended up in terms of Home Depot being a big advantage. But we felt good about each other right from the outset."

They ate lunch together nearly every day. Even if Arthur's domain was primarily financial matters, Bernie consulted with him on all kinds of issues that affected the stores. At the time, Handy Dan was one of a handful of regional chains that controlled the home improvement market. There were Rickel and Pergament in the east, Scotty's in the south, Pay 'n' Pak in the Pacific Northwest, and a host of others. Under Bernie's direction, with Arthur at his side handling financial matters, Handy Dan was the most profitable. Alas, the man overseeing the chain at Daylin headquarters, the diabolical Sandy Sigoloff, was not so appreciative of the efforts of his managers.

"He had a sign on his door that said 'Ming the Merciless' [an old villain from the Flash Gordon comics]," remembers Bernie, "and he acted the part. He was a vicious guy, a nasty guy."

As the sign on his door indicated, Sigoloff had a reputation for running his companies by fear. According to Bernie and Arthur, he actually began his career as a nuclear engineer, but had found his way to the executive path and become an expert in turning around struggling companies while destroying anything in his way. If he fired someone, Bernie says, Sigoloff wanted them to really suffer, so that people who still had their jobs would think twice before crossing him. The most frightening story that I've heard about him came, not surprisingly, from Bernie, who can be prone to an exaggeration or two, even when telling legendary tales.

"He killed people—he literally put people in the grave," Bernie told me. "I'm not kidding you. He gave a guy a heart attack on the phone. The guy literally dropped dead right there. He was a good friend of ours. Sandy fired him on the phone and then canceled his insurance. I went to see him, and I said, 'Sandy, the wife is penniless, how can you do this?' 'I can do anything,' he said. He was Ming the Merciless."

And there was no one he wanted to intimidate more than the guy who was getting the credit for the success of Handy Dan, Bernie himself. According to Bernie, as Handy Dan flourished, it drove Sigoloff to more and more hostility, outrage, and jealousy.

"I went to a Daylin board meeting," Marcus remembers. "They invited me to the meeting because they wanted me to do a presentation on Handy Dan. And when we finished the presentation, I said I'd like to leave the room, and a couple of the board members asked me to stay. And all of a sudden the agenda turned to who was going to succeed Sandy. And he was in the room. And I got very hot, and I started to sweat, and one of the board members said, 'Why are we wasting our time with succession? We already know who the successor is,' and he points to me. I take a look at Sandy, and I say to myself, This is not good. This is not going to work out. And from that day on, I knew this was death." And he was right.

Sigoloff may have thought he was saving himself by rejecting Bernie, but he obviously was not serving the company

well. Jealousy and envy are powerful forces, never in the interest of the people that are plagued by them. But it is not unusual for these unconscious drivers of personality to cause
leaders to force out those who threaten to upstage their own
stature. CEOs who don't realize the value of their talented
executives, think weak executives make them look strong,
and favor sycophantic colleagues end up as the victims of
their own bad actions, actions drawn from ego-enhanced
stupidity.

Nobody ever said all successful businessmen and -women
have wisdom or common sense. Of course, most do, but just
like everybody everywhere—politicians, professors, laborers,
doctors and lawyers, architects and contractors—people are
people, and some are not only unwise but, frankly, screwed
up. That's the human situation. At Disney or Paramount or
ABC, when we had a personnel problem of serious propor-
tion, at some point in the unpleasant process of dealing with
the issue, I'd sometimes comment, "Well, let's solve this as
quickly as possible, but remember, if our whole executive
population was completely normal, adjusted, reasonable,
happily married, content, and socially mature with 2.5 perfect children, then we'd be quite unusual, and if the world
wasn't a little messed up emotionally, what would there be to
make movies and television about?" That was my own process of accepting the interpersonal drama of running an organization. At all levels of a company, emotional instability
must be guarded against as much as plain stupidity. Those
who act based on this kind of foolishness—like Sandy Sigoloff—are ultimately doomed in the long term. I remain convinced that Goethe's observation that "there is nothing more
dangerous than ignorance in action" is true.

But in the short term, it was Bernie and his close lieuten-
ants who were in trouble. And sure enough, a few months
later, Marcus was called into a conference room in California and fired for a minor labor law violation that typically
wouldn't have cost someone their job. In another room down
the hall, Blank was let go along with him, as was Blank's lieutenant, a man named Ron Brill. They were supposed to be
at the top of their careers, but instead, they suddenly had
to consider new career options. Bernie's reward for turning
Handy Dan into maybe the country's best home improvement store was possible bankruptcy (he had much of his
money tied up in the company). He feared that for Sigoloff,
actually firing someone was often just the beginning of ruin-
ing the person's life.

Back in New York, however, another man heard what had
happened. And as Bernie Marcus was frantically calling his
lawyer and making sure he had enough cash on hand to live
for a few months, this other man couldn't have been more
excited.

■ ■ ■

Ken Langone is the kind of guy actors study when they want
to portray an unforgettable character. Now in his seventies, he looks at least a decade younger, in large part due to
an entire room of Nautilus equipment he keeps in his New
York City office. He talks with a classic New York accent,
loudly, profanely, and unapologetically. If his name sounds
familiar, it might be because of his involvement in the controversy over Richard Grasso's compensation from the New

York Stock Exchange a few years ago. Langone was part of the group that defended Grasso, and if you ask him about it, he isn't afraid to tell you exactly why. Langone backs down from no one—not Eliot Spitzer, the New York State attorney general who pushed that case; not the group of corporate titans who eventually had to testify that they had willingly approved Grasso's compensation; and not the media that was quick to condemn Grasso's side. In the end, Grasso and Langone won that case.

I visited Langone on a rainy summer day, and, a few minutes early, I was checking my BlackBerry in the lobby when he came up behind me, returning from a meeting. He complimented my shoes (actually, sneakers that I was still wearing thanks to my previously broken foot), and told me how happy he was I'd come by. Ken Langone loves to talk business, and he was especially happy to talk about the most successful investment he ever made.

"This was a company that was meant to be," he said when we sat down in his office, and then told me the story of how he got involved.

In the mid-1970s, Langone was an investment banker who happened to have a client in Philadelphia who ran a small chain of home improvement stores. During a meeting, he asked about the industry, and asked who the best operator in the country was. The answer was Bernie Marcus of Handy Dan out in California. That night, Langone looked into it, and was astounded by three things: the store's volume of sales, the discovery that Daylin owned only 80 percent of the chain—the rest was publicly owned—and the fact that the remaining shares could be had for a tremendously low price.

He immediately got his client to put him in touch with Marcus. On the phone, holding nothing back as always, he told Bernie that Handy Dan was one of the most impressive companies he had ever seen, that he was going to start buying up the public stock, and that he wanted to meet with him.

"Okay," Bernie said, taken a bit aback. "When you're out here sometime, come by and see me."

"I'll see you tomorrow for lunch," Langone barked back into the phone.

(You're getting an idea of how Ken operates.)

"I took a seven a.m. flight," Langone remembers, "and met him in a diner, and he brings another guy with him. Turns out it was his lawyer—I had so frightened him the night before, he brought a lawyer! We talked, and then as I get up from the banquette—one of these plastic seats—and I couldn't get up. I'm saying, what the hell's wrong with my ass, I couldn't get up. Well, there was a wad of bubble gum stuck to my ass. I said to myself, that's a good luck omen—it's like stepping in shit."

There was 19 percent of the stock outstanding—over the next several months, Langone would eventually buy 16 percent. The remainder was owned by an order of Catholic priests in Brooklyn, whose financial adviser, a man named Father Ray McCarthy, spoke with Langone when the banker wanted to buy the stock.

"Langone," the priest said. "That's an Italian name. Are you Catholic?"

"Yes, I am," Langone said.

"Then tell me—what in the name of hell should I do?"

"Keep it" was the laughing response. "Don't sell."

Even without that last chunk, Langone eventually made a huge profit on the stock, and even with minority ownership, he had the ability to make his presence known to Sigoloff. Sure enough, he soon did, in a variety of ways. The already paranoid Sigoloff had no interest in hearing from a minority owner, and quickly began making plans to buy Langone's shares back. But Ken, being a savvy businessman, wasn't going to make that so easy. A few months later, Langone heard from his new friend Bernie Marcus.

"Do me a favor," Marcus told Langone. "Sigoloff wants to buy you out."

Though his boss was a nightmare, at the time, Bernie figured getting Sigoloff off his back about Langone was the right move. His friend knew better.

"I said to Bernie," Langone told me, "'If I sell, I'm signing your death warrant. You'll be a dead man walking.'"

But Bernie didn't change his mind, and Langone went ahead with the plan and made another small fortune. Sure enough, though, the clock was ticking, on both Bernie and Arthur. And a few months later, Bernie and Arthur were both escorted out of the office. Marcus's first call, not surprisingly, was to Langone.

"Bernie was then beside himself," Langone remembers. "He had no money, no stock. I said, 'Bernie, relax. When can you get to New York?' He comes, I meet him at the Waldorf the next morning. He's got a labor lawyer with him, Jerry Glassman. I turn to Jerry and ask, 'Jerry, is he going to jail?' 'No, he's not going to jail.'" It was never a possibility.

Bernie was nervous that Sigoloff, as was his style, would push this minor labor issue to actually put Bernie on the sidelines forever.

"Okay," Langone continues. "I say, 'Bernie, you just got hit in the ass with a golden horseshoe. Remember how you said there was an Achilles' heel in this business? Let's do it.'"

He was referring to a conversation several months prior, when the banker had joined Bernie at an opening of a new Handy Dan store in Kansas City. As they took in the scene, Bernie had slyly mentioned something to Langone.

"Kenny, you better be careful. If somebody figures out the Achilles' heel of this business, we're dead."

"What do you mean?" Langone had responded.

"I'm not telling," Bernie had said.

Now, out of a job, it was time to tell. Remember, Bernie had started in the discount retail business. Today, names like Wal-Mart, Costco, Target, and others dominate that sector. But one of the founding fathers of the discount principle—"sell more for less"—was a man named, fittingly enough, Sol Price. Price had founded FedMart in San Diego in the 1950s, and later created the pioneering warehouse membership store, Price Club. Bernie had spent time with Sol, who had first flicked on the lightbulb for him—that the home improvement business was ripe for a takeover by discount-minded merchants. All those regional chains across the country—including even the well-run Handy Dan—sold items at high margins with a narrow assortment, and with little emphasis on service. And that was what shaped the Home Depot model.

"It's all Home Depot was," Ken Langone says today. "A three-legged stool: low prices, high service levels, and a wide assortment."

Well, yes. That created a blueprint. But the success also came from Bernie's partnership with someone else who would bring very different tools to the store.

■   ■   ■

Arthur Blank had a couple of options after he was fired from his job at Handy Dan. He was offered a position as president of the Wickes home improvement store chain. For a while, he entertained the idea of moving his family to Palm Springs and opening a private accounting practice there. But Bernie had a bigger idea—the home improvement store of the future. And he didn't want to start figuring out the plans for it without the man who'd become indispensable to him at Handy Dan.

"I am an entrepreneur," Marcus told me. "My life is entrepreneurial. But the entrepreneur has a weakness, and the entrepreneur's weakness is that they know no boundaries, they don't know any restraints. And so I always say, if you're an entrepreneur, you've got to find yourself somebody who is financially oriented, and whose judgment you can trust. You don't let them stop you—you only let them slow you down. That is really what you need. And with Arthur, I found that."

This was 1978. I was at Paramount at the time, and we had been very successful, even ranked number one, through realizing that in movies and television, creativity had to be encapsulated in that financial box. Rules and restraints, sense and stability, downside protection and designs for upside returns, all had to surround the imaginary box that contains enthusiasm, instinctual thinking, and volcanic imagination. We reminded our executives all the time that both profits and quality are good and go together, that profits are a good thing, that profits make investors dance and let the company continue operating, and that profits actually impress newspaper critics. Profits are good for everybody. They fuel the growth of the middle class and the labor movement, create taxes, and improve the general economy. Even in Hollywood, profits are not something to be ashamed of.

In the home improvement business, meanwhile, Bernie Marcus had discovered the need to surround his entrepreneurism with a partner with a sharp pencil. There was also something else very telling. At this new company, Bernie didn't want Arthur working for him, as had been the arrangement at Handy Dan—he wanted Arthur working with him. To provide the financial box that would surround his own set of creative ideas.

"Arthur and I have the same beliefs in lots of things," he says, "and when it came time to start Home Depot, I decided I didn't want to hire him—I wanted to make him my partner. I wanted him to feel strong enough that he was going to be equal to me in every respect.

"Let me tell you: I believe that people who think they are the smartest people in the world, that they don't need anybody else, I think they're assholes. I mean, that's my personal opinion, that's how I feel about them. Everybody needs somebody, and why not give them the credit for what they do? There's a Yiddish word, *kuva*, that means happiness. Why not give them a little *kuva* and let them feel how important they are? With Arthur, I think it was a combination. I think he wanted it, and I think he needed it. You have to remember, we had just both been fired."

So they went to work—together—meeting at that coffee shop in the City of Commerce several times a week, and even forming an operating company, MB Associates, for Marcus/Blank. And as Bernie was convincing Arthur to improve the numbers on his profit models and projections, someone else was working the phone for them back in New York. Ken Langone believed in the project as much as anything he'd ever seen in his career, and he was going to do everything he could to raise capital for the opening of the new store. All across the country, he was selling the idea of a discount home improvement chain to anyone who could listen. After a few months, he got Ross Perot, the founder of EDS and future presidential candidate, on board for a potential 70 percent interest, but when the men went to Dallas to work out a deal, it fell apart. Bernie was talking to Perot about an issue related to payments on his car, a Cadillac (which the new company would help pick up), and Perot flatly objected, saying that in his company, everyone drove Chevrolets. There was also the issue of Perot's strict no-facial-hair policy, which Arthur, wedded to his trademark mustache, was prepared to battle. Bernie and Arthur took these as signs that they might have another Sigoloff on their hands, and passed, creating one of the great what-ifs in business history. Eventually, Langone ended up where he had started, getting his own investment group to provide seed money for the store. Just as important, though, he was playing another role—cheerleader, providing enthusiasm and a boost of confidence for Bernie and Arthur as they determined the best place to start the chain (Atlanta, Georgia, where the market was ripe and real estate was cheap), what to call it (an investor named Marjorie Buckley came up with the name when the word *depot* occurred to her as she drove past a restaurant made out of a former railroad car), and how they'd get the first stores finished in time for a grand opening in June 1979. Bernie and Arthur were attached at the hip and the head, but they had, undeniably, a third partner of a different sort in Langone.

"Kenny was like a guru on the outside," Bernie told me, "and I could always turn to him if I had a problem or a situation, and I knew he was going to be objective. And he would come in and give us advice."

As I listened to what Bernie told me, and then when I met with Ken, the sense of déjà vu continued to impress me. Retail, especially home improvement retail, is a completely different business from entertainment, but I had the same kind of figure in Sid Bass, the Disney investor whose support of Frank and me had been critical when we got our jobs, and whose guidance and wisdom was invaluable to me during my two decades at Disney. Just as Ken had given Bernie the confidence to start the Home Depot, Sid had given me confidence when he supported my becoming CEO. And once the job started, in a different way from Frank, he had also been a partner for me, perhaps not in the hands-on, day-to-day running of the company, but as a steadying presence ready and willing to act as an ombudsman whenever I needed him. And just like Ken Langone at the Home Depot, for Sid Bass, it wasn't just a case of a guy protecting his investment. It was a good man who enjoyed getting his hands dirty once in a while and solving problems. Great partnerships can be propped up by these types of involved men and women. Along with Sid Bass, another adviser and guide that I've been privileged to call a friend and partner for over three decades is a man named Irwin Russell, a lawyer, sole practitioner, now an octogenarian, and my moral compass still available to me 24/7, still working six days a week, twelve hours a day, and who would be a great subject for his own book.

Like Sid Bass and Irwin Russell, Ken Langone largely stayed in the background at Home Depot, which was fine with him, particularly when those first stores in Atlanta ended up being incredibly successful, opening a path to expansion and, eventually, a public offering that made the company one of the great American business success stories of the 1980s and 1990s. Bernie and Arthur made fortunes, and were on the cover of newspapers and magazines, as admiring writers praised the success of their partnership. But as an additional partner, Langone didn't get nearly as much press, nor did the contributions of the other important figures in the company, like Ron Brill, the financial wizard who had been fired along with them at Handy Dan, and who had become one of the Home Depot's first employees. And then there was Pat Farrah.

"In my opinion," Arthur says, "Pat was the third leg of the stool. Without Pat, I don't think we would have had a Home Depot the same way that we did."

"The guy was totally a genius," echoes Bernie. "And what happened to us on a retailing side and merchandise side, happened because of Pat Farrah."

With a huge head of hair, a collection of strange outfits, and a variety of gold chains around his neck, Pat Farrah certainly stuck out in a crowd. He also stuck out in the competitive marketplace of the home improvement store business in California in the late 1970s. Farrah had been operating a store in Long Beach, California, that in many ways was the original Home Depot. There were big boxes everywhere, big assortments, low prices, great service, with forklifts operating during business hours, professional customers, and so forth. The only problem was that as brilliant a merchandiser as Pat was, he had little interest in details like paying his bills. Accordingly, his store was going bankrupt. Enter Ber-

nie and Arthur, who recognized his talent and convinced
him to abandon his one-store operation and join them, even
giving him equity, which technically made him a partner of
sorts. And in the fledgling first months of the Home Depot's
existence, make no mistake—it was Pat Farrah who introduced many of the chain's signature flourishes and found
ways to lure customers into the stores, even from towns
and cities more than an hour away from Atlanta. He was
the salesman who dared to price items super-low—and then
proudly watched as they sold out. He was the merchant who
actually bought empty boxes and empty paint cans to stack
to the ceiling in the first stores, to give the illusion of huge
supplies of stock.

"He was crazy," says Langone. "The first time I went to the
store, he had a mountain of Coca-Cola. I said, 'What are we
doing with soda in the store?' He said, 'It brings people in.'
He was a showman. Pat was a merchandising genius."

"Someone like Pat Farrah or Ron Brill brought in different
skill sets," says Arthur. "It's not just the partnership at the
very top. I think when you create one partnership, it sends
a message throughout the organization that partnerships are
important. So we had lots of subpartnerships—Farrah and
Brill, for example—and each one left to their own devices, in
their own little discipline, they were fabulous. But without
egos, and without walls being built—instead, just a 'Let's just
get this thing done' attitude. These guys worked together in a
way just like we did at the top—there was no ego."

Looking back decades later, the results speak for themselves. In 1981, roughly three years after the opening of the
first stores, the company went public. Everyone in the inner
circle—Bernie, Arthur, Langone, Ron Brill, and Pat Farrah—

became fabulously wealthy. But a willingness to share credit and subvert ego doesn't alone create a company like Home Depot. There will inevitably be bumps in the road. Partnership was the integral element in navigating those bumps.

■   ■   ■

Bernie Marcus talks a good game. But in the beginning, he confessed to me, he had trouble sharing power at the top. A few months into the launch of the company, he was in a meeting with Arthur Blank and Pat Farrah, who were disagreeing with a decision he made.

"At the end of the meeting," he remembers now, "I basically said, 'Screw you, I'm the CEO of the company, this is what we're doing, and if you don't like it, you can get your ass out of here, and that'll be the end of it.' "

That night, at 3:00 a.m., Bernie woke up with a start, and suddenly couldn't stop replaying his response in his head.

"It was the first fight I'd ever had with Arthur," he told me. "And that night I thought, 'Here I am on the verge of personal bankruptcy. Why did I bring these guys in? I brought them in because I thought they were the brightest in the world, and here I am, not giving them even an opportunity to argue with me.' I had come in with a preconceived idea of how to do this, and I wasn't listening to them."

So the next morning, he immediately brought his partner and their top employees back into the conference room.

"I said, 'Guys, I want to apologize for last night. I want you to explain to me what you were trying to explain to me yesterday.' And so I listened, and I'll be a son of a bitch—they made sense. What they said was one hundred percent right, and I was one hundred percent wrong. And that had an effect on everything after that. I learned how to listen."

And as he listened, the company began to thrive, and grow. Pat, a natural freelancer at heart, was given more free rein to implement the sales strategies he wanted. And Bernie stopped drawing a line between himself and Arthur, once his employee but now his partner.

"What happened," Arthur told me, "was that people would go to Bernie to ask a question, and then me to ask a question. And after a while, they realized—these guys, ask them a question, they're both going to say the same thing. So why bother? So that political stuff—going to him to get certain answers, and me to get other certain answers—we never had that. And that was a tremendous strength at the company, because we didn't have that political infighting at the top. Associates would call us 'BernieArthur,' like we were one person. The world viewed us that way, and it was fine for us."

The idea of being consistent and not letting those who work for you, supply you, finance you, or support you in any way try to get different answers from two partners is extremely important. And it's certainly not easy. Talking so much, and looking at things from different angles, will result in a plethora of different thoughts. But it's about managing those conflicting thoughts within the partnership before they turn into wider conflict throughout the executive suite or the company. Did Arthur Blank and Bernie Marcus, Frank Wells and I, or Barry Diller and I always agree on everything the first time we talked? Of course not. But in each case, we talked so many times a day, shared so much, and trusted each other so much that once we came to a conclusion, nobody was able to get us to differ, to be inconsistent, to be contrary. We basically acted as one, but in each case, one plus one added up to at least three.

■　■　■

"Bernie and I shared a common bathroom for thirty years—as long as we worked together," Arthur Blank says. "We built our offices at Home Depot to be this way. And we put all the good articles written about us in the bathroom, hiding them from everyone else, because we didn't want to believe our own bullshit."

As their company grew at a blistering pace throughout the 1980s, spreading all across the country, that link—their shared commode—provided an assurance that they would rarely be too far apart.

"We would just walk into each other's offices I don't know how many times a day," Blank said. "We'd plop down and say, I got a phone call from Langone, I got a phone call from this person, I got a phone call from this store, or I have some issue with someone, and we'd just sit down and talk about it."

Earlier, Ron Howard told me he and Brian Grazer view the world differently, but arrive at the same conclusions. He could also have been talking about Bernie and Arthur.

"We are like night and day," says Bernie. "Arthur is the most meticulous guy—I would walk into his office, and there would not be a drop of dust. I used to collect dust, and go in and sprinkle it on his desk, and then in the bathroom between our two offices, I would stand behind the door and wait for Arthur to come in, and watch him see the dust, the guy would go crazy! That was Arthur. And me, I'm like a schlepper. It was like the odd couple. We were the absolute odd couple, except that we believed exactly the same thing. And the fact that we were the odd couple meant that we always looked at a situation differently."

"It was a great yin-yang," says Arthur, "and a very good balance between the two of us. And being different—not in terms of our conclusions in business, but our personalities— also was very important to the company. Because that sent out a message to everybody that if the founders are like black and white in so many ways, it's okay to have lots of different people in our company."

But occasionally, even in a company that values freedom of opinion and empowers employees to make decisions and act on their own, problems arise. And in the Home Depot's case, perhaps its biggest problem came from its most important individual, Pat Farrah.

Bernie Marcus was supposed to be the merchandising genius, but even he took a backseat next to the guy who proudly called himself a "sales radical." But Pat's energy, admittedly, sometimes came from alcohol. "I wasn't real good at moderation," he told *Fortune* magazine in 1996. "I worked more than I should have. I drank more than I should have. I did everything to the extreme." He once even got in a forklift and drove it through a store wall—"just to make a point."

And so by the mid-1980s, Home Depot may have been flying, but Pat Farrah was sinking.

"He was going to kill himself," Arthur says. "Pat was the kind of guy—he'd have to go into a store and fix it personally. If something wasn't right in a store, he'd take all the merchants, go in there and fix it. After the first fifteen or twenty stores—it became very difficult to do that. It became very frustrating. And he started drinking more, and didn't sleep, and his marriage was suffering. And the inability of being able to fix everything as opposed to working through people and becoming a teacher and trainer was a very difficult transition for him."

So, after an intervention, Pat Farrah left Home Depot in the mid-1980s. He quit drinking, used his money to buy a house in Hawaii, and—as driven as ever—got into competitive sailing. By this point, Home Depot was almost on autopilot in its growth, and while Pat's talents as a merchant were no doubt missed, the company cruised for about a decade. But it had become somewhat stagnant creatively, and finally that started to catch up with them. In the mid-1990s, Wall Street suddenly started taking notice—the stock had reached a plateau.

By this time, Pat had settled down a bit, and thanks to the efforts of Arthur and Ken in particular, he had remained close to the Home Depot family, still talking frequently with executives and offering advice. Eventually, those talks led to conversations of returning to the company, and in 1995 Pat came back as essentially a merchandising expert at large, reporting to a vice president, but obtaining tremendous latitude to try and bring a spark back to the company. It worked—though eventually Pat again burned out.

Still, Bernie and Arthur had gotten a lot out of a guy who they had discovered running a bankrupt store in California in the late 1970s. And their partnership, I think it's fair to say, played a big role in their ability to manage such a unique asset.

"I think that from time to time, Arthur and I changed

roles [dealing with Pat]," says Bernie. "That sometimes I just couldn't tolerate it anymore, and he would be the good guy, and then some other times, I would be the good guy. Pat was such a difficult guy, and he was such a complex individual. He was so brilliant. He had a mind that was so fast, so quick, and he just blew it."

Having a partner to manage Pat, though, kept him around for a long time, thanks to Arthur—who Bernie says is a "much nicer person than I am, much more tolerant." He also says Ken did what he could to handle situations when Pat created problems, and thus stave off his dismissal from the company. Bernie exhibits anger and frustration in his appraisal of Pat, but there's also sadness.

"I brought this guy on board against everybody's will," he says. "Nobody wanted him, because he was totally irresponsible. But I recognized his genius. The guy was totally a genius. You can give people so many chances, and then after a while, tough love says, Listen, this is your last shot, if you don't make it this time, then time to move on.

"He totally wore me out, and today, we have very little contact, but that doesn't mean I don't give him credit that is due to him."

■　　■　　■

With the exception of Disney, and Berkshire Hathaway, which of course largely let its subsidiaries run themselves, the Home Depot is the largest corporation profiled in this book. And more than any other partnership I've looked at, Bernie Marcus and Arthur Blank exemplify the value of a pairing at the top that sets a tone for an entire company, whether it was about dealing with important people near the top like Pat Farrah or managing the hundreds of thousands of employees (associates, they call them) at their stores across the country.

"We developed this inverted triangle," Bernie explained to me. He drew an upside-down triangle in the air. "At the top of the triangle were the people in the stores. In the scheme of importance, they are the most important people. And when you go all the way to the bottom, the least important people were the CEO and president. We got most of the money, because we had to make decisions. But when it came to taking care of customers, I was the least important, because I was the most far-removed from the customer. And on this, Arthur and I—our brains were on the same line. We always believed in the same thing: number one, taking care of our customers; and number two, taking care of our people."

Their principles were well-known, and the company thus attracted a high quality of applicants to become employees (associates) who believed in the company and wanted to work at Home Depot. Success comes more from how you hire than how you train. Home Depot did both well. It all, of course, went back to a philosophy first coined by Sam Walton. "There is only one boss, the customer. And he can fire everybody in the company from the chairman on down simply by spending his money somewhere else."

Inside Home Depot, to keep every employee on the same page, and to maintain a sense of partnership between different parts of the company, a series of very creative tools were used. For example, if they were hiring a lawyer in the human resources department, the attorney would have to go through a vetting period surely unlike anything he'd ever dealt with at a law firm.

"We would sit him down and he'd have this wonderful résumé," remembers Bernie, "and then we would say to him, 'Oh, by the way, you're going to have to work in the stores for four to six weeks.' And he'd say, 'Great, that's wonderful.' And we'd say, 'We don't think you understand. You're going to work with an apron on, you're going to start in the warehouse, and you're going to unload trucks.' And the guy might say, 'I'm a Yale graduate. Are you kidding me?' But our response to that was if we have a situation with an employee where he hurts his back, or something happens to him, if the lawyer doesn't understand what it's all about, then he can't be there for that person. We want you to represent him; we don't want you to be antagonistic to him. In most companies, the HR people and the lawyers are especially antagonistic."

Not at the Home Depot, where working together and doing the right thing was entrenched in the culture from the highest levels. One of Bernie's favorite examples involves a store's conundrum in the 1980s, when a manager called him upset about a problem: a woman had come to a store, asking if there was anything they could sell her for five dollars to plug a leaky roof. She couldn't spend any more because she didn't have any more. The solution was simple: with Bernie and Arthur's encouragement, the manager sent a team of his staff to the woman's house and repaired the entire roof for free.

"They did it," Bernie recalls, "and the entire store went crazy. All of a sudden, the whole personality of this store changed because of what they did for this woman. And Ar-

thur and I thought, this is great, we're teaching them a little
tzedakah [the Yiddish word for charity]. And so it became corporate culture—every store was told they had to do things
like this. And the more they did it, the better they felt about
themselves, the better they felt about our customers, and the
better they felt about the Home Depot. And it became about
'I love working at the Home Depot.' We both believed in it,
and we both pushed it, and this is why the success came. And
remember, this comes from people who are totally opposite.
Absolutely diametrically, totally opposite."

Their devotion to their partnership, a partnership that inspired an entire company, always kept them together. There
was just one problem: What in the world would come next?

■   ■   ■

For nineteen years, Bernie Marcus held the title of chief executive officer of Home Depot, and Arthur Blank was the
president. Perhaps, as Arthur told me, "the titles didn't really
make a difference—people viewed us much more as a partnership." But nonetheless, it still meant something to him
when, in May 1997, he was named CEO, while Bernie took
the title of chairman, scaling back his time at the office.

"I didn't want to work the way I was working," says Bernie. "I was seventy-something years old, at that point, and it
was fifteen-hour days, and it was enough already, it was just
enough. I had a foundation already, and that was taking a lot
of my time, and I couldn't be CEO at this time anymore."

They still worked together for the next few years, but the

partnership was obviously scaled back. For Arthur, it was a chance to be a different kind of leader, but soon, a problem became apparent to both of them: What was going to happen when Arthur wanted to step away from the company? Who would take over? Certainly not Pat Farrah, the third leg of the stool. Many others who had been in the executive suite alongside them, it seems, just got too comfortable with Bernie and Arthur at the helm.

"We had prepared five to seven people to take our place," says Arthur, "but they had made so much money, they had just lost the eye of the tiger when it came time. So when I look back on the one thing we failed, my opinion is that we didn't succeed at providing the succession for the company for the two of us."

There is certainly an irony here—the two guys who were fired from a job because their boss was concerned about them succeeding him now had a succession crisis of their own. In this case, though, it was because people liked working for them so much, they got used to it. Still, changes also needed to be made. Yes, the partners had instilled a tremendous culture throughout their now massive company, but that had also created some problems.

"People didn't fear us," Bernie explains. "They all loved us because of the way we treated them. So they would try and hide things from you because they didn't want to hurt you. It was a situation where our stores were out of control. We had entrepreneurs in the stores, and you would tell them to do something, and they would do their own thing. I'd walk in the store, and people would tell me, 'Bernie, you always said to do what's right for the store.' So we had twelve hundred stores, and guys just doing what they wanted to do. So I thought a guy from GE would have the ability to put systems in, and to get us where we needed to go. That's really why Nardelli came in."

In the late 1990s, Robert Nardelli had been one of three executives in line to succeed the legendary Jack Welch at General Electric. When he was beaten out by Jeff Immelt, who succeeded Welch (James McNerney, the other candidate, went on to become CEO of the 3M Corporation, and later CEO of Boeing), Nardelli became a great candidate to come to Home Depot, with the ability to apply a new emphasis on efficiency in management to shore up what was beginning to be a problem at stores within the company. But the problem was that Nardelli, like all the top-level candidates to come in as potential heirs to the Depot throne, wanted—not surprisingly, and not inappropriately—to be the CEO, and not anyone's number two. The candidates were largely coming from places where they had been second in command, and not in a way that made them part of any partnership. And so the founders, along with the board, made the decision to bring Nardelli aboard as CEO, with Bernie and Arthur stepping aside. It wasn't the most pleasant process, but the founders went along with the plan for the sake of the company.

When I spoke with Ken Langone, he told me Nardelli did some great things to address the issues in the company, and streamline a lot of the confusion in a company that had resulted from the freedom that store managers were given.

"Home Depot didn't use e-mail until 2003," Langone said. "We had such freedom of movement that we had 152 separate and distinct evaluation forms across the United States. It was free-form."

(Arthur says Ken's recollection of the e-mail is correct, but the policy was intentional, explaining that the company did not use e-mail as a primary communications tool because they wanted store managers on the floor with customers, not spending their time communicating with executives.)

Under Nardelli, the chain saw its revenues and net earnings increase 50 percent. But Home Depot had always been more than simply a company that made money. It was a place where people loved to shop. That had long made it a great place to work. But with a new leader, there were new priorities, and a new tone being set. And to the founders who still bled orange, it was upsetting.

"For however many years Arthur and I were together, it was never about ego," Bernie told me. "It was always about the business. Whenever we did anything, the question was, Is it good for the business? Will this have an effect on our employees? Everything we ever did, we had the same thoughts over and over again."

The point he's making is clear: Nardelli didn't have the same style of management. He didn't want to be anyone's partner, and he certainly didn't want to hear from the men he'd replaced, even if they might have been the best people to give him advice.

Bernie leaned forward in his chair to elaborate.

"One of the people I was out with last night sold his business," he told me. "And he said to me, 'Bernie, can you explain something to me? How come I ran a business for twenty-five years, and I was brilliant, and I made a lot of money, and now, these people that bought my business want nothing to do with me? From the day I sold them my business, I said to them, I will help you any time you need me, I will come in, offer myself, won't charge you, will share anything with you.' This guy says from the day he sold the business, they haven't spoken to him. Why is that?"

He then turned the story back to Home Depot.

"How could I be so brilliant for such a long period of time, and then end up being such a schmuck? How does that work? That was Nardelli. I stayed in the building with Nardelli. Because I said I could move out, or I could stay here. I said if I stay here, I'm going to try and help you. Anything I see, I will come to you, and I will not go to anyone else, and I will bring to you everything I find wrong. For the first six months, it was like paradise. Everything I brought to him, he would institute. Then all of a sudden, boom boom boom, it started to go the other way. And then one day, I said I had to move out of this building, because the guy would not listen to anything."

I'm sure Bob Nardelli would see it differently. You might think CEOs would be the smartest men and women in the world, but—believe me—they are as fallible and capable of being foolish as anyone. Former CEOs hope new CEOs will need them, just as new CEOs frequently ignore the value of experience of those that came before them. It's best to traverse a middle ground. A new CEO does need to set his or her own path. At the same time, predecessors can be of invaluable assistance. Even the last few U.S. presidents seem to have understood this—George W. Bush developed a relationship with Bill Clinton, and Barack Obama invited all the living presidents to the White House early in his tenure. The people who have been in your office before you can help you out. Bernie Marcus was in his seventies when Nardelli took over, and he wanted desperately for Nardelli to succeed. But it seems, at least from one perspective, that ego got in the way. And it was ironic to Bernie and Arthur: they had a succession problem above them with Sandy Sigoloff at the beginning of their partnership, and with Bob Nardelli replacing them at the end.

"I just had the same conversation coming over here today," Marcus concluded in his office when we chatted. "My driver said the same thing, because he worked for Nardelli. With you, it was always Home Depot. With Nardelli, it was Nardelli."

(Needless to say, when I spoke with Nardelli about his years at Home Depot, he didn't see it this way at all. We decided to speak off the record, but I think it's fair to summarize our conversation by noting that he recognized the great partnership Bernie and Arthur had.)

Eventually, the powers that existed at Home Depot felt that Bob Nardelli had worn out his welcome at the company, and that he was isolating himself at the top. He left the company in early 2007 and was replaced by the current CEO, Frank Blake. Not only is Blake's management philosophy much more in line with that of Bernie and Arthur, but he makes a point to keep the founders in the loop on company business and consult them on problems that arise. Even today, Blake occasionally walks through the stores with Bernie, still smartly picking the brain of the man who discovered the Achilles' heel of the home improvement business.

"I love him," says Arthur of Blake. "He's a terrific guy, and he understands the company's core values."

A company can last for years by riding on the creativity

and innovation of the past, and by relaxing on the reputation built by its founders and visionaries. But it's only a matter of time before that company caves if it ignores its core strategy—in this case, customer service.

Not having a strong succession plan in place certainly ended up being a blow to Home Depot, but the corporate culture was strong enough to reemerge. Today the company has reclaimed the reputation the founders worked so hard to build—of a great place to shop, and a great place to work. Meanwhile, Bernie and Arthur are still friends, even as they pursue different post–Home Depot interests. As close as they were on a day-to-day basis at the office, beyond that, they made a pact to limit their personal relationship when they were working. In the retail business, Bernie had seen partners get too close, families get too close, and then relationships—and companies—go up in smoke. If it sounds sticky, it isn't. When I spent time with them separately, they reaped praise upon one another throughout our conversations, and talked of continuing to counsel one another on their current pursuits like the aquarium in Atlanta and the Falcons football team.

"Obviously you have to have a shared vision of the business," Arthur said as he walked me out, reflecting on his partnership. "If you're thinking about different things, that's not healthy for anybody. But also, work with somebody you like. It is a marriage—we spent a lot of hours together, and you want to have fun doing it.

"It's a really great model—a great story for how a partnership can work," he concluded. "Though our philosophies were similar, our skill sets were different."

On their own, Bernie Marcus, Arthur Blank, Ken Langone, Pat Farrah, and many of the thousands of people who became part of Home Depot would probably have been very successful in life no matter what they did.

Teaming up, though, gave them a chance to make American business history.

8

SUSAN FENIGER AND MARY SUE MILLIKEN

"A good partnership has to allow for a certain amount of separation."

Too many cooks in the kitchen."

It's a phrase heard in any number of places in the business world, and a phrase, if you think about it, that runs counter to the concept of the virtues of partnership, describing people unable to figure out their roles and work together. It's ironic, then, that I found one of the most intriguing partnerships in this book in a kitchen. Two women who are partners, friends, and even married to the same man. (Well, not at the same time.)

I'll start the story in early 2009, with a new restaurant, called Street, opening in downtown Hollywood, about fifteen minutes from my office. Almost every well-known restaurant has a Web site these days—typically artfully designed, with basic information, a menu, sometimes some good reviews—but the Web site for Street is a bit more ambitious. There, you'll also find a series of Web videos starring its owner and founder, and chronicling the panicked and stressful months leading up to the opening of the restaurant. As part of an opening sequence edited together to emphasize the haywire and frantic process of getting things off the ground, chef Susan Feniger is shown doing a dozen things at once, talking on the phone, talking to people in the kitchen, cutting food, tasting food, even jumping off a table. And as the video goes on, Susan explains her vision. The menu features creative takes on urban street food—it is clear that her personality and identity is very much part of the restaurant's personality and identity.

"It's exciting, it's challenging, it's crazy," she narrates. "And it's got my name all over it!"

Yes, Susan Feniger's Street is the actual name of the restaurant, which makes sense as a business decision. Feniger is a well-known name on the Los Angeles eating scene, with two decades of tremendous success and popularity in the area that's translated into a television career and several cookbooks. But to people who might see the name on the restaurant, or stumble onto the videos on the Web site, what's missing might be just as striking as what's there. At Street, Susan Feniger is without her longtime business partner, Mary Sue Milliken. After the success of their collaborations—the restaurants City, Border Grill, and Ciudad; the television shows; and the cookbooks—two decades of triumphs along with the failures, and even a shared husband (with several years between their marriages), apparently it is time for a change.

Susan is doing this restaurant on her own.

■ ■ ■

There are all kinds of contradictions in the restaurant business. One has to do with atmosphere, a huge part of a successful eatery. Some are romantic, some are quiet, some are purposefully bustling with energy—but with all the good ones, an incredible amount of thought, care, and effort goes into making them just so. Then there's what's behind the kitchen door; with all the attention put on the product going out into the dining room, little heed is paid to the quality of the atmosphere by the grills and fryers and stainless-steel countertops. Sometimes it's controlled frenzy, often it's all-out frenzy, but it's always packed with pressure. The successful chefs somehow find comfort amid the madness—they're like athletes who say the game slows down for them in the biggest moments. But it takes a certain type of talent to perform an already difficult task in an atmosphere where so much can go wrong so quickly.

Another contradiction revolves around an outdated cultural stereotype that today has become a rallying cry for aspiring female chefs. For many years, even as women proved them wrong, "Women belong in the kitchen" was the mantra of a male-dominated society, even as so many women proved them otherwise. Though it's still a sarcastic retort for male chauvinists to dust off once in a while, a piece of irony was

perhaps lost on the narrow-minded: historically, women actually haven't been welcome in professional kitchens. Beginning with the classic tradition of French haute cuisine in the
nineteenth century, through the expansion of fine dining all
over Europe and the United States, cooking professionally
has been a man's job. Working in a kitchen at a restaurant is,
in fact, very physical, a life of lifting heavy pots, arms frequently burned by scalding water, fingers often cut by sharp
knives. In addition, the hours—working nights, weekends,
and holidays—are brutal, and certainly most brutal on someone trying to raise a family and nurture children. In today's
more egalitarian world, people tend to work around these
difficulties more than they did, say, in the late 1970s, which
meant it was a very unlikely occurrence one day back then
at the famed Chicago restaurant Le Perroquet, when a young
woman barely in her twenties walked in to ask the owner for
a job.

"It was the best restaurant in Chicago then, by leaps and
bounds," Mary Sue Milliken remembers today. "I show up
and say I want a job in the kitchen, and he laughed me out
of the interview. He fixed me a cup of tea, and told me forget
it—he asked me if I wanted a job as a hatcheck girl. I was just
devastated, and I cried all the way home. And then I started
this letter-writing campaign. I wrote him a letter every three
or four days for a couple weeks. Then I started calling him,
and finally he said, 'Are you going to sue me?' And I said, 'No,
all I want is a job. I just want to work for you.' And he said,
'Okay, come in tomorrow, $3.25 an hour, it's minimum wage,
you can peel shallots.' "

It wasn't a glamorous offer, but it was all she wanted. Mary

Sue had grown up in Michigan, where she had acquired a love of food and cooking at an early age.

"I had a moment," she remembers today. "I had been in home-ec classes that I loved in high school, and I loved to cook with my mom. But when I was sixteen, I met this great guy who was a very passionate cook. He was a friend of my sister's, and he invited us over to dinner, and we went over to his apartment, and he wasn't there yet. And then he comes up the stairs with these two grocery bags, and goes into the kitchen and just starts chopping, and at that moment, I just said, That's what I want to do. I want to be a chef, and hold a knife like that, and cook that fast, and be that proficient. It was this one moment. He made chicken paprikash, and just handed me a shrimp appetizer that he'd made after he'd only been in the apartment twelve minutes, and I said to him that day, I want to be you. I want to go to chef school."

So after she graduated high school, she moved to Chicago and went to the Washburne Culinary Institute. Two years later, she talked her way into the kitchen of the best restaurant in Chicago, where she quickly began outworking all the men around her.

"I'd come in early—my shift started at eight, and I'd come in at five thirty," she remembers. And soon the owner who'd so reluctantly hired her took a liking to the employee who seemed more passionate about the food business than anyone else in his kitchen. The Chicago restaurant legend Jovan Trboyevic and his twenty-year-old shallot peeler began to bond.

"People like Jovan, older generation European chefs and

restaurateurs," she remembers, "they were so tickled to have somebody that fascinated and tickled with the profession that they would just give everything. It was such flattery for those guys. You just give them a lot, and it gets you a lot."

You have to go to law school to become a lawyer, and medical school to become a doctor, but any good member of either of those professions will tell you their real-world education begins in the office. Similarly, Mary Sue may have gone to trade school to learn how to be a chef, but her real education was just starting.

"There were only like five restaurants in Chicago at that time of that character, and really Le Perroquet just blew everyone else out of the water," she says. "Totally ahead of its time. It was on the second floor, and you had to get into this little velvet-walled elevator to go up, and then Jovan, this courtly Yugoslavian, really old-school restaurateur, would greet everybody. He didn't want food critics in the restaurant. You'd get those little *amuse-bouche* when you'd sit down, and everything—they way they made the coffee, the way they made the salad—was just amazing."

Trboyevic's eyes had also been opened—to the fact that a hard worker was a hard worker in the kitchen, man or woman. And so six months later, when another woman showed up at his door asking for a job, she didn't have to embark on a letter-writing campaign. Instead, twenty-five-year-old Susan Feniger was hired on the spot.

Mary Sue was no longer all alone in the kitchen. But she couldn't have known how much the new woman would impact her life.

■   ■   ■

Susan Feniger can talk. There is a spirit and a charm to her that would make even the shyest of diners smile at her enthusiasm. As I sat next to her and Mary Sue Milliken when we met on an afternoon in Los Angeles, enjoying an unending parade of food courses that would render dinner (and breakfast the next morning) unnecessary, I thought about what it must have been like for Mary Sue Milliken when Susan came to work at Le Perroquet for her first day on the job. For one thing, I didn't get a sense that any competitive fires were stoked—when you graduate chef school from a class of sixty with only one other woman in your class, there is a real thrill when another one suddenly materializes in the kitchen.

"They brought her around to show her the place," Mary Sue remembers, "and I thought to myself, What if they hire her? Wouldn't that be great? Another woman!"

Susan, she soon learned, was also from the Midwest, having grown up in Toledo, Ohio. She had gone to college, but soon dropped out and gone to live with her high school boyfriend on a farm in Vermont—in a tepee on the farm's land. Her boyfriend worked on the farm, and she worked for a cabinet maker. One night, presumably freezing their behinds off in the tepee, the young couple decided enough was enough, and went back to college—this time in warmer California. And then, in another right turn, Susan decided she was going to go to culinary school.

"I was working in the school cafeteria," Susan remembers excitedly, as if it were yesterday. "And the guy who was the cook there, who ran the cafeteria, said to me, 'Why are you in school? Why don't you go to culinary school? Why aren't you doing this—this is what you should be doing.' And he was right—I absolutely loved it. I loved the dish room, working in the dish room—there was this woman who was like eighty pounds, she smoked cigarettes and washed pots and pans, and I loved her. When I worked in the dish station, I loved it, when I was slicing ham on the slicer—everything about it, I loved."

After two years at the Culinary Institute of America in New York, Susan reunited with her boyfriend, Josh, in Kansas City, where he was attending architecture school. Soon they were married, she was working at a great restaurant, and life was great. Until she came home and made a confession to Josh: she was leaving him—for a woman she had fallen in love with at the restaurant. A few months later, she moved to Chicago with her new girlfriend and got the job at Le Perroquet. And very quickly, while cleaning vegetables, stirring chicken stock, and steaming broccoli, Mary Sue heard the story of her new friend's whirlwind last few years.

"We became such fast friends—it was immediate," Mary Sue says. "We had the same work ethic, we both wanted to come in earlier than everyone else."

Further, Susan inspired Mary Sue with her passion; this wasn't the kind of woman who went into anything—her romantic life, her professional life—halfheartedly.

"When I first met Susan," Mary Sue continues, "she told me she wasn't reading any more novels. She was only reading cookbooks. I thought, Holy cow, I will never be that driven."

That drive, though, meant that inevitably Susan would get restless and want to continue her training at another restaurant. After about a year working at Le Perroquet, Susan broke up with her girlfriend and decided to move to Los Angeles, getting a job at Ma Maison, Wolfgang Puck's first restaurant in the United States. It is the way of life of aspiring young chefs, going from city to city, learning from different masters, improving their own skills. For her part, Mary Sue briefly tried to open a café in Chicago with some other friends, but it quickly became clear the venture wasn't going to work, just as her own relationship with a boyfriend was beginning to crumble. Yovan, the owner of Le Perroquet, had become her mentor, and he suggested she turn her eyes across the Atlantic—to the culinary capital of Paris. Thanks to some of his connections, she got a job at a restaurant in the city. But before she left, she called Los Angeles to let her old kitchen friend know where she was going. Or maybe in L.A., Susan called her. Neither can exactly remember, but when they spoke, they found out something strange: they were both starting jobs in France the following week.

Their experiences were very different. Mary Sue was an off-the-books employee at a bistro in the city, and while she learned a lot, she had a lonely year there.

"I had taken French in high school," she says, "but that didn't help, because they were speaking as fast as they possibly could. They would say things like, 'Can you put a pot of water on to boil?' in French, and of course I wouldn't know what they meant, and they would giggle and laugh at me, saying, She doesn't know how to boil a pot of water!"

(I can relate. I took French in school, went to Paris with my wife on our honeymoon, and once decided to spend a couple of days at Le Cordon Bleu, the top French cooking school. The chef/professor spoke French [fine, that was appropriate], but when he held up ingredients, his hand purposely hid the labels so we had no idea what he was saying [not so appropriate]. We lasted one day.)

Susan, on the other hand, was in a small town near Cannes and loved it. When Mary Sue went down to visit Susan on the Riviera, ready to complain about the French to her friend, she discovered café owners walking by and happily greeting her! "Susan! Susan!" Still, when the tourist season ended, it was Susan who came up to stay in Mary Sue's tiny apartment, where they split up the bed by putting the box spring on the floor, fooled with recipes, drank wine, and talked about the future.

"Around the second bottle of wine one night," Mary Sue remembers, "there was a rainbow outside the window, and we said, You know, we should go into partnership, and we shook on it. Literally did the handshake."

"We had been drinking, but there was a rainbow," Susan corroborates. "And we said, We should open a restaurant together. Where should we do it? And so then, we started naming cities. Austin, Dallas, oh—I heard Phoenix was a good place. . . ."

If only it was so easy, even for these free spirits. Mary Sue went back to Chicago, and Susan back to Los Angeles, where they got different jobs. It was fun to talk about the possibilities of the future, but not easy to immediately turn the future into the present. Susan, however, was not going to give up on the idea.

"The thing about Susan," explains Mary Sue, "is that she's so persistent. She just doesn't take no for an answer. So it just gradually wears you down."

Susan began calling Mary Sue, pestering her to come to Los Angeles and join her at this new, small café, where she saw all kinds of possibilities—and freedom.

"I'm going to move out of my apartment," she told Mary Sue, "and you can move in, and you can just stay the summer. How about just commit to two months?"

And since Mary Sue hated her new job at the time, finally, she did. She came out to L.A., they put a stove in the café the weekend she got there in 1981, and City Café on Melrose Avenue was born.

■　　■　　■

I hadn't heard the story of Mary Sue and Susan before I began researching this book. When I talked to a few people who knew them, everyone told me the same thing: they finish each other's sentences, complete each other's thoughts, and answer each other's questions even before they're asked. Wolfgang Puck even told me that he remembered Susan as an "adventurous, interesting" young chef in his restaurant whom he called "Brownie," because she always had a tan, and "who would make it if she found the right business partner." When I met them, I quickly saw what their friends meant, and immediately understood how they worked so well together.

Why then, I kept wondering, was Susan starting a restaurant on her own?

We met at Ciudad, one of the pair's three restaurants. It's in downtown Los Angeles, a longtime popular lunchtime spot for people looking for a unique business meal as well as a destination on weekends. The menu is inspired by cuisines from all over Latin America, with recipes originating in the Caribbean, Central America, South America, and more. When I sat down at the corner table with the pair, I took a look around the place, and it struck me how far the chefs had come, not only from peeling shallots in Chicago, but also from the original City Café.

"City Café was a cool little space," Mary Sue says. "Nine by eleven feet, eleven tables, thirty-nine seats altogether, including the ten seats at the bar."

And in the back, in the tiny kitchen, it was just them, along with a dishwasher who doubled as a busboy. There was a hot plate, and then, in the parking lot behind the small café, a prep table and hibachi for cooking fish. That's right—they would get an order for grilled fish, and one of them would run outside into the parking lot to grill the fish. It didn't endear them to the city health inspector, but the fish apparently came out well. Following their apprenticeships in a series of expensive restaurants, at their little café, Mary Sue and Susan had found the perfect place to mature themselves.

"We were learning how to run a restaurant," Mary Sue says. "We didn't know what we were doing. There were two waitresses, Holly and Iris, and then there was the dishwasher, Jose Luis, and we would write the menu on a blackboard every morning."

And every night, the lines would stretch down the block. City Café became one of the most popular spots in the arts scene that was emerging around the neighborhood. Mary Sue and Susan had gone from being kitchen grunt workers to having a hot (if small) restaurant in Los Angeles in less than three years.

"What felt genuine and authentic," Mary Sue says, "was

that we shared the kitchen equally, and we were both really passionate and driven, with a strong work ethic, and we complemented each other."

"We collaborated on food all the time," Susan continues.

"It's funny," Mary Sue picks up. "In the beginning, we did everything almost as one person. I'd do the produce order, she'd check it. She'd do the produce order, and then I'd check things off. We basically did a lot of things right on top of each other—and everything together."

The cramped kitchen and the pressure could have either driven them apart or brought them closer. I think it's fair to say it was the latter of the two because, simply, these two wanted it so badly. They wanted to succeed, for the women who hadn't had the opportunities they had, and for their own opportunities in the future.

Sure enough, once the reviews had been published and the cash continued to flow in, Mary Sue and Susan began fantasizing about their next dream—a bigger restaurant. They began looking around Los Angeles for locations, and soon found a carpet warehouse that appeared perfect. They'd call it City—to keep the spirit of the City Café name. After successfully negotiating with the owners to take over the space, the next step was figuring out how to design a restaurant. Susan was all over it—she had an old friend, an architect, whom she desperately wanted to hire to design the restaurant. It was Josh, her ex-husband, who she had tried (sometimes in vain) to stay close to after they'd split up several years earlier, calling him every several months to check in. He would take the calls and listen to Susan—remember what Mary Sue says, she doesn't take no for an answer—but understandably, Josh wasn't super interested in staying close to the woman who'd left him.

"But when we decided we were going to do City," Susan says, "I called him and said we're going to open up this big restaurant, and you have to come in and design it."

Josh was noncommittal. But a few months later, Mary Sue was out front in the café when a man walked in and sat down at the bar.

"I went back," Mary Sue remembers, "and said, Susan, go out there, I think your ex-husband's here."

They hadn't seen each other in five years. Mary Sue, meanwhile, was surely fascinated about meeting a guy she had heard all about for so long. The three began to talk about the possibilities of the larger restaurant. It was several months away from a point where Josh could even begin the designing process. He was happy to stay in Los Angeles to wait. Perhaps improbably, perhaps predictably, he had felt an instant spark with the woman who had become his ex-wife's business partner and best friend. Three weeks later, Josh moved in with Mary Sue. They've been together ever since.

Yes, Mary Sue is married to Susan's ex-husband. And Susan couldn't be happier about it.

"Susan would say, 'You should meet my ex-husband,'" Mary Sue remembers. " 'You'd love him.' I didn't have a boyfriend the whole time I had lived in L.A., and Susan kept saying—"

"She kept dating these total loser creeps," Susan jumps in. "It was like, Why are you dating that guy, he's such a creep."

"It was so true. Guys like the bad guy from the *Mad Max* movie."

Eventually, years later, Susan would be at the hospital (once in the delivery room) for the birth of Mary Sue and Josh's two children. In the short term, meanwhile, the women had an architect for their new restaurant.

■   ■   ■

Designed by Josh Schweitzer, City was 5,000 square feet, with 125 seats—four times the size of the original City Café. The menu was, in essence, of the city—a combination of Asian and Latin American and Indian foods, cuisines of many of Los Angeles's biggest ethnic cultures. Soon they opened a new restaurant, the Border Grill, a Latin American restaurant with recipes and dishes inspired by many of the Latino cooks and busboys the women had worked with over the years, but with a twist.

"We looked at the Mexican kitchen like we did the French kitchen," Mary Sue once recalled. "We took our French training and took the basic core of what people were doing for hundreds of thousands of years. The idea is there, we're not changing it. Mainly, it's just changing the technique."

It was, again, a success. A few years later, the women moved Border Grill to a larger spot in Santa Monica, and when City closed in the mid-1990s, the Latin American kitchen became their flagship. The economy was suffering, and Mary Sue and Susan were content to have one great restaurant in a great city. Until in 1995, the fledgling Food Network invited them to guest-star on the show *Chef du Jour*. Even before the network had started, of course, going back to Julia Child, chefs on television had been popular. But no one had ever seen two chefs like this, with a chemistry that made viewers wonder if they shared a brain. Soon, the Too Hot Tamales, as they called themselves, had their own show. Cookbooks, radio shows, and appearances at cooking shows across the country followed, as did new Border Grills elsewhere in L.A. and also in Vegas, as well as Ciudad, the restaurant I met the pair at. The cooking world fell in love with the short, spunky, aggressive Susan and the taller, somewhat milder, somewhat calmer Mary Sue, very different women who (a few people knew) had married the same guy and (more people knew) had grown up together in the restaurant world. They became two of the most recognizable chefs in the food world, a veritable mini-industry unto themselves.

No one had really seen a lasting restaurant partnership like this—between two chefs—in the restaurant world. Sure, there are often business collaborations, but few if any cases where partners essentially started from scratch together and stayed attached through years of expansion. The stories of any others have tended to end in dramatic explosions. Yes, as we spoke, Susan was headed to her own establishment, Street, but I didn't exactly observe this partnership to be broken. Their other three restaurants were staying open, and it was hard to find tension between these two women as they laughed about their early days and finished each other's sentences. The partnership certainly continued to exist, even if, at the same time, Susan was embarking on her own endeavor.

Looking back, maybe because of the original uphill battle they faced breaking in, their bond was stronger. Maybe they were predisposed to join forces more than the average chef. A few years ago, a handful of women founded a trade organization for women chefs, largely intended as a support and advocacy group.

"I remember in the meetings," Mary Sue says, "talking about how we had all gravitated toward our own small businesses, rather than fighting through the ranks to get more money, or better positions. We wanted to call our own shots.

We went through hell to get this education and we started in this tiny restaurant with a couple of hot plates because we just didn't want to hit that ceiling and have a boss—a guy— determine our fate."

Perhaps just as important, they're just a really good match—years ago and today; in the kitchen, and then also back in the restaurant office.

"I think it's interesting that from the first time we got in the kitchen together," Mary Sue says, "we gravitated to different sides. Susan loves chaos—when there's a huge mess, and the waiters are screaming, and the cooks don't know what to do, and everybody's in a big horrible kind of catastrophe mode. That's when Susan is the happiest, in the middle of that. I'm about precision and planning and not being caught in that."

"Mary Sue would lean toward pastries and the pantry and things that are way more predictable," Susan continues.

"What really makes me happy is creating as many systems that won't let [chaos] happen."

If both women were into precision, it wouldn't work—they probably would have driven themselves crazy. And if they were both into bedlam, it also would have failed.

In Susan's view, "That balance has worked for us, because I tend to be more one way, and Mary Sue tends to be the other way, and so I think we have both learned that in the middle, we come up with this balance that works."

But balance isn't as easy as they might make it sound, in a small kitchen or a much bigger one. In the business world, there is much more room to operate—physically, and creatively. Behind the restaurant's swinging doors, all the focus is on the food. Everything about the partnership—the sharing of duties, the pace of preparations, the problems that come up—is much more pressure-packed, making balance that much trickier. Meanwhile, all this intensity makes everything else outside the kitchen—not just the television work and radio work and cookbooks, but managing a handful of restaurants and making more traditional "business" decisions—that much easier. Apparently, if you can work in a tiny kitchen with someone, it makes running a business a lot easier.

"I think we're both very entrepreneurial," says Susan.

"Susan pushes more than me for sure," counters Mary Sue.

"No, we talk it out," Susan continues, "like when we opened in Vegas. I really thought we should do Vegas. Mary Sue might have been more hesitant, but the hesitancy forces us to look at it, and ask, Why is it a good idea? So I think that really balances for us, and then [in other cases] convinces me it's a bad idea, and we don't do it."

At the core of all this, of course, is something very simple but not so easy; at the core of every partnership profiled in this book is trust. Going into business with someone takes trust. Growing that business with the same person takes even more trust. Marrying your best friend's ex-husband, no matter the circumstances, takes an incredible amount of trust as well.

"I think that's been the strength for all of these years," says Susan. "I think there is this complete trust."

Mary Sue: "When I'm out, the decision's going to get made as if I were here. I totally and fully trust that."

Susan: "I feel the same."

Mary Sue: "I don't think if we were any more alike, it

would have ever worked. And the fact that we're as different as we are . . ."

Her voice trails off for a second.

"There have been plenty of times over the years when we said to each other's face, you know, questioning whether I want to keep in this partnership, and I've let myself wonder about it for a week or two, and then it's come to me that it's worth it, because I'll put up with that stupid whatever-it-is-that-you-do that drives me crazy, in order to reap the benefits."

Searching for the roots of their openness, Susan raises another point.

"I think in being two women, one thing we have always done is always keep a very open communicative company. We don't have tension between the front of the house and the back of the house. Our kitchens are playful and friendly and warm, and any time we've ever had a chef who's an asshole, they haven't lasted. We don't tolerate this stuck-up nature— the nature of what chefs have always been."

In some partnerships, because of the dynamics as much as the individuals, doubts are inevitable. What is certainly not, though, is the partners' willingness to deal with the doubts head-on.

"We've been to therapy together," Mary Sue almost proudly admits. "Like, if we weren't able to decide on growth—like Susan's appetite for growth would be more than mine, and would create tension. I think we've made a conscious decision to talk about things a lot."

In the past year, there's been plenty to talk about.

■   ■   ■

They are sitting in front of me at the table at Ciudad, the plates finally cleared, stomachs more than full. I'm ready for tension as I broach the subject of separation, to read between the lines of what might be said.

"After we closed a Border Grill in Pasadena, and then Green Valley," Susan says, "those were two losses. Plus, I had all this family loss. I lost my oldest, closest friend to a horrible disease, and then three months later my mother passed away, and then like four months later our fourteen-year-old dog passed away, and then three months later, my dad. So it was just a miserable eighteen months. And I think it felt, for me, like I wanted to do more. I don't want to feel like I'm afraid to do it—I was really ready to do it."

But wouldn't a time like that be a time when you'd come together with your partner, not go out alone? Mary Sue jumps in.

"Well, I have two kids, and I don't have the same appetite, because I have so much of my life taken up with that. And I didn't want to hold Susan back. I thought a good partnership has to allow for a certain amount of separation. We would literally blow each other's noses and check each other's work at the beginning of this partnership, and it seems like this long, slow separation, and kind of this individuation, if that's a word." It is.

"I think it's been the most difficult of any decision," Susan says. "We were fifty-fifty on everything, no matter what."

Mary Sue: "So even if Susan would do a project without me, we would split the money fifty-fifty. But then there also came a point where that wasn't going to work anymore, and we were still trying to figure out exactly what does work."

So, in their fifties, in a phase of life completely different from where they started, partnership has, as much as
anything, become about understanding each other's needs.
On one side of the coin, Mary Sue and Susan's three restaurants—the two Border Grills and Ciudad—are as strong as
ever. On the other side, clearly their passions have begun
to diverge. After three decades of sharing everything, Susan
needed a new challenge that didn't involve Mary Sue. And
in fact, the best thing Mary Sue could do as a partner was to
let her go off and take that challenge. After we met, Susan
was going to Street to spend the afternoon and evening at
her new place. Mary Sue, meanwhile, was actually headed
backward—to Michigan to participate in a cooking show with
her old mentor Jovan, now eighty-nine years old and retired.
They e-mailed me separately after we talked.

In Mary Sue's e-mail, she wrote that it was "great to talk
partnerships yesterday," and offered one of their restaurants
for a book party in Los Angeles.

Wrote Susan, meanwhile: "Street's given me an outlet to
continue to grow, to discover more about myself, to question
some things I've grown comfortable with, and it's validated
many things I've learned over the years. But in many ways,
it was freeing to make decisions without Mary Sue and our
whole small corporate structure. It's been incredibly inspiring and so satisfying that I can only describe it with saying
it's made my heart full and almost giddy. That's pretty fantastic after thirty-plus years in a career, how lucky I feel!"

She is alone, but she is still a partner. Apparently it is possible to be both.

9

JOE TORRE AND DON ZIMMER

"Hit and run."

The baseball had been hit about as hard as you can hit it, and was rising as it rocketed into the gap between right and center field at the old Fulton County Stadium in Atlanta. It was a Thursday night, October 24, 1996—Game 5 of the World Series between the Braves and the Yankees. The series was tied—Atlanta had won the first two games at Yankee Stadium, and then the Yankees had come back with two victories on the road. Now, with two outs in the ninth inning, the Yanks were up 1–0, but the Braves had put the tying run on third base and winning run on first base, runs that appeared destined to score courtesy of the line drive headed to the right-center field gap.

In the Yankees dugout, Joe Torre sat and watched the ball take off with everyone else. After more than three decades in major league baseball, Torre was enjoying his first trip to the World Series. He had played eighteen seasons for three different teams, making nine All-Star teams and winning a Most Valuable Player award. Then he'd become a manager, and after three mostly unremarkable stops over fifteen years, had landed with the Yankees. When he'd been hired in his hometown of New York before the 1996 season, he'd brought with him a hardly inspiring career managing record featuring more losses than wins, and after his introductory press conference, one of the headlines in the city tabloids had read "Clueless Joe." Now, less than twelve months later, he'd led his team to a first-place finish in the American League East division, and then victories in the playoffs to take them to the Series against the Braves. Torre would be the first to tell you his sudden success was first and foremost due to the talents of his roster, a combination of rising stars like Derek Jeter, Mariano Rivera, and Andy Pettitte, and experienced veterans like Wade Boggs, Tino Martinez, and Paul O'Neill. But Torre had also thrived doing something few managers were willing to do, particularly in the fishbowl of New York, and particularly with an impulsive owner like the late George Steinbrenner constantly looking over his shoulder. All season, Torre had made bold decisions that left him vulnerable to second-guessing by newspaper columnists, radio-talk-show hosts, and fans.

Game 5 of the 1996 World Series was littered with examples of such aggressive but debatable moves. Some had worked out while others threatened to backfire. Just a few moments earlier, in the top half of the ninth inning, the Yankees had had two runners on base with a chance to get a few extra runs before the Braves' final turn at bat. But Torre had decided to let his young starting pitcher, Andy Pettitte, hit and remain in the game. As expected, Pettitte had been retired at the plate, ending New York's rally, and then, when he took the mound in the ninth, had given up a leadoff double before being relieved, a hit that now threatened to cost the Yanks the lead. Before the game as well, Torre had ignored conventional wisdom when making his lineup. A right-handed pitcher, John Smoltz, would be on the mound for the Braves, and typically, left-handed hitters do much better than righties against right-handed pitchers. But rather than go with the percentages, Torre had elected to look at other factors as he decided who'd play Game 5. At third base, he'd chosen the right-handed-hitting Charlie Hayes over his lefty counterpart Wade Boggs, reasoning that Hayes was superior defensively, and with Pettitte on the mound, there would be a lot of ground balls to the left side of the infield. Sure enough, Hayes had played a solid third base all night, and already in the ninth, had made a strong play for the inning's second out. Torre had also put righty Cecil Fielder in the starting lineup at first base, rather than Tino Martinez, figuring, damn the percentages—Fielder had been swinging the bat well. Fielder had driven in the game's only run with a fourth-inning double.

He'd also intended to put righty Tim Raines in right field to replace Paul O'Neill, the gutsy, intense team leader who'd been battling injuries all season long.

"I don't just write a lineup and put it out there," Torre explained to me in Los Angeles years later. "I call these guys in one at a time. I said to Boggs, 'I'm playing Charlie Hayes today.' 'Okay.' He walks out. I call in Tino. 'I'm going to play Cecil today.' He was mad, and he walked out, respectful but angry.

"Then I call in Paul O'Neill because he was struggling. You know, he's been hurt most of the year. I say, I'm going to play Tim Raines. He puts his head down, and he walks out. Zim is sitting right there."

"Zim" is Don Zimmer, Torre's bench coach and closest confidant on the team, who sat in the manager's office for meetings like this.

"So he walks out," Torre remembered, "and Zim says, 'You know, he's been playing on one leg all year. I think he deserves to play.' " And then Zimmer walked out of the office to give the manager a chance to think about it.

Torre did just that, and called O'Neill back into his office.

"Manager's prerogative," he said. "I have the right to change my mind. You're playing."

Now, three hours later, the baseball was rocketing into the right-center field gap. And Paul O'Neill, running on one gimpy leg, was lumbering toward the wall after it. Baseball can be a complicated game, but looking back at those few seconds of uncertainty, it's easy to flash through all the decisions Torre had made up to that point that had led him to this dramatic juncture—not just the decisions of Game 5, but the decisions in the playoffs, the regular season, and even spring training. At the moment, the biggest decision of them all seemed to be putting Paul O'Neill in right field. But everything had been decided in the same fashion, either in the manager's office or in the dugout: all with Don Zimmer sitting next to him. Zimmer's input on the O'Neill call was obvious, but his influence on all the others was also undeniable. Paul O'Neill, of course, caught the ball, sticking his glove up at the last possible moment, just before he ran into the outfield wall. The Yankees won the game, and the next one, to win the World Series. They'd win three more over the next four seasons. All with Torre at the helm, all with Zimmer at his side.

"That was about the most dramatic game I've ever been involved in," Torre told me when I asked him about it. "I get goose bumps talking right now. That's where Zimmer gave me the courage to do something that was against the grain. And we wind up winning the World Series. He was definitely my partner. And as we get into this, you'll see how he changed me."

■   ■   ■

The sports world is certainly filled with different types of partnerships, especially in individual sports. Golfers and caddies, boxers and trainers, figure skaters and coaches. Olympic fans are familiar with the beach volleyball tandem of Misty May-Treanor and Kerri Walsh, who have won two straight gold medals, and who have said they "hit the jackpot" when they found each other, and realized how perfectly complementary their playing styles are. In tennis, twin brothers Bob and Mike Bryan have been the most successful doubles team on the circuit for much of the last decade, and may well have been born to play together.

But managing or coaching a sports team is different. In fact, it's not much different from managing a company. Often when I was talking to the people I worked with at ABC, Paramount, and Disney, we even used sports metaphors. Sometimes while we were making movies or televisions shows, basketball became a reference point. Take good shots, from inside the key—namely, near the basket. Don't shoot the ball from half court—the odds are too slight. Being selfish and hogging the ball doesn't win games. Well-thought-out and reasonable attempts pay off. Frankly, these are all common sense. Sometimes in making acquisitions or difficult decisions, hockey could even come up. Being offsides gets you nowhere—you can't score. Playing by the rules is necessary in sports and essential in business. Shortcuts lead to short profits and worse. In all team sports, leadership and selflessness and talent drive you in the right direction; so, too, in business. In both cases, groups of individuals are put together to achieve a common goal, and personal agendas sometimes clash with that goal. In business, employees can't be faulted for looking out for themselves and their own career paths, and in sports, as much as we like to idealize the values of team play, professional athletes can't be faulted for being concerned about their playing time and the terms of their next contract. But businesses need strong leaders to handle these dilemmas, and so do ball clubs. The New York Yankees are no exception.

From even his playing days, Joe Torre was fingered as manager material by people in baseball circles. He started his career as a catcher, a position that breeds leaders and, quite often, managers. On the field, the catcher is the anchor of the defense, intricately involved in every at-bat, and charged with handling the delicate psyche of the pitcher. In the clubhouse, meanwhile, Torre was one of the most well liked guys in the game, combining a cool demeanor with an ability to reach out to teammates.

"I was very sensitive to players," he told me. "I've been through some counseling and stuff, and I think maybe it was my upbringing. I grew up, my dad was abusive to my mom, and I was the baby in the family, and my older brothers and sisters were always whispering, and I thought maybe I was doing something wrong, causing all these problems in the family . . . that I found out later they were trying to protect me from. But I learned to listen to people."

At the plate, Torre could hit—he won a batting title and MVP award in 1971—but he didn't have great timing with everything else in his career, including his luck. He made his big-league debut with the Milwaukee Braves in 1960, just after they appeared in two straight World Series, and then was traded to the Cardinals in 1969, just after their two straight World Series appearances in 1967 and 1968. By the time Torre was traded to New York after the 1974 season, his skills on the field were fading, but the lowly Mets did see other kinds of potential in the Brooklyn native. While still playing at age thirty-six, Torre took over as a player/manager midway through the 1977 season, and a few weeks later retired and made managing his full-time job. He lasted five years with the Mets, learning the job as he went, and then went back to the Braves to manage in Atlanta, where he won the division his first season in 1982. But the team was swept out of the playoffs in three games, and after a steady decline the next two seasons, Torre was let go again.

"So I get fired, and I get fired," he recounted to me. "I get very sensitive. I think, I guess I didn't do a very good job. I went on, broadcast games for six years, went to St. Louis, managed five years there, got fired there. Then I interviewed with the Yankees, and they offered me the general manager job after the '95 season. I said, 'No, I can't do this, my wife's pregnant, I can't be working for George Steinbrenner as a general manager.' You have no days off, and I can't do this—

my wife's expecting in two or three months. But ten days later, they call and ask if I'm interested in the manager job, and I say sure. So I'm taking on this job, after with all these other jobs, it was like, 'You weren't this, you weren't that, you weren't this.' People have to find reasons to fire you. It's not like, 'We want to try something different.' It's because you couldn't do this, they have to justify the fact that they fired you to somebody."

Torre talks about all this disappointment now with a confident detachment, confidence you'd expect from a manager who's led his teams—in New York and Los Angeles—to the postseason every year from 1996 to 2009 and, and as of press time, counting. But back in '96, he was hardly as secure with his abilities. Communicating with players would be no problem, but it would get him only so far.

"You get sort of sensitive to everyone telling you how you can't win, because you never won," he said. "You lie in bed and say to yourself, 'I should have done this or that.' It's so easy to say, as a young manager, I should have done something else, because what I did didn't work, or I should have been smarter than that. I beat myself up early on as a manager. Winning is the ability to wear a World Series ring. It's the bottom line. And I'm sure it's consistent in any number of areas in business. It's the bottom line—whether you're good, bad, or indifferent—that's what you're judged on."

New York, Torre knew, was the wrong place for a manager who was insecure about his ability to win. The Yankees were in the midst of their longest drought without a World Series appearance since their first title in the 1920s, when Babe Ruth patrolled the outfield. Any slipup, and the press, the fans, and George Steinbrenner would be ready to pounce.

Torre had the players, but he needed to approach the season with something else—confidence. Little did he know he'd find it thanks to the indispensable help of a colorful baseball lifer nicknamed "Popeye."

■   ■   ■

"You know that thing you always hear about Lou Gehrig being the luckiest man in the world?" Don Zimmer asks as he sits at the dining room table of his condominium in St. Petersburg, Florida. "Well, he's got a tie. Because that's the way I feel. No matter what happens to me. And the eight years in New York just put icing on the cake."

Zimmer is seventy-nine years old now, living in Florida with his wife of nearly sixty years, a few miles from the Tampa Bay Rays spring training complex. In the *Baseball Encyclopedia*, he's still listed at his playing weight, 177 pounds, even if most fans today know him as the rounder, cartoonish-looking game elder statesman who was a staple in dugouts for four decades. Today, he works for the Rays as a consultant, and is still closely attuned to what's going on in the game he's been around for more than six decades. Don Zimmer was one of the biggest high school stars in the Cincinnati, Ohio, area in the late 1940s, equipped with a tremendous throwing arm, and was recruited by the legendary coach Bear Bryant to play quarterback at the University of Kentucky. Zimmer visited the school merely because it was his first chance to ride on an airplane; he always intended to play baseball, his first love, and was signed by the Brooklyn Dodgers out of high school in 1949.

Zimmer's rise to the big leagues was delayed when he was hit in the head by a pitch as a minor leaguer, which left him in a coma for a week, but he eventually made it with the Dodgers, and was a member of the famous 1955 Brooklyn team that won the World Series. But like Joe Torre, Zimmer had his own troubles with timing—he was a shortstop in an organization with the great Pee Wee Reese at the position, which meant he didn't get a chance at the full-time job for several years. Eventually Zimmer was traded to the Cubs, then taken by the Mets in the 1962 expansion draft, and bounced to a few other teams before his playing career ended in 1965. He quickly got into coaching with the encouragement of his former general manager in Brooklyn and Los Angeles, Buzzie Bavasi, who hired him as a third-base coach with his new team, the San Diego Padres, in the early 1970s, and then promoted him to be manager of the team halfway through the 1972 season. As a manager, Zimmer quickly earned a reputation for not being afraid to do the unexpected.

"Buzzie Bavasi in Brooklyn," Zimmer says, "gave me some advice. He said, 'I'll tell you something that might help. You'll play and coach for a lot of managers. Take two good things that each manager has, and two bad things that he has, and bury them, so when it's time for you to manage, you'll know.'"

From Casey Stengel, Zimmer learned the magic of the double steal. From Billy Martin, the safety squeeze. And so forth. Put it all together, and the result was a manager who made decisions by the seat of his pants, relying on a combination of instinct and the lessons of his mentors.

"When I explained it," Zimmer says, "I'd tell them who I got it from. I don't want somebody to think I'm the smartest guy in the world—because I'm not."

With an appetite for aggressiveness and creativity, Zimmer would do things few other managers dared try.

"I didn't give a damn if I got fired tomorrow. If a guy hires me to manage, I'm going to manage. And I'm going to do it my way. And every time I did something, I thought it was something that would help the ballclub win. I wasn't trying to be a genius—these are things that I picked up from other people, put them all together, and that's why I did it."

That kind of thinking took Zimmer from San Diego to Boston, where he managed for five seasons, and then the Texas Rangers for three years, and then the Chicago Cubs, where he won Manager of the Year honors in 1989 en route to his only first-place finish. After he was fired in Chicago, Zimmer was offered a different job with the expansion Colorado Rockies, the role of bench coach for rookie manager Don Baylor in 1993. Baylor was, like Joe Torre with the Mets years earlier, a respected, recently retired veteran, chosen to lead the young Rockies for his leadership charms. For more fundamental dugout decisions, like pitching changes, double-switches (replacing a pitcher and a position player at the same time), and other strategies, management decided Baylor would need some help, so they hired the seasoned Zimmer to be, in effect, his dugout tutor. The arrangement lasted well for a few seasons, until Zimmer sensed Baylor had had enough of the tutoring. As ever, the bench coach decided he'd make his own kind of exit—in the fifth inning of a June game in 1995—so as to avoid media attention and what he deemed as unnecessary fanfare. He walked to the end of the dugout, tapped his manager on the knee, said, "Good luck the rest of the way," and made his way to the clubhouse, where he showered, changed, and left without any further good-bye.

He spent the rest of the summer with his children and grand-children, quite content if uncertain of his baseball future at age sixty-five. Then a few weeks after the season ended, the phone rang.

"I didn't know Joe Torre real well," Zimmer says. "I knew him managing against me, and when I managed when he was a player. So when he called me, and said 'This is Joe Torre,' there was only one thing that went through my mind. I thought, He is going to ask me about some player I might know about that he doesn't know. I said, 'How you doing?' He said, 'How *you* doing? How's your health?' 'My health is all right.' 'How's retirement?' 'Well,' I said, 'I didn't exactly retire, I just left.' And it went on and on and I'm still wait-ing for him to say something about this player that I think we're going to talk about. And then he says, 'Do you want to be the bench coach of the New York Yankees?' It blew my mind. That's the last thing that I thought would ever happen. I said, 'I'll get back to you in a week.' I called him back in twenty minutes, and told my wife, 'I'm back in baseball. I'm the bench coach.' "

Zimmer and Torre had played in an age when a man-ager generally hired just four coaches: a first-base coach, a third-base coach, a pitching coach, and perhaps a bullpen coach. If you look back through the annals of the early days of baseball, teams occasionally had assistant managers, or other nebulously named positions, on staff, but those four positions were largely the norm. Gradually, in the 1980s and '90s, as the game became a bigger business than ever, further specialization took hold, with additional hitting and pitch-ing instructors working at all levels of the organization. And though no one's sure exactly who the first actual bench coach was, by the 1990s, they became fairly regular presences inside dugouts, offering a consigliere-like presence for managers during games, as well as before and after them. In his most recent job with St. Louis, Torre had enjoyed working with a Cardinals Hall of Fame legend, Red Schoendienst, and was interested in hiring someone to play that role for the Yankees as soon as he got the job.

"I had a list of people," Torre told me. "Different people's suggestions. And then it just clicked for me—Don Zimmer. I had talked to him, but didn't know him that well. I respected the fact that he managed in both leagues twice. He had also coached in New York, so he knows what that scenario is like. Because New York is unlike any other place to do what I was about to do."

Torre had as many friends in baseball as anyone in the game, but in selecting his coaching staff, he decided to go a different route, with men he respected from a distance, many of whom, like the first-base coach Chris Chambliss and the pitching coach Mel Stottlemyre, were former Yankees.

"I had to separate myself from the friends I wanted to have dinner with, and hire the people who were going to help me do my job," he says.

He handled his coaching staff as any good manager would handle any staff—by delegating, and maintaining a priority on clear lines of communication to the players. If there was something dicey to be dealt with, Torre wanted to handle that himself.

"I told every single one of them," he says, "'I want all your opinions. If there's something you think you can do better, tell me. I have the right to ignore what you might tell me, but I want to hear it. But I don't want anybody going directly to the player.'"

There were two exceptions—two coaches who were allowed to go the players directly—the pitching coach and the bench coach. Stottlemyre, the pitching coach, would become an integral part of Torre's success, guiding a staff that became a critical weapon for the team with both strong starting and deep relief. But no one he hired, it turned out, would be more important than Don Zimmer.

■ ■ ■

Before I continue with more about Joe Torre and Don Zimmer, I think it's important to give a little Yankee history as background. And the man at the center of Yankee history for the last nearly four decades was George Steinbrenner, who will go down in baseball history as one of the most influential—and controversial—people ever to have control of a ball club. Steinbrenner made his fortune after taking over his father's shipping business, and bought the Yankees from CBS in 1973.

(A brief side note on media companies owning businesses: I worked at CBS in the mid–1960s, when the company owned the team, managing it poorly—which usually happens when a corporation owns a team. I remember being shocked when I heard they sold it for $10 million, a memory that came back to me when Disney bought the Anaheim Angels in 1996. Gene Autry had been talking about moving the team, and as a company, we wanted to make sure they stayed in Anaheim alongside Disneyland. We also began a professional hockey team—the Mighty Ducks—around the same time to play in a completed arena that the city council had built with no prospect of a team. On one hand we wanted to support Orange County, but we didn't want to enter sports ownership with promises to the community that we couldn't keep. The CBS failure with the Yankees was a warning example. After we won the only World Series in Angels franchise history in 2002 against San Francisco, and that same year got to the Stanley Cup Final with the Mighty Ducks, we decided to sell the teams with one condition: the new owners couldn't move them to another city. Owning ESPN and ABC Sports was our primary sports business. Owning teams was, conversely, a distraction and no-win situation. If we spent wildly on the team, we'd be applauded by the fans and would be the darling of the *Orange County Register* and the *Los Angeles Times* sports section, but excoriated by our shareholders and the business sections of the same papers.)

Back to the Yankees: when Steinbrenner bought the team from CBS in 1973, the team was in the midst of a down period, and he immediately ratcheted up the expectations of fans by aggressively pursuing free agents, or veteran players who, thanks to new rules in the game, were free to sign with the highest bidder when their contracts expired. Four years later, in 1977, led by the biggest free agent signing to that point in history, Reggie Jackson, the Yankees were back on top, winning the World Series, and then winning it again the next year.

Though the Bronx Bombers made it to another World Series in 1981, which they lost to the Dodgers, as the 1980s continued the team began to decline again, and the franchise became known more for Steinbrenner's bluster, impulsiveness, and unpredictability than anything else. In his first twenty-three years of ownership, before Joe Torre came aboard, Steinbrenner hired and fired managers twenty different times, including Billy Martin five times alone. Nonetheless, when Torre arrived for his first spring training as Yankee manager in 1996, he was excited.

"I basically came in," he told me, "at a point of, 'Okay, I'm gonna find out if I can do this thing.' You know, we have good players, I know George is going to spend money, but I know going in that my job is going to have a lot to do with being able to deal with George Steinbrenner."

In any business, managing up—knowing how to handle your superiors—is often just as important as managing down. The Yankees were no exception. On one hand, Torre seemed a perfect fit for the job—a calm, steady hand who could charm even the bullying Steinbrenner. But on the flip side, someone not willing to make strong decisions with the potential to backfire wouldn't work in New York. Torre couldn't be gun-shy, and there would be little time for missteps once the season started. The Yankees had made their first postseason appearance in over a decade in 1995, and the owner was expecting even bigger things in 1996. It's easy to forget now, but then, the reality was, if Torre got off to a bad start, a deathwatch on his job would have begun quickly.

"I knew I had to basically put blinkers on," Torre said, "and go into this job without concerning myself with 'What is he thinking?' "

Fortunately, the manager who had for so long been afraid of failure was now matched with a partner—Don Zimmer—

who "never gave a damn" if he got fired tomorrow. It was always the same, from the beginning, in the dugout. Torre sat with Stottlemyre, the pitching coach, on his left, and Zimmer on his right. Zimmer, unafraid and uninhibited, was immediately comfortable with his role. As a game went on, he'd offer suggestions freely, concisely, and frequently. "This pitcher's done," "steal," "bunt"—whatever he thought the situation called for.

"After ten days of working with him," Zimmer says, "the first thing I said to him was, 'Joe, I'm controversial baseball-wise. There's only one boss here, and you're it, but I don't sit like a mummy. I'm going to make suggestions, and you'll never hurt my feelings if you don't take them. You're the boss, you've got to answer to the media. I don't. But when I've got things on my mind, I'm going to run them by you. And I'm not going to be afraid to run them by you.' And in two weeks' time, I come home from spring training one night, and I said to my wife, This will work. I just knew that we hit it off good. I could say things to him that I wouldn't say to a lot of managers I'd be working for. And I just felt comfortable running anything by him that I wanted to."

For Torre, though, it took a few weeks to get completely comfortable with someone sitting next to him, on one hand very aggressive about his suggestions, on the other hand claiming he wouldn't take it personally if those suggestions weren't taken. Again, a scenario that sounds a lot like a more traditional office.

"It took us some time," Torre says. "Especially me with my sensitivity to people—when he made a suggestion, I wanted to do it, because I didn't want him to think that I didn't want his input. So it was a fine line in there—I was trying to figure out how to handle not doing something that he suggested I do."

But eventually the sensitive kid from Brooklyn got the hint that, take them or leave them, the suggestions were going to keep coming.

"I remember one time," Torre says, "Luis Sojo was hitting for me. And what Zimmer noticed that I really never noticed was the fact that when Luis Sojo swings, he doesn't very often miss. He might foul the ball off, but he doesn't swing and miss very often. But at that particular time, I was thinking bunt."

"He says to me," Zimmer remembers, "I think I'll bunt. There were men on first and second. I say, hit and run. I love hit and run with men on first and second."

"So I did the hit and run," Torre recalls, "and he hit the ball down the right field line, and the guys started running around the bases. Well, he's already built up the equity now."

Zimmer's recollection of the play excites him more than a decade later: "He puts on the hit and run, and it works. Now Joe's a strong guy—and in the dugout, he's so happy, he banged me on the leg! Bruised it! Another time—Joe Girardi, our catcher, was on first base. And I know Girardi—he played for me as a rookie in Chicago. I'm watching this pitcher, and I know this catcher, and I say, 'Girardi can steal second off this guy.' He put on the steal and stole second. Maybe a week and a half later, Girardi did it again."

Girardi stole thirteen bases that year, a high number for a catcher.

"He banged my leg many times," Zimmer says with a laugh.

"We're fire and ice, basically," Torre adds. "I mean, I'm a little more conservative, he's a little more of a risk-taker. And that's where he changed me. He got me in situations to think outside the box a little bit, and take more chances. And just sort of read individuals a little bit more than just making conservative decisions."

"The media would say to Joe, 'That was a hell of a squeeze play,' " Zimmer remembers. "Joe would give me credit in the papers—he was great. He would say, 'You know, I'm a little more conservative. But I've got a maverick on my right.' He said that in the papers many times."

With half a dozen newspapers covering the team, and local all-sports talk-radio hosts ready to pounce on every decision he made, it would have made sense if Joe Torre became even more conservative than he had been at previous stops, retreating further into a shell of self-doubt. Not incidental was the already burgeoning baseball statistics industry, with many managers swearing by big books of numbers and analysis to make their decisions. Instead, though, with Zimmer at his side, Torre went the other direction, buoyed to rely on a feel for the game in the dugout as much as any matchup numbers for making decisions. With a partner, he began to manage more confidently.

It all is strikingly familiar to the business world—and both of my experiences with great partnership. At Paramount, Barry Diller was the boss, with his job on the line every day with the parent company and the media. For me, the second in command, I had little to lose. So Barry was naturally more conservative, more careful, more deliberate, and I was less so in all those categories—sometimes even off the wall with my suggestions and ideas. The combination of the two of us turned out to be the right mix of risk-averse decision-making with theatrical bravado. In the end, we both agreed on everything, and came together with strong financial protections balanced by interesting commercial and quality endeavors. It made us the leader of the industry for eight years, and we never lost money on any movie. Then at Disney working together with Frank Wells for ten years, it was the opposite. I was relatively conservative when my butt was on the line, while Frank was much more of the "Let's swing for the bleachers" type of guy. He was off the wall compared to me (even though, as I said earlier, nobody believed that). The result was again the right combination of two people coming together with a common purpose to create huge success. Great partnerships—in Hollywood, and on New York baseball fields—rise to the occasion where often the number two can make the number one so much better.

And so it was with Torre and Zimmer. Sure enough, the Yankees took first place at the end of April 1996 and didn't relinquish it for the rest of the season. Today, the Yanks are known—happily by their fans, jealously by fans of teams elsewhere in the league—for being a juggernaut filled with high-priced All-Stars, many of whom they signed or traded for. Back then, though, the team really had no ultra-high-priced stars. Instead, players like Jeter, O'Neill, Tino Martinez, and Bernie Williams led a team that was greater than the sum of his parts, and that took well to aggressive strategy.

"I told Joe when we left spring training," Zimmer recalls, "that we didn't have a typical Yankee ball club—the kind that hits home runs. We had a different kind of club. We were going to have to manufacture some runs. We must have squeeze-bunted about six or seven times that season. But that's the way our team had to play. And we had a lot of guys that executed what we wanted them to do."

Along the way, those guys also took the lead of the example being set in the dugout, and a manager who had no qualms about getting help when he needed it.

■　　■　　■

"There is jealousy, and . . . envy is a good word. There is a lot of that in our game," Don Zimmer says, sitting in an apartment that's filled to the brim with mementos of a life spent in that game. "I've known third-base coaches who have told me that they should be managing the team, and tell me the manager doesn't know what the hell he's doing. That's a terrible thing. If I'm smarter than the manager, I'm trying to help him. That's what I'm there for. I want him to be the best he can be, and I want to be a part of it if I can help him."

When Joe Torre hired Don Zimmer, he knew he was getting an experienced baseball man not afraid to go with his gut. What he didn't know was that he was getting something much more valuable—as loyal and honest a friend and partner as he's ever had in his career.

"He's so loyal," Torre says, "loyal to a fault. And he's just honest. That I didn't know about him, that kind of shoot from the hip and shoot from the lip and, you know, almost too much honesty. But he had no other aspirations or sensitivities other than 'We need to win, and I need to contribute what I can.' "

Recognizing that his bench coach had no hidden agenda

was just as important as recognizing that when Zimmer suggested a hit and run, he knew what he was talking about. Zimmer was sixty-five in 1996 when he took the job, five years removed from his last managing job. He'd had a small health scare a few years earlier when he was with the Rockies, but was obviously well enough to travel for the Yankees, and admitted when we spoke that if another managerial job had come calling at that time, he might have bitten, since, well, "You still want to be the boss." But as the devotee of an old-school baseball code, with the Yankees, all the focus was on helping his team, and his new friend, win.

"You know, I've been in places where I've had coaches that I've confided in," Torre said. "But when I was managing before, I was guarded, maybe because if I asked someone a question, maybe it shows that I'm weak. You know, that I don't know what I'm doing. So unless you trust in that person, it's tough."

Once he got trust and faith in Zimmer, though, he was changed forever as a manager.

"I did it alone, and it wasn't fun," Torre continues. "In New York, though, as long as I had somebody to talk about what just transpired, I didn't care what anybody else thought, because I knew we knew what we were doing. That was more important to me than what was written in the paper the next day, or what was being talked about on radio and stuff like that. These are the people that are in the foxhole with you, who know what you're trying to accomplish, who know how you're going to try and do it, because you've talked about it. And if it blows up on you, it's nice to have these guys sitting there and we're all in the same boat, even if it's a failure."

But not only was it not a failure in New York that first season, but the tone set by the partnership in the dugout trickled down to the rest of the clubhouse.

"You're right about the envy thing," Torre says. "It's what I try to project to my team. You know, we're here to reach this goal, and I really don't care who gets the credit on a daily basis. I'm going to make right decisions and make wrong decisions. We all have to be in this thing together, and find a way to get it done—and it doesn't always have to be pretty."

"We had a group of guys that really were a team," Zimmer adds. "Team. Team. T-E-A-M."

Torre tells the story in his memoir, *The Yankee Years*, of his first postseason series in 1996, against the Rangers. As pitcher Kenny Rogers was getting hit hard in the second inning, Zimmer turned to him in the dugout and said, "You might want to get someone up in the bullpen." The manager was surprised—it was just the second inning.

"You can never let these games get away from you," his friend warned.

They yanked Rogers, who had given up just two runs, and the Yankees came back to win the game. Rogers surely wasn't happy, but as Torre put it to me, "my loyalty is to the twenty-five, not the one."

A lesser-known example of the mind-set of those Yankee teams came in that same series, when Torre had to make a decision on which of his veteran sluggers to start at designated hitter, Darryl Strawberry or Cecil Fielder.

"Strawberry was the first guy to come in the clubhouse that day," Torre recounts, "and he had some good numbers against John Burkett, who was going to pitch. And I say, 'Straw, come on in here, I have a dilemma.' And this is something I learned, too, over the years—that, you know, you're not infallible here. Let's get information, and have players know that it's not easy to do what you do—that you don't have all this predetermined bullshit going on."

Decisions are made with your head and your heart.

"So I say to Straw," Torre continues, "'I'm not sure who to play here, you or Cecil, at DH.' Strawberry says, 'Play Cecil, because I think I can handle sitting on the bench.' I say, 'Thank you for that, but you're playing.' And Cecil wasn't happy about it, but that was fine. And then it winds up later on, in that game in the World Series, we play Cecil over Tino Martinez, and he knocks in the only run. And that was a tough decision, too."

Torre and Zimmer led a team with brains and compassion, believing that "a true hero isn't measured by the size of his strength, but the strength of his heart," a line uttered by Zeus in Disney's animated movie *Hercules*. The movie, incidentally, came out in 1997, in between the Yankees' first and second championships under Torre.

As the manager put it to me, "You can't win the Derby on a quarter horse," and ultimately, his Yankees won four World Series titles in five years because of his players. But given a stable of Thoroughbreds, he and Zimmer rode them nearly perfectly.

■   ■   ■

Joe Torre barely gave it a second thought that Don Zimmer and George Steinbrenner—his prospective right-hand man and his boss—had known each other for twenty-five years when he picked up the phone to offer Zimmer a job before the 1996 season. They had first met when Zimmer was coaching for the Yanks during one of Billy Martin's stints as manager, and then the two longtime residents of the Tampa area became friendly acquaintances at the local racetrack. If anything, Torre saw it as an asset that his bench coach was familiar with the owner's mercurial ways.

Torre became perhaps the most successful skipper in team history at dealing with "the Boss," who'd frequently call the manager's office to complain about a loss, or a slumping player, or even a decision made during a game. Torre was patient, never yelled back, and had a way of assuaging the owner's concerns without actually acceding to any of his impulsive, ill-conceived, and ultimately empty demands.

But in the spring of 1999, Torre was diagnosed with prostate cancer. Fortunately it was caught early, and with treatment, a full recovery was expected. Still, the manager would have to miss most of spring training and the start of the season. Zimmer was the natural choice to take over the team on an interim basis, and for a few weeks, everything went smoothly . . . until a pitcher named Hideki Irabu, a highly touted Japanese veteran who the Yankees had signed a few seasons before, and who'd been a disappointment, had some problems at the end of spring training. Steinbrenner was furious, and famously called the pitcher a "fat toad," which, as you'd expect, made headlines in every paper. He also called Zimmer and demanded he pull Irabu from the rotation, which Zimmer did not intend to do.

"I had a sense that shit was going to fall down here somewhere," Torre says. He had been keeping tabs on the team through frequent conversations with Zimmer and occasional visits to the ballpark. "And I remember calling Zim and saying, 'Do me a favor. When George calls and says something, just say okay. And then do what you want. Because George never really tells you what to do.' "

To me, this was clearly something Torre learned at the foot of his own abusive father.

"But I knew," he says, "even when Zim said okay and hung up the phone with me, there was no chance he was going to have George Steinbrenner yell at him and not respond."

Sure enough, he responded. When he was thrust into the top spot, it became quickly apparent that Zimmer's style of confronting the boss, and reacting to his bullying, was different than Torre's, and soon Zimmer's friendly relationship with the owner became a feud that would fester for years.

"Hell, George was my friend for twenty-five years," Zimmer says now. "He would sit in Joe's office, maybe after we lost one or two straight games, and he'd be sitting in there like a bulldog. And I'd walk in and say, laughing, 'How's your personality today, boss?' And he'd start shouting, 'Oh, you son of a bitch!' I'd just walk out. I had a great relationship with him at that time; it's a shame that it happened the way it did. But everybody has their own reasons to do things."

You see, before Torre and Zimmer arrived in New York, Steinbrenner had been used to being the king of the Yankees. He could say whatever he wanted in the newspapers, and whoever he was talking about—managers, coaches, players— would be powerless to respond. But Joe Torre was different. First, as I've discussed, he was better at managing up—dealing with his boss—than anyone else before him. Even more important, though, was all his winning. Steinbrenner really couldn't criticize Torre to the media—how could you threaten to fire someone who had been so successful right from the start? So instead, when he got frustrated, Steinbrenner picked on others, including Torre's coaches, and including Zimmer.

Though Torre would say things to deflect the criticism, his style was not to say much—which is often the best strategy when dealing with a bully. Zimmer, as you'd expect, had different ideas of how to handle Steinbrenner. It wasn't that big of a deal in 1999, when the Yankees won the World Series, or in 2000, when the team beat the cross-town rival Mets in 2000 for their fourth title in five years. There wasn't much to criticize. But starting in 2001, when the Yankees lost in dramatic fashion in the ninth inning of the seventh game of the World Series to the upstart Arizona Diamondbacks, the situation started to worsen. The following year, thanks to Disney's Angels, they failed to make the Series for only the second time since Torre had taken over. As the purported "failures" mounted—the Yanks were still dominating during the regular season, but coming up short in playoff series where even a touch of bad luck could be dooming—Steinbrenner turned the heat up. Again, Torre was able to avoid a lot of the criticism because of his track record—or at least not be bothered by what came his way. But Steinbrenner continued to say things to reporters to indirectly lob shots at Torre, and one way to do that was to make insulting comments about his coaches. And even though Torre continued in vain to tell him to ignore it, for a proud man like Don Zimmer, the abuse from above eventually reached a tipping point. Following a bizarre incident in the 2003 playoffs, when the seventy-two-year-old Zimmer was tossed to the ground by Red Sox pitcher Pedro Martinez during a brawl, and then, embarrassed but not seriously injured, got emotional during a press conference, rumors

mounted that, despite his affection for Torre, he was planning to leave. Sure enough, after the season, he left.

"He started treating me like a dog," Zimmer told the *New
York Times* in 2004. He said that Steinbrenner had criticized
and questioned coaches' work in the media, and canceled a
bobblehead doll giveaway promotion scheduled in his honor.
"It was in his own way, never face-to-face, and I got tired of
it. This was a decision I made with my heart."

"Joe didn't believe I was going to walk out," Zimmer told
me six years later. "It's not so much what Steinbrenner did to
me—just little things. I got tired of it, and I said who needs
it. So I left."

In Torre's eyes, Zimmer's departure was actually an il-
lustration of his friend's profound loyalty and honor. Zimmer just couldn't stand Torre and his fellow coaches being
unfairly criticized, and the only option was to leave. It didn't
affect the friendship at all; they still speak often, and get together several times a year during the off season with their
wives. On the field, meanwhile, Mel Stottlemyre, Torre's
trusted pitching coach and other partner, soon also left after his own cancer scare. A new generation of coaches came
in, most of them less experienced; and in a role reversal, it
was Torre often tutoring them. Zimmer had permanently
changed him; winning had given him the confidence to make
bold decisions on his own without stressing too much about
the consequences. But with a new horde of players, many of
whom had become stars on other teams and then been lured
to the Yankees by big contracts, the Yankees became a different team. Gone were veterans like Darryl Strawberry who
would volunteer to sit out games for the benefit of the team,

and in were new, big-money acquisitions who weren't bred to put the team first.

The Yankees never won another World Series with Joe Torre as manager. Sure, they had four more playoff appearances, but not the ultimate prize. Torre has since taken two Dodgers teams to the playoffs as well. Is he still one of the best managers in the game? Without question. But in 2004, when the Yankees began to crumble with a 3–0 series lead against the Red Sox, Don Zimmer wasn't sitting beside him to offer up some strategy that might have stopped the bleeding. In 2007, when gnatlike bugs descended on the pitcher's mound in a game in Cleveland, Torre didn't have someone next to him to tell him to pull his players from the field (a decision he's said is his biggest regret as a Yankee manager). In so many instances in so many games, surely Torre wondered, "What would Zim say?" And in all of those instances, after so many years with Zim at his side, he was certainly well equipped to guess what he might say. But in all those instances, it was just a guess.

"He's the best guy I ever worked with, that's all there is to it," Zimmer fondly says today. "We got along so good. He was comfortable with me, I was comfortable with him. And I think that was a big thing."

"He made a huge difference in me," Torre says. "A huge difference."

Which is exactly what a great partner does.

10

JOHN ANGELO AND MICHAEL GORDON

"Smart as hell . . . and scrupulously honest."

I spent roughly a year interviewing the partners profiled in this book. The final two interviews took place just after Labor Day, in a familiar building on Park Avenue in New York, just north of Grand Central Station. I got off the elevator, walked into the office I'd visited at least a dozen times before, and was greeted warmly by the receptionist, who knew who I was here to see.

"I'll tell Mr. Angelo's assistant you're here," she said.

Mr. Angelo is John Angelo, my oldest friend.

"Actually," I replied, "you can tell Mr. Gordon's assistant also. I'm here to see them both."

Mr. Gordon is Michael Gordon, John's longtime business partner at the company they built together from scratch into one of the most respected investment firms in the world, managing more than $20 billion. For twenty-three years, their names have shared space on the door of the office I was entering. But until I had begun exploring partnerships all across the business world and beyond a year earlier, I hadn't given my friend's successful arrangement at Angelo, Gordon & Co. too much thought. Now, though, as I researched the topic, I had suddenly grown more curious about how John, whom I know as well as perhaps anyone aside from my own wife and children, had managed to build such a successful firm in tandem with someone with whom, at least from what I'd observed in a handful of meetings over the years, he had little in common.

More than a year earlier, just as I'd begun my interviews for the book, the American—and consequently global—financial industry had collapsed. Lehman Brothers, a venerable presence on Wall Street for more than 150 years, had gone bankrupt; thousands had gone into foreclosure on their homes; and people's faith and confidence in the financial system had evaporated. Even if most people didn't fully comprehend what exactly had happened, the scathing newspaper and magazine appraisals that appeared for months afterward, particularly following the indictment of Ponzi schemer Bernie Madoff, made clear that there had been a fundamental loss of trust in the securities business. It all was striking to me for countless reasons, including the fact that a glance at well-known investment banking institutions over time revealed so many partnerships, at least in name: Lehman Brothers, Goldman Sachs, Bear Stearns, Merrill Lynch, and so forth. And beyond that, banking and investment banking had interlocked with each other and caused the collapse, or at least were a systemic part of it.

"You may be able to name those partnerships," John Angelo had told me once, "but you don't know that they got along." My suspicion is that they did, but of course those original partners are long since gone.

I did know, however, that John Angelo and Michael Gordon had gotten along, and grown tremendously close, over their twenty-three years of partnership. I also knew, through personal and professional experience, that they were extraordinarily successful at what they did—making money. And they had emerged from the ugly downturn of 2008 firmly intact, and actually set with opportunities for new growth because so much of their business involved a wide variety of alternative investments like bankrupt businesses and distressed debt. I also had learned from others who knew the securities industry better than I did that Angelo, Gordon & Co. is different in another way: they are respected not only for being successful but also for being conservative, reasonable, and ethical, attributes more critical than ever in financial circles. They are an enterprise doing it right in an environment where so many other companies are doing it terribly wrong. They understand that trading and banking are separate functions. Hopefully by the time this book is published, so, too, will the U.S. Congress.

I had a feeling that the partnership between John and Michael might have had more than a bit to do with this. What I ended up discovering was even more familiar than I expected.

■   ■   ■

Though I've tried to make any praise I give Angelo, Gordon & Co. in this chapter totally objective, I acknowledge there might be reasons for the reader to question that assertion. Dating back nearly a century, my grandparents, Rita and Milton Dammann, and John's grandparents, Ethel and Frederick Bach, were close friends. My mother, Margaret Dammann Eisner, was best friends with John's mother, Judy Bach Angelo. They went to the same schools and the same college, lived three blocks apart in Manhattan, and in the 1950s, had one of the first telephone interconnection, or intercom, lines, from East Eighty-ninth Street to East Eighty-sixth Street. They were extremely close, so close in fact that when John's father died in World War II, his mother found out at our house. When Judy's second husband, Arthur Cowen, died, her first call was to my mother, and about a decade later, when my father died, my mother's first call was to John's mother. So John Angelo and I grew up three blocks from each other; we went to the same school on East Seventy-eighth Street, Allen Stevenson, and the same camp in Vermont, Camp Keewaydin; and as fate would have it, we married a pair of college friends from St. Lawrence University, Jane Breckenridge (Eisner) and Judy Hart (Angelo), whom we met when they were living together on Fortieth Street in Manhattan. It continues today: John's son shares an office in Los Angeles with my son, and my son's son Noah, and John's son's son Julian, although less than three years old, play together. If you've lost count, that's five generations and counting of close friendship. There's an old Chinese saying once adapted by Germany's "Iron Chancellor," Otto von Bismarck: "The first generation creates wealth, the second manages wealth, the third studies art history, and the fourth degenerates." I guess Noah and Julian, the fifth generation, are on their own.

In the midst of the timeline, some forty-plus years ago in the mid-1960s, John and I entered the working world together. John, following in his father's footsteps, had spent two years in the service in Korea, while as I've mentioned, I had spent a few ill-conceived months in Paris trying to become a playwright. When I returned to New York, I became a page at NBC, and soon got a job programming Saturday-morning television at CBS (well, okay, putting the commercials in the shows). John took another kind of job downtown in 1966—as a clerk on the bond floor of the New York Stock Exchange.

"It was a forty-foot-square room, with a brass rail in the middle, surrounded by telephones," John remembers. "Clerks would pick up a phone, take an order, write it on a piece of paper, and then run it to the brass rail, where you'd give it to the broker, who would execute the trade."

There were only nine Wall Street firms who had licenses to sell bonds at the stock exchange, and John's employer, Cowen and Company, was one of them. Cowen had three clerks, including John, who worked in an atmosphere somewhere between a frat house and a full-fledged carnival. Some firms hired pro athletes in their off-season to work as additional clerks and provide the muscle to get from the phones to the rail, while other brokerages actually retained midgets to sneak underneath the scrum, as well as stand on the countertops and make hand signals across the room. Cowen and Company did neither.

And amid the chaos, an introduction to the financial world wasn't John's only education.

"I went to the bond floor and found out certain things about myself that I had no clue of," he says. "I learned that I could multitask, that I could hear things that other people couldn't hear, that I could look at a person's eye and tell if he was lying to me. And I learned that I was a good negotiator."

In this case, negotiating means clerking on the phone, getting someone to move a price bid on a bond a fraction of a percentage point, and making that much more off a particular sale. Among the familiar names John took orders from—and negotiated with—were two future U.S. Treasury secretaries: Robert Rubin, then at Goldman Sachs; and William Simon, then at Salomon Brothers. John did it well enough in his first year as a clerk to make $100,000, which was not only an incredible amount of money in those days but more than five times what I was making in the media business. (No wonder John—a sports fanatic—didn't listen when I kept telling him that I'd connect him with Roone Arledge at ABC Sports to help him get a job there. But maybe entertainment isn't for everyone.)

"So I was having the time of my life," he says, "and I was as good as they had on that floor, and then, in April of 1970, eighteen months after I got there, there was a sign on the bond floor of the New York Stock Exchange: 'As of May 1, the Bond Floor Will Cease to Exist.' Followed up by: 'The Clients Are Better Served If Bonds Are Traded Upstairs Rather Than Downstairs.' This was not true. The reality was, they wanted more space for stocks. So they threw us out and moved the stocks in there."

Either way, brokers would now be trading bonds directly with clients on the phone, meaning clerks were no longer needed, and John was out of a job. Fortunately, he had developed relationships with his clients, including bankers at Bear Stearns, who offered him a job doing arbitrage and put him at a desk in between a pair of banking icons, Cy Lewis, who was a managing director of the firm, and Alan "Ace" Greenberg, who would later become its CEO.

Arbitrage was John's introduction into the world of securities beyond bonds—any and all of the many different instruments that represent financial value. He would buy and sell, or sell and buy, for profit all day long, making Bear Stearns lots of money, and resume earning his impressive $100,000 salary. Until again, a year later, this job was essentially rendered extinct as well, thanks to a new tax law and improving global telecommunications that cut out the need for middlemen in the types of transactions in which John was engaging.

Fortunately, he found a more permanent home in the offices of another venerable Wall Street firm, L. F. Rothschild, doing a different kind of arbitrage. John has explained the nuts and bolts of what he did at Rothschild to me, and how things changed throughout his tenure, but since the goal here is to tell the story without delving into too much financial jargon, I think the most important theme can be summarized by John himself: "I found areas where there was a real niche, and where I could really make some dough for the company."

From his stories of moving between different niches, I know he interacted with famous—and infamous—names in the financial sector, including Jimmy Goldsmith, Ace Greenberg, Gus Levy, Cy Lewis, Michael Milken, T. Boone Pickens, Jacob Rothschild, and Michael Steinhardt. He traveled around the world to meet investors overseas and negotiate

deals. Tough, charismatic, and with a confidence in his abilities first forged on that bond floor, John worked at Rothschild
for over a decade, eventually becoming a partner at the firm
and one of the heads of the arbitrage group. The group—sell-
ers, traders, analysts—all sat in a large room, surely an oven
burning with ego and cutthroat competitiveness. But a few
desks away from John's, there was one guy who stood out, for
being everything most other bankers weren't.

■   ■   ■

For months and months after the collapse of the financial
system in the fall of 2008, business writers tried to explain
what had happened in newspaper and magazine articles.
Then came a spate of books and documentaries that did the
same. The loss of faith and trust in banks and financiers was
staggering, and continues to this day. Investment insiders
are now looked at by many warily at best, and scornfully
at worst. But then there's Angelo, Gordon & Co.—a place, it
turns out, defined by the conscience of an investment outsider, even if that outsider has really been on the inside for
nearly half a century.

Michael Gordon came to New York City in the fall of 1969
knowing nobody. The son of an optician, he had grown up in
a Boston suburb, gone to Colby College in Maine and Boston
University Law School, and then decided he'd try and get a
job on Wall Street. He answered want ads and knocked on
doors for three months, and then was hired to work as an
analyst at L. F. Rothschild. As he shook hands with the man

who hired him, he couldn't believe his luck—getting hired without any experience—and couldn't help saying out loud, "I can't believe you're hiring me. I'm going into business with a law degree." The man replied, "I didn't go to business school either, and it didn't stop me." And the next day, Michael began working as an oil analyst, researching the industry—oil companies, oil supply companies, and oil services companies—and advising the investment bankers in the firm on their oil-related deals.

"Michael made his reputation saying 'There's no oil here,' " John told me. "There's an old saying—the definition of an oil well is a liar standing on top of a hole."

"It was a joke I used," Michael says. "Most oil wells then, when you drill for an exploratory well, you'd hit one out of ten, maybe, if you were lucky. And so then, when there'd be a company drilling, I'd say, simply, There's nothing there. And there'd be nothing there, and people thought I was a genius, but it was just that there was never anything there. A lot of analysts don't have opinions—they say just yes, no, maybe, never. Traders used to call me all the time about oil deals and stuff like that, and we'd have conversations, and I always had opinions about things. When somebody asked me a question, I would actually give them an answer."

After about ten years as an oil analyst, he had impressed enough traders in Rothschild's arbitrage division with those answers to get transferred into their office, where he had a desk not far from John Angelo's. He eventually rose to become the arbitrage department's director of research. And a few years later, he began joining John at the firm's partner meetings as a managing director of the firm. Over the next decade, John, Michael, and the arbitrage group made millions of dollars for Rothschild, and the two men got to know each other better.

"I had been at the department three days," Michael remembers, "and John came over to me to ask a question. I started to give him an answer, and he started to walk away. Because John has no attention span."

He laughs.

"And I said, 'What the hell is this?' This guy comes over to ask me a question, and as I'm about to answer it, he starts walking away."

John simply knew after three words what he was being told, but eventually he learned to at least pretend to be a better listener—at least when Michael was doing the talking. Everything changed, though, when the bottom fell out of Wall Street on Black Monday, October 19, 1987. Though arbitrage had made the firm steady money, not enough of the capital had been stored up, and in a scenario that repeated itself at plenty of banks that fall—and two decades later at Bear Stearns and elsewhere—nervous clients quickly began to move their accounts elsewhere. The arbitrage department now had no money with which to trade, and no real future at the company. L. F. Rothschild was in big trouble, which meant that Michael Gordon—who had taken out a several-hundred-thousand-dollar loan to buy into the firm as a partner—was also in big trouble. Nearly all of his net worth was in untradable Rothschild stock.

"I was going to pay off the loan with my next bonus," he says. "But suddenly, I had no money, I had a house and three kids. This was not a good thing. So I had to look for a job."

Stock options are problematic if, when you exercise them,

you don't sell enough to pay the taxman. And even today, at firms like Rothschild, the management either doesn't let you sell company shares or frowns on you doing so. It's a horrible policy (and one I wouldn't allow at Disney), forcing the executive to borrow the money to pay the tax. This is what happened with the housing bust over the last few years: people owned houses that had less value than their mortgage. And Michael Gordon learned this lesson early—his remaining stock wasn't valuable enough to pay off the loan.

But fortunately, one day, he was approached by John Angelo.

"He said, 'We're going to start our own firm,' " Michael remembers. " 'We'll raise money, and have our own firm.' I said to him, 'You might be able to raise money, but I don't know anybody. The only guy I know is the cleaner around the corner.' I had no friends in the business, and I've never had any friends who had any money. John knew everybody, he grew up in New York, he's terrific and well liked, articulate, and a great salesman. I'm from Boston, not New York. 'So if we're going to raise money,' I said to him, 'you can forget me.' "

John didn't, though. In fact, he lent Michael the money for him to become a partner in the new venture, which in turn soon made it possible for him to pay back the large loan that was hanging over his head. John, meanwhile, raised the $50 million to start Angelo, Gordon & Co.—a name I encouraged him to use, reasoning that so many other places on Wall Street had done well by putting their names on the door. They took sixteen people with them from Rothschild, which in the meantime had been sold to a group of bankers in Kansas. The new owners were happy to lose the overhead and let the group leave. L. F. Rothschild soon became a name of the financial past. Twenty-two years later, however, Angelo and Gordon remain two in the present.

■   ■   ■

To understand why John Angelo wanted Michael Gordon to be his partner, and to understand why their partnership has been so successful, you have to understand what Angelo, Gordon & Co. does. And what they do remains an original form of investing and making money, even in a climate that's completely changed since their first years as a firm.

Angelo, Gordon & Co. has grown the $50 million it started with into $22 billion. The firm has persevered and thrived through the savings and loan crisis; the rise and fall of long-term capital management; the "tech wreck"; the Enron and Adelphia fraud cases; and the biggest recession the nation has ever seen. And after losing a small amount of money with the rest of the world in 2008, with just 3 percent redemptions (clients asking for their money back), the firm was up an estimated 50 percent in 2009. Without getting too bogged down in financial terms, the firm has made its money investing in a markedly broad range of things; they refer to themselves as "specialists in nontraditional investments." In the 1980s, working in different parts of the arbitrage business gave John, Michael, and their associates a wide breadth of exposure to sectors that, particularly back then, weren't popular targets for investors. Their most notable target was distressed securities—that is, companies either in default or bankruptcy, or headed in that direction. But along with "distressed," the firm also has long invested in private equity, venture capital, real estate, and more. If a hedge fund, defined in the classic sense, hedges the market based on a specific investment strategy, Angelo, Gordon's strategy is to work in a variety of sectors that may not necessarily be related.

"If you give your money to a hedge fund to invest," John explained to me, "it can be anything. It can be five guys sitting in a room who are smart. Here, if you give money for us to invest in distressed, it's not just the seven guys working in the bankruptcy department. It's also the thirty other people working everywhere else for us. And they get all paid from the same pot."

So in a sector that's supposed to be about nothing else but the bottom line—profit—for Angelo and Gordon, it's actually about synergy.

"Let me give you another example," John says. "Chelsea Market, in lower Manhattan. A bankrupt building that we bought when it was essentially empty, suffering from high vacancy rates. In the rest of the investing world, real estate people typically stay away from bankruptcy people. Well, our bankruptcy group bought it, and walked down the hall to our real estate group, and said, 'Let's do something here.' We secured high-profile tenants [Major League Baseball, the Food Network, and a few others] who coinvested to renovate the property. We made hundreds of millions of dollars. It all comes from a philosophy and a culture of making certain that every group works together."

As much as this sounds like common sense, it's not so common in the investing world. At many huge places like Goldman Sachs, and the late Lehman Brothers, and Bear Stearns, the firms are so big, there is an inevitable lack of communication, and at times there is infighting. Angelo, Gordon & Co.

uses its small size to keep everyone on the same page, even as it remains big enough to support a series of strategies that are, importantly, not market-dependent. When the economy is going strong, small firms make money along with the rest of Wall Street. But when it isn't, John, Michael, and their group position themselves to take advantage of others' mismanagement. It's commonly estimated that there have been ten thousand hedge funds started since alternative investing became popular. From 1982 to 1999, the market was up tenfold; if you could raise $100 million to invest, it was, in some ways, difficult not to make money. But from 1999 to 2009, thanks in large part to the disaster of 2008, the market remained flat. A large percentage of those hedge funds lost a lot of people's money, and are gone today. Angelo and Gordon, however, is still around, and still very profitable.

But it's not just because of their intelligent strategy. It's about the ethics behind it.

■   ■   ■

The main section of Angelo and Gordon's office is a large, bullpenlike area, with analysts seated at several rows of desks in front of computer screens, presumably monitoring the day's market activity. Along the far wall is a large office, connected to a conference room, which is where John Angelo spends his days. John wears a suit and tie to the office every day, and though the suit jacket comes off as soon as he arrives in the morning, the tie is never loosened. Befitting of his "fast-moving" attention span, he is on the move the entire day, talking on the phone constantly, having lunch with a client or potential client nearly every afternoon, and often traveling for other meetings and presentations for the firm.

Michael Gordon, meanwhile, has no office. He can be found in the bullpen, with his desk at the front, facing the analysts, almost like a teacher's desk in a classroom. He also wears a suit and tie to work, but loosens his tie to almost a half knot by mid-morning, making him look like a somewhat rumpled English professor. He rarely leaves his desk, even for lunch, preferring to let John take the bulk of the meetings and represent the firm.

"We're fiercely close," John says. "But very different people."

As I sat in the conference room adjacent to his office, John paced the room, answering my questions. Beyond the glass wall, I could see Michael at his desk the entire time. And after I'd heard him retell the story of how they met, I was most curious about one thing. If John was able to raise all the money himself, why did he want a partner so badly that he was willing to lend the guy money to come aboard?

Well, first, it made sense from an investing perspective: John and Michael had different, and complementary, specialties in arbitrage, and John wanted to keep doing the same thing he was doing. But there was also something else.

"I'd been with him ten years, in this small room," John says. "I knew he was smart as hell, and I knew he was scrupulously honest."

That honesty was clear from the moment they drew up their partnership agreement.

"I had never been partners with anyone before," Michael told me later. "And it came to the provision of what happens when John and I disagree about something; how is it going to be resolved? And I said to the lawyer, 'What's typically the provision?' And he says, 'Well, there's arbitration.' And I said, 'That's ridiculous.' I said, 'You know what, if it comes to that, there's no partnership. If we disagree on something so seriously that we have to go to arbitration to resolve it, then this partnership is over. So either we work out our problems if there are any, or the firm ends.' So there is no provision in the partnership agreement about arbitrating disputes between John and me."

But that hasn't been a problem.

"Michael Gordon and I have never had an argument," John says. "If we have, I mean, maybe there are two times I can remember—he said, 'Okay, fine, I'll give in—you'll give in the next time.' And that's it."

There is nothing in the firm's business that they do not decide together, and as in all the other partnerships I've explored, one plus one adds up to more than two.

"Whether it's a new employee," Michael says, "or whether we should get into a certain business, or if we should have a partnership with someone on the outside—he comes at things from a different perspective than I do. He brings a different skill set. He's a trader, and I'm an analyst, and personality-wise, we're very, very different. He's very good at marketing and selling and giving speeches, and I would never want to follow him on the podium. He's very, very good, and I'm not good at it, and I don't like it. He's very different than I am."

But from the beginning, that's exactly why John asked him to be his partner. And an early decision where Michael prevailed has been at the core of their success.

John remembers: "I said to Michael, 'We have a lot of mouths to feed here. Why don't you lever up the portfolio?' "

Levering in the funds—or using debt to provide additional money to invest—was something John wanted to do in the first few years of the firm. It's a euphemism for borrowing, and borrowing money is fine if it is done wisely, reasonably, and affordably—something that didn't happen all over Wall Street and beyond in the years leading up to the financial bust.

"We could get a little more juice and be able to pay our employees a little more," John remembers. "And Michael's answer to me was 'Okay, yeah, I know, I'll do it.' But thirty days would go by, and nothing. And I'd come back and say, 'C'mon . . . ,' and he wouldn't do it. And finally, months later, he said to me, 'Look, if I'm leveraged, I can't sleep.' And that's how that happened. And we're known for that. For not using leverage. And the reason is, he can't!"

Heavily leveraged firms—and individuals—were what the financial collapse of a few years ago wiped away. Angelo, Gordon & Co. remained standing. Michael Gordon can't sleep when he's leveraged, because he thinks as much like a client as he does a banker. It may be because he's always viewed himself as an outsider in the industry. It may be because of his own experience as an executive, borrowing money to pay for his L. F. Rothschild stock, a move that put him in serious personal debt and almost ended his career. But more than anything, it's because Michael thinks it's the right thing to do.

"I think your reputation is important," Michael says. "John's name and my name are on the door, and we don't want to do something that's bad, or looks bad, or even something that people are going to say is bad. We're tough negotiators in deals, but I think we have a good reputation, and at the end of the day, that's all there is. So when we hire people, we tell them—you know, you can lose money on a trade. You may not like it, but you can. But if you do anything to besmirch the reputation of this firm, you're gone. And that's the way it is."

His philosophy on deals, even in the difficult area of distressed debt, where the firm is negotiating with sometimes desperate companies, is no different.

"We have always felt like a good deal is when you make a good profit—and leave something on the table for the next guy," he says. "It's very important that people want to do business with you, that they trust you, and that they want to come back for more. And when we negotiate for bankruptcies, we're tough but reasonable. A lot of people sue simply because they can sue; even if they have no foundation for the lawsuit, they can delay something three years. We would never do that. And we've been accused by everybody else as willing to take less than everyone else. To us, it's a deal, and I'm not going to scrounge around for a year to make another two percentage points. It makes no sense."

"To this day," John says, "Michael asks, 'Is it fair to the client? Is that the right thing to do?' He said it then, and he says it now. He always puts his client first."

"I sold eyeglasses," Michael says. "I worked in my father's store for the summers and on holidays, and I waited on people to sell them eyeglasses at eighteen, nineteen, twenty-three dollars a pair. And my father always said, 'Treat the customer well. Think about the customer. You make a great product, and treat the customer well, and you'll be fine.' And I think we do a very good job with our investors. We're open, we speak with them all the time, we're accessible, and I think we do the right thing."

That should always matter on Wall Street, just like it should matter on every street in America. This firm is one place where it definitely does.

■　　■　　■

A *Dr. No* movie poster hangs over Michael Gordon's desk, because, the joke goes, any idea that anyone takes to him—anyone from John Angelo to a first-year associate—his response is always the same.

"Anything you say to him," John says, "he'll say no. [Sounds like Charlie Munger.] You want to be interviewed for a book by Michael Eisner? No. Why? I don't know. People go to him, and they say, We want to invest in such-and-such. Now Michael's going to say, Have you thought about this? Have you called so-and-so? Do some more work. I don't disagree, but I think you need to do some more work. The analysts love him for that. And it's a very important quality, very important. I called up last week with two ideas, and he said, Those are good ideas. I was shocked. Shocked."

Similarly, by the early 1990s, John and Michael had raised enough money and gotten enough experience to open a signature fund—a portfolio of an assortment of different investments that took advantage of their knowledge of so many different sectors. John had told me about it, and wanting to help out, I had instantly begun brainstorming possible names for the fund. It was late January, and the Super Bowl was the next weekend. Call it the Superfund, I told him. He later told me that Michael had turned white when he shared the suggestion—at the time, there was a lot of controversy over hazardous waste sites in New Jersey that were coincidentally known as Superfunds, and in addition, he was afraid that if the fund performed poorly, people would call it the Mediocre Fund. In any event, John trusted my marketing instincts, talked Michael into it, the name stuck, and the fund did incredibly well (and still does).

"I once described to someone who I was," Michael says, "and it actually sounded pretty good. You know the show *Law and Order*, and the old DA, Adam Schiff? That's who I am. I harrumph a lot. The analysts say they're going to do such-and-such, and I say, 'Well, you better do it right.' I envision myself as Adam Schiff, or he's Michael Gordon, one of the two."

Even as he plays the role of sage for everyone in the firm, Michael finds it a constant struggle to remind them of what matters and what doesn't matter.

"You worry after a period of time," he says, "when someone has done so much, why they have to be as avaricious as they are. It is all about insecurity. The only way they can determine their self-worth is by how much money they have. And you see it here: if you go out and tell a guy he's going to have a five-million-dollar bonus, he shrugs and says, 'Well, what is that?' 'Well, it's a lot of money.' 'Well, I deserve more.' And I say, 'What if I told you that the guy who sits next to you made four million dollars?' 'Then I'd be thrilled. I'd be happy I made more than he did.' That's what drives Wall Street— jealousy and competitiveness. They know they're overpaid, and they don't know how to value their own self-worth and being, for the job they do, unless it's money. That's the only way they can do it.

"So I told one of the guys, go home and tell your wife about this conversation. Tell her how much money in bonus you got—and you've earned it, I didn't give it to you—but tell her how much. And tell her how unhappy you are that it isn't a bigger number. So he comes in tomorrow, the next day, and he doesn't talk to me. And I say, Come here. Did you tell your wife what your reaction was? Yes. And what was her reaction? She said I'm an asshole."

They don't typically teach lessons like that in business school or on Wall Street. Maybe being an English major and reading Oscar Wilde would be productive for business executives. "In this world," he wrote, "there are only two tragedies. One is not getting what you want, and the other is getting it."

"I never dreamed in my life that I was going to have as much money as I do now," Michael says. "This is just unbelievable what we fell into. We didn't plan it—the business grew up around us, and we did well, and we took advantage of it. When we started, we never dreamed that the business would turn into what it turned into."

Despite the millions of dollars he's made, he is still the son of an optician from middle-class Newton, Massachusetts, who came to Wall Street without knowing anyone. John Angelo, who has as much ability, charisma, and salesmanship as anyone in his field, was smart enough twenty-three years ago to recognize that the guy across the room at L. F. Rothschild was different from everyone else he'd met in his journey through the investing world, and John's been smart enough to keep listening to Michael's distinctive perspective as they've built up their partnership.

We had grown up together three city blocks apart, our families intertwined for generations before and after us. And while John Angelo and I had gone into different careers, when we found ourselves intersecting once again, we discovered the same thing.

In so many ways, we both succeeded because we found the right partners.

HAPPINESS

You have probably never heard of Jeff Meckstroth and Eric Rodwell. They are in their mid-fifties and live in Tampa, Florida, though they frequently travel around the country and the globe together as part of their job. They are the best bridge players in the world, and they have been partners for over thirty years.

Eric and Jeff are separate individuals, but in bridge, they are one. You would think that since partnerships are required in the game, there would be dozens of well-known, elite, long-term teams in competitive bridge. But in fact, there are very few of them—and none as successful as Meckstroth and Rodwell, who are known in the bridge world as "MeckWell," and who have won multiple world championships and other major titles together.

"We've learned so much from each other over the years," Meckstroth says. "We both approach the game in very different ways, and met in the middle and found the best of both worlds. I've adapted his strengths to my game, and vice versa."

"Jeff has a tremendous ability psychologically to perceive and read what his opponents are thinking, and get them to do what he wants," says Rodwell. "Then there is a large technical aspect to the game—what we call a system. And that's been primarily my thing."

The game, as Meckstroth put it to me, is a game of mistakes.

"We always make mistakes," he said, "and when we do, we look at it and try and figure out what we could have done about it."

"My number one thing," Rodwell adds, "would be that you've got to use the energy constructively. You really want to try and keep egotism in check because egotism does not produce good logical action. If you want to validate your ego, you're going to falter."

It is a familiar refrain. Like business, bridge is a pursuit that combines intelligence with strategy and creativity and perseverance. The central difference is that you have to play bridge with a partner—you have no choice. But why, then, haven't more successful long-term partnerships emerged in bridge than this pair? The short answer is that it's hard.

With any union of two people, different combinations work for different reasons. And the ten partnerships profiled in this book demonstrate that dramatically. But trying to use the stories told here to come up with the perfect formula for partners is not only impossible, it's fruitless. It's like a calculus problem with an infinite number of variables.

Still, if I didn't write this book to find the perfect partnership, I did try to pick ten stories that appealed to me, that

fascinated me from a distance, and that I wanted to understand as completely as possible. And through the variety, I
did find unmistakable common threads, a set of conspicuous
attributes that great partners share. First and foremost, as
Warren Buffett noted, partners cannot be envious of each
other. They must value trust. They have to discover how to
keep their ego in check. They must put a premium on not
just brains, but human decency.

A quality partnership also allows you to recognize your
own weaknesses, and draw on a partner's strengths, without being uncomfortable about that vulnerability. That self-
knowledge gave Joe Torre the willingness to rely on Don
Zimmer to help him make decisions, and, conversely, allowed Giancarlo Giammetti to be happy as the supporting
member of his partnership with Valentino.

Then there's being comfortable with the way that someone else views the world. Charlie Munger looks at every possible business deal skeptically, always looking for a reason to
say no. Warren Buffett uses that to his advantage—he tries to
find ways to convince his partner to say yes. Michael Gordon
and John Angelo find themselves in a similar situation. Gordon is the skeptic, Angelo the optimist. Together they move
forward effectively. When Barry Diller asked why, I pushed
back and said, "Why not?" "Maybe" was rarely in our lexicon,
but we always found the right solutions for us. Meanwhile,
at Disney, Frank Wells would often play the devil's advocate
on a range of issues (well, actually every issue). In all cases,
working together is successful because the partners have so
much respect for each other. That kind of mutual admiration
allows a partnership like Susan Feniger and Mary Sue Milliken to continue to flourish even as one partner goes off to

work on a new project. (Even if the fact that they each married the same man probably pushes the limits of collaboration!)

The chefs' partnership continues. Meanwhile, there are others profiled in this book that ended not in explosions but in retirements—Joe Torre and Don Zimmer, Arthur Blank and Bernie Marcus from the Home Depot—as well as Bill Gates's working relationships with Paul Allen and Steve Ballmer. In each of these cases, all these former partners remain friendly. Breakups in business are not supposed to be easy. But with these partners, it was different—again, because of the strong sense of history, friendship, and accomplishment that these individuals all shared. They entered their partnerships without an exit strategy, and that may have been the biggest reason their ultimate exits were without any drama.

I have always believed that when you're making a partnership agreement, there should not be a provision on how that partnership ends. Even if there are obvious exceptions where it is impossible, I don't believe in buy/sell agreements, arbitration agreements, or anything else that would suggest a potential end to the relationship. (I also don't like the idea of prenuptial agreements—at least for the first marriage.) The fact Ron Howard and Brian Grazer have been fifty-fifty from day one is really smart. The fact that Ian Schrager and Steve Rubell didn't have a negotiated end to their relationship probably was a positive. And the fact that Michael Gordon wouldn't consider any type of arbitration to settle disputes was very wise. When a problem comes up in a partnership, solve it then. Anything other than that sets the wrong tone. This is a strategy not practiced very often and not very popular. Nevertheless, it is the correct strategy.

■ ■ ■

The list of recognizable characteristics of these relationships goes on, and their success has a common root: a real sense of ethics. Today in business, ethics are more important than ever. And as the country slowly pulls itself out of a super recession, it will be ethical people in business and in government who will be needed to redirect a moral compass that got turned in the wrong direction. For generations, the majority of public servants, business entrepreneurs, small business owners, and corporate executives have always done things the right way. The minority has also been there, doing bad things, milking the public, shorting even the shortcuts—but nothing like the last business cycle. As the twentieth century turned over, something changed. Suddenly gambling, self-dealing, crossing the line, conflicts of interests, and favors became accepted practice. Fortunes were built on foundations of Jell-O. The country was brought to the edge of a financial cliff by an endemic sense of entitlement wrapped in greed, coupled with a system that created perverse incentives and may have even encouraged rogue behavior.

As the dark shadow cast by the banking and real estate industries recedes and the long-term social consequences are being absorbed, it's time for us to demonstrate that we have learned the error of our ways, and to move past the small group of individuals—the bad seeds dominating the news—who nearly destroyed everything for all of us. Even as minimum-security jails have replaced upscale restaurants for the notorious, it's time to rearrange the *Tischordnung* at those eateries. Will all the bad sorts go away? Nope. But maybe we won't honor them anymore.

Partnership can be a major part of the change that needs to occur. Another voice in the room can often intercept and prevent bad choices. Risk is fine, but a partner will point out when a risk is over the line financially or legally or ethically. A partner saying that something doesn't smell right could prevent embarrassment, failure, or even a trip to jail. Now, could two people working as a pair wreak evil together? Certainly that could happen—but it's much more likely to go the other way. If two people are malicious and criminal, and decide to team up, eventually they will betray each other; it's in their DNA. Eventually—and probably sooner than later—that kind of partnership will fail. (Steve Rubell and Ian Schrager are the exception that proves the rule. They were caught cheating just twenty months after Studio 54 opened, sent to jail, and emerged as legitimate businessmen whose loyalty kept them together through the toughest of adversity.) The existence of a partnership is not what makes it work; it's the people who enter into it. The characteristics of a good partner are the characteristics of a successful person. And the individuals who find ways to make partnership successful, and who understand the value of teamwork and collaboration, and who can avoid ego and selfishness, are much more likely to be good people than bad. Two minds, two endurances, two personalities, tied to a common cause works.

■   ■   ■

Perhaps the greatest challenge to increasing the presence of partnerships is the long-held fascination with single heroes—in and out of business. For generations, the titans of industry, icons of progress, have been individual figures. That's the story the media wants to tell, the story the public wants to hear, and, quite frankly, the fantasy that ambitious young executives conceive for themselves. They want to be the next Andrew Carnegie, the next J. P. Morgan, the next Rupert Murdoch, the next Jack Welch. Sharing those aspirations with someone else runs counter to the way they are bred to achieve.

I have let the grand success of the partnerships do most of the arguing here. But to bring partnerships into the central lore of business history, there are changes that can be made. If high schools, colleges, and graduate law and business schools spent more time teaching the subject of business ethics—and it's all too frequently forgotten about in these settings—the virtues of partnership could be integrated into these curricula. In business schools, working in groups has long been a common teaching tool. Maybe classes should take that even further, and encourage students to seek out partners in projects and assignments.

Even large companies can foster partnership among employees and executives by pairing individuals. Bernie Marcus and Arthur Blank also showed at Home Depot that having a partnership at the center of a company's culture can foster cooperation, productivity, and ethics throughout an entire organization. At Disney, we used corporate retreats (called Disney Dimensions) to encourage members of different parts of the corporation to get to know one another, learn from one another, and work together. That was how we achieved true synergy—different people from different parts of the company partnering on projects that benefited everyone.

Nonetheless, after some 279 pages spent advocating for

partnerships, I'm still very much a believer in the need for leadership by one person and ultimate accountability. Individual leadership and partnerships are not all mutually exclusive. Companies, organizations, and governments do need a single individual to make final decisions, someone with whom the "buck stops," a senior voice. But if that senior voice has a strong partner, all those decisions will be wiser, and probably better. In fact, review most lists of iconic business leaders, and I'd venture to say that every one of them has or had someone else behind the curtain. You just haven't read about them. Maybe it is a second in command. Often it is a spouse. (Never underestimate the power of "pillow talk.") In the end, everyone needs someone else for balance; anyone who walks past a mirror and has the need to look at himself also has the need for a partner to set him straight. Otherwise, entitlement creeps in, stubbornness metastasizes, balance is lost, and tripping and finally falling occurs. Someone has to tell the emperor he has on different-colored socks.

And another reminder to the rising executive: it's usually best to acknowledge your partner—best for the relationship, and best for the success of your enterprise.

■   ■   ■

A few times when I've talked about this book, skeptics have raised an intriguing point: that the main reason these partnerships worked is because of the extraordinary success that they enjoyed. In other words, while it's all well and good to have good ethics and no egos, if the businesses failed—if Warren and Charlie never made any money, if Ron Howard and

Brian Grazer's movies stunk, if Joe Torre and Don Zimmer's Yankees didn't win any games—the partnerships would have crumbled along with them.

Does the partnership cause the success, or does the success sustain the partnership? The answer is that both are true. There are thousands and thousands of successful partnerships in all kinds of businesses, from multinational corporations to the smallest of companies managed from home, from profitable enterprises to the nonprofit world, from education to medicine to, frankly, everything. In all of them, partnership can lead to success—and success can also sustain partnership. It is no accident that the individuals profiled in this book have had remarkable success, but it is also no secret that this success has been multiplied many times over because of partnership. Ron Howard is a great director on his own, and Brian Grazer is a great producer on his own, but only together have they built such a successful company. Bill Gates would have started a foundation, but would it have been as much of a force without his wife? I doubt it (and so would he).

But even if the success of these partnerships is persuasive, and even inspiring, the skeptics persist: What about the surely countless failed partnerships that have also been part of the history of business? What about people who have gone into partnerships, and for some reason or another, it hasn't worked out? Well, they happen; I can tell you from experience. It should be as simple as two unique people finding each other, and working well together, but it isn't. But that's why this book is interesting to me. If a partnership doesn't work, the response should be to keep looking for one that does work. You learn from the experience, and search for a better partnership. Just look at the ultimate partnership in our society, marriage. We know the odds of having that work—they say it is 50 percent. I'd take those odds in business.

But there's something more. Take the list of partnerships profiled in this book and put it alongside a list of individuals who have had similar success on their own. On paper, everything might line up—the dollar figures, the stock amounts, the titles and the companies. But dig deeper, and you'll find something else, something far more important, and by far the most compelling argument for working together.

Happiness.

Partnerships all made these people happy, and happier than they would have been had they worked for their success alone. They had someone else with whom to experience the challenging lows and the ecstatic highs; another person in the trenches, another person to pop the champagne. Not too long ago, the *Atlantic Monthly* published a Harvard University study in which over 250 men had been interviewed every five years since the 1940s, to determine what really makes someone happy. To summarize the results, there was just one overriding cause of happiness: sustained relationships over a long period of time. Wealth and social class didn't mean anything, and even exercise helped only so much. What mattered was having real communication with someone, love, and friendship—all of which you get through a sustained loving marriage or significant relationship, strong continued contact with your siblings, extended communication with grown children, and satisfying business partnerships.

In the study—and it is among several that have shown the same conclusions—having real relationships was what led to other factors that were common among happy people: passing wisdom down to future generations, and being adaptable and able to bounce back from disappointments. These come with partnership. I am not surprised some of the happiest people I have known for years include the people profiled in this book. John Angelo is as happy now as he was when we were eight years old. And I am happiest when I am collaborating on a project with someone else, as I did on this book with Aaron Cohen. The highs and lows, the successes and the failures, the feeling of being with someone you know is smarter than you are, all the while confident they think the same way.

Working together is much better than working . . . alone.